Dancing Across the Page

Dancing Across the Page
Narrative and Embodied Ways of Knowing

Karen Nicole Barbour

intellect Bristol, UK / Chicago, USA

First published in the UK in 2011 by
Intellect, The Mill, Parnall Road, Fishponds, Bristol, BS16 3JG, UK

First published in the USA in 2011 by
Intellect, The University of Chicago Press, 1427 E. 60th Street,
Chicago, IL 60637, USA

A catalogue record for this book is available from the
British Library.

Cover designer: Holly Rose
Copy-editor: Integra Software Services
Typesetting: Mac Style, Beverley, E. Yorkshire

ISBN 978-1-84150-421-6

Printed and bound by Gutenberg Press, Malta.

Contents

List of Photographs and Figures

Mihi

Hei tīmatanga māku, ko te mihi nui ki te mauri o tēnei whenua me ngā tai e ngunguru
   nei ki Aotearoa nei.
Ka mihi nui anō hoki au ki ngā iwi o Tainui.
Ka huri aku mihi ki ngā iwi o te Ao, ki ōku tūpuna kei tāwāhi, kei Kotirana me Kānata
   hoki.
I whānau mai au i konei, i Aotearoa nei.
E noho ana au i konei i raro i te mana o te Tiriti o Waitangi.
I tipu ake au i te rohe o Maungamangero, i te pūtahi o ngā awa o Mangaotaki me
   Waitanguru ki Piopio nei. I tōku tamarikitanga kai ake ōku karu ki ngā pae maunga
   o Maungamangero ka tū tūtei ake mai e whakamakūkūtia ana e ngā awa kōpikopiko.
   Ka huri rā taku titiro ki ngā tomo i noho mai ai hei āhurutanga mōwai mōku.
Rongo ai au i konei, taku piringa ki tōkukāinga.
Ina rongo ai au i te tangi mai a te ruru i te pō, ka hoki tika tonu atu au ā-wairua nei,
   ki te wāhi kei roto i tōku whatumanawa, ki te wāhi e kīia tonu nei e au, ko tōku
   kāinga.
E noho ana au i Hamutana ināianei, i ngā tahatika o te awa o Waikato. He piko, he
   taniwha.
Ko Barbour me Hunt ōku hapū.
Ko Karen Barbour taku ingoa.
Tēnā koutou.
Ki taku tama;
'He tihi pekehā ki te moana, ko Ngāti Ira ki te whenua.'

Acknowledgements

I would like to acknowledge my family and friends for their support throughout the process of writing of this book. In particular, I acknowledge my partner Arana, my son Tahukiterangi, my ever-present mother Mary and sister Julie. Some of my wonderful family and friends appear within my narratives as 'characters' – I could not write about my experiences without writing about them too. I appreciate their love and their willingness to be part of my living and writing.

In the following pages you will meet my generous and insightful friends who have also been participants in the research projects that underline different chapters. My narratives feature solo contemporary dance artists Raewyn Thorburn and Jan Bolwell, along with Susanne Bentley, Bronwyn Judge and Alison East. Their insights ground my articulations of embodied ways of knowing. Being a passionate teacher, I wished to include a wonderful group of students with whom I shared the studio: Holly, Wiremu, Courtney, Desiree, Barry, Elaine and Whetu. These students taught me so very much as we shared our experiences. I also introduce my friend and colleague, contemporary artist Kristian Larsen, with whom I explore performance improvisation and with whom I continue ongoing debate and discussion. And finally, dancers I regularly choreograph and perform with are present in various moments within the narratives. These are some of the central 'characters' who dance with me throughout these pages and who are part of my community in Aotearoa.

My family members, research participants, friends and close colleagues have been invited to read and comment on my writing. I thank them for their consent to write about them, their time and insight in reading draft chapters.

Acknowledgements to Jane Strachan, Pirkko Markula and Jim Denison who initially helped me to find my voice as a writer during my time as a doctoral student.

My heartfelt thanks go to my colleagues in the Department of Sport and Leisure Studies, who have more recently offered valuable critique as I experimented further with writing styles and organizing the content of this book. Thanks particularly to Bob Rinehart, Toni Bruce and Debbie Bright.

With much respect I acknowledge Nātana Takurua for his generosity in sharing his time and knowledge to help me to gain insight into te Ao Māori. Special thanks to Te Kāhautū Maxwell for his valuable assistance.

The University of Waikato's, Faculty of Education Research Committee has provided financial support for varied research projects included in this book, without which I could not do what I do.

I wish to acknowledge the photographic artists I am privileged to work with, and particularly those photographers whose images appear in this book: Cheri Waititi, Robert Fear and Marcia Mitchley.

Thanks to my aunt Sarah for her excellent editing assistance. And finally, thanks to the reviewers and editors at Intellect Books for believing in my ability to dance across the page.

I dedicate this book to Tahukiterangi.

Chapter 1

Being: Introductions

Writing at my computer now as a dancer and writer, a feminist researcher, teacher in tertiary dance education and mother, I wonder how you will connect with me, with my different experiences, ways of knowing, cultures and environment. I share my experiences with you in this book – a narrative exploration of embodied ways of knowing as a means of living creatively in the world. I feel deeply in my bones that the specifics of my embodiment as a woman and a contemporary dancer living in *Aotearoa*[1] are integral to my engagement in qualitative research. My embodiment is crucial to the ways in which I understand my personal experiences in relation to the social and political world around me. My contention as a feminist is that the specifics of my embodiment are pivotal to epistemology too, just as the specifics of my cultural, social, discursive and geographical context are also integral to what I can know. Consequently, this book contains a collection of specifically located, personally embodied narratives and *autoethnographies*[2] based on lived experiences.

Recollections

A remote rural area of *Te Ika a Māui, Aotearoa*[3] (the North Island of New Zealand) was my first home. Surrounded by native bush, rugged farmland and cool fresh rivers, my days were clear blue and full of adventure, and my nights alight with family discussion and the imaginary worlds of books. My sisters and I ran barefoot, playing in the rivers, exploring caves, climbing hills and building tree huts, watched casually by our parents. We knew the deep, quiet pools and the secret space behind the waterfall, the route up the limestone cliffs to where we could see over the whole valley, the best spots for gathering watercress and picking wild plums, the places glow-worms lit and the calls of the *Ruru* (Morepork owl) in the night. School was a long drive away, our bus crawling along familiar dusty roads and picking up neighbours every few kilometres before reaching the little town. Some summers our spring would run dry and winter storms could leave our valley isolated and without electricity for days. We learned to live with the seasons and we made our own fun.

As a naive but precocious young girl, my parents took me to see popular Limbs Dance Company[4] perform in the local community theatre. I remember sitting near the stage, my eyes wide as dancers transformed into reptiles, moths and all the fancies of my young imagination. Enraptured with the strength, fluidity and charisma of the dancers, I knew then that contemporary dance was what I wanted to do. After pestering my parents for months, I had my first real contemporary dance experience in the big city of Auckland.

My 11-year-old body was filled with nervous anticipation as I set out for my first morning of the ten-day Limbs dance workshop. After catching buses from my aunt's house to the central city, I walked through the tumbledown houses and boarded-up buildings of the early 1980s inner-city suburb of Ponsonby. Climbing eagerly up the creaky wooden stairs to the third floor of the old Limbs Dance Company building, I arrived at last. Dressed in my new black footless tights, leotard and T-shirt under my street clothes, I was ready to become a dancer. To my elation, I was greeted by one of the marvellous dancers I remembered seeing perform, and from then on I imagined myself one of them. I remember distinct things from that first workshop, like the smell of one woman's perfume and the absolute thrill of moving in new ways. Though always in awe of those around me, somehow I also felt at home too.

That first dance workshop and those clear blue days of adventure are some of my fondest childhood memories. Or at least, these are what remain in my memory anyway, because after this, the realities of being a young woman began to sink in. The days seemed to get shorter and there was not enough time for wandering and adventuring. Saddened, I noticed the hillsides scar with landslides in the winter storms after the farmers began logging more forest. Our rivers changed too as the water was contaminated with silt and with animal effluent from increased livestock. As time went on, my outside play reduced to running and swimming for competition rather than for pleasure. Study for exams also meant that I did not get to attend many dance workshops and I had to make do with leaping around my bedroom and imagining I was dancing in Limbs Dance Company.

The books in front of me morphed from novels to textbooks and study ate steadily into our family discussion time. I suppose that I was well prepared for my tertiary education, but I still reflect sadly on this inescapable change from childhood to adulthood. Inevitably I left my remote home environment and family for the city and university, choosing to study philosophy and psychology because dance was not offered in tertiary education in those days. By the time the tertiary dance programme in Auckland city became established, I had completed my Master's degree in philosophy. Enrolling in dance training at long last, I immersed myself in the dance world, my childhood dream of professional training and performance coming to fruition, albeit briefly. It was not long though, before I traded in the struggle of professional dance and returned to the academic environment in search of a more sustainable career and lifestyle.

My nostalgia for both the seemingly uncomplicated rural life of my childhood and my naive dream of a career as a dancer are balanced now with a much greater awareness of the political, social and artistic context of Aotearoa, and by my experiences travelling internationally.

Dance in my footsteps

As the short vignette above illustrates, I share my own lived experiences in this book, beginning by providing some context through the autobiographical vignette above and extending my writing style throughout the book to more substantial narratives. Within these pages I develop richly descriptive, visceral and kinaesthetic methods of writing to deliberately draw attention to the constructed, contextual and embodied nature of my experience and research. I believe that, as a member of the dance community and social context of Aotearoa that I study, my own dance-making experiences and research with others should be represented to convey lived experience as fully as possible within written forms. Thus, I consult my own embodiment for understandings and I search for evocative words to articulate my understandings. My hope is that I can inspire you to engage kinaesthetically and empathetically with my experiences, so that you can 'dance in my footsteps' through these pages.

Throughout my chapters I engage in practices of feminist research, narrative inquiry and dance making, drawing on the words of academic writers who have influenced me. I weave these academic words with my own experiences and with the voices of research participants and friends. In a number of chapters I weave these creative feminist narratives together with short excerpts from more traditional academic texts, such as sections from my doctoral thesis literature review, and from research proposals and conference presentations. In this weaving I demonstrate the range and forms of texts I need within my multiple roles as dancer, writer, researcher, teacher and mother. While I reveal the challenges I have in writing both narratives and traditional texts, my passion lies in crafting personal narratives of embodied experience.

Within feminist research there is a particularly strong history of use of personal experience and representation of lived experience through autobiographical writing. According to Nicola Armstrong and Rosemary Du Plessis, feminist researchers[5]

> write themselves into their texts as a way of making explicit their positioning as readers, as interpreters, and as constructors of theoretically informed stories [...]. The researcher is identified as actively constructing research narratives, rather than as engaged in the transparent transmission of 'authentic' or 'true' accounts of 'real' experiences [...]. (1998: 109)

As individuals, we make our experiences into narratives in our everyday lives, by telling stories that relate causal links, justifications, characters and interactions between characters, and explanations of why things happen for us (Richardson 1997). Writing such stories is a representation of our perspective on our experiences in the world, and a construction within which we interpret these experiences. Writing narratives can also provide an understanding of the lived experiences of others (Richardson 1997). In areas of enquiry such as sociology, this approach to writing narratives of personal experience is called autoethnography, what Carolyn Ellis describes as

> writing about the personal and its relationship to culture. It is an autobiographical genre of writing and research that displays multiple layers of consciousness [...]. Back and

forth autoethnographers gaze: First they look through an ethnographic wide angle lens, focusing outwards on social and cultural aspects of their personal experience; then, they look inward, exposing a vulnerable self that is moved by and may move through, refract, and resist cultural interpretations. (2004: 37)

So I write to reveal myself to you as a person in this book, using my various voices and experiences as a dancer, researcher, writer, teacher and mother. Each narrative makes links to wider philosophical, cultural and social theorizing, reaching outwards to understand and articulate my experiences. Each narrative is also locally situated in my everyday life, whether in the context of preparing a guest lecture or conference paper, travelling around the world, writing in my office or at home, dancing in the studio or performing. In this process of writing narratives or autoethnographies I am also discovering myself, writing to know and to reveal the multiplicity of my experiences. Laurel Richardson writes that such narratives of the self are

highly personalised, revealing text in which an author tells stories about his or her own lived experience. Using dramatic recall, strong metaphors, images, characters, unusual phrasings, puns, subtexts, and allusions, the writer constructs a sequence of events, a 'plot', holding back on interpretation, asking the reader to 'relive' the events emotionally with the writer. (1998a: 356)

Within my text I represent the voices and experiences of dance research participants, family members, friends and colleagues. Together we are the 'characters' that inhabit these narratives of lived experience.

In writing about my life, about research participants and intimate others, I am particularly mindful of ethical issues that can arise.[6] In addition to the requirement that all my research be approved in terms of ethical conduct and methodology before being undertaken, I also consider relational ethics. 'Relational ethics requires researchers to act from our hearts and minds, acknowledge our interpersonal bonds to others, and take responsibilities for actions and their consequences' (Ellis 2007: 3). Writing personal narratives and autoethnography are ethical practices – practices in which I must work with a feminist ethic of care and constantly consider the impact of what and how I write on all those real people I include as characters, on our relationships, on myself in the future and on readers of my work. As Carolyn Ellis (2007) writes

No matter that we might feel differently now than then and see ourselves as changed from the characters presented in the story, this portrayal of ourselves is edified in print. An important element in writing autoethnography then is considering the ethical responses to one's own story by readers. A second is considering the people in your life who might be distressed by your revelations. (2007: 22)

Photograph 1: In *Dancing Through Paradise* (Barbour 2010). Photograph by Marcia Mitchley.

As a consequence of my commitment to considering relational ethics, all research participants, and each of my family members, friends and colleagues who feature as characters, have read, had the opportunity to comment and consented to appearing in these pages.

As I develop my narrative approach to research through the following chapters, I draw from the excellent practices argued so eloquently and demonstrated so clearly in the work of Carolyn Ellis, Laurel Richardson, Pirkko Markula, Jim Denison, Norman Denzin, Yvonna Lincoln and others. Carolyn Ellis' (2004) wonderful book *The Ethnographic I. A Methodological Novel about Autoethnography* sits in pride of place on my bedside table, guiding me in progressing my writing through new research projects. As I edit these pages to share with you, her words remain a solid voice of support. Underneath Ellis' work on my bedside table are two other significant books. Firstly, *Possession* by AS Byatt (1990) and, secondly, *The Spell of the Sensuous* by David Abram (1996). Both continually remind me that writing can be moving and rigorous, conversational and theoretical, poetic and academic, and that there are multiple ways to engage in writing practices.

Throughout my chapters I engage with a range of authors whose words provide philosophical and methodological understandings that help me to theorize and articulate my experiences as a dance researcher more fully. Listening to their voices helps me to understand my political and social context, and in particular, to express my feminist commitments. Maxine Sheets-Johnstone, Iris Marion Young, Judith Butler, Elizabeth Grosz, Mary Belenky, Blythe Clinchy, Nancy Goldberger and Jill Tarule are all key feminist authors with whom I engage. Not surprisingly, I am also inspired by a range of dance researchers and writers. Sondra Fraleigh, Sue Stinson, Ann Cooper Albright and Susan Foster are dancers whom I admire for their ongoing scholarship and pedagogy. Other researchers are professional artists and insightful writers, such as Carol Brown, who I see as a catalyst in the development of creative practice as research. In seeking to understand my social, political and bicultural experiences within Aotearoa, I make connections to writing by feminists Ngahuia Te Awekotuku and Avril Bell, as well as historian Michael King.

I introduce a range of academic and philosophical terms throughout my chapters. For fuller definitions/discussions and links to other pages where terms are explored, you can refer to endnotes. I make use of *ngā kupu Māori* (Māori language words) throughout my text. I offer contextual interpretations of these words in parentheses on the first use of each word (except where they appear within a quotation) as well as in endnotes when further discussion is required (drawing on the Ngata Dictionary 2007). Endnotes also provide links between my discussions of underlying themes in the book that span different chapters. Photographs of dancing add further detail alongside my words and suggest more of the aesthetic of the dancing I describe.

Finally, to help guide you as a reader, I provide an outline of each chapter below. Each chapter has a specific narrative focus on articulating a topic of interest in terms of narrative and embodied ways of knowing. However, read in sequence, the content of the chapters accumulates, as experiences do in life, to offer a detailed engagement in embodied ways of knowing.

Reading your way

In Chapter Two – Becoming: Feminist choreography and dance research – I share some of the main influences that shape my solo dance making and refer to a specific choreography – *This Is After All the Edited Life* – as I introduce feminist perspectives, postmodernism and contemporary dance. Framed within the context of preparing and presenting a guest lecture, I embed my narrative in tertiary dance education in Aotearoa. I draw from my embodied experiences of crafting movement in the dance studio and of performing this solo dance. As I share in this narrative, travelling away from home prompted me to consider the themes of home and journey, and how both weave through my solo dance making and research. These themes resurface as I reconsider identity and culture in later chapters.

I specifically explore issues concerning representing dance research through narrative and autoethnography in Chapter Three – Dancing across the page: Representing research through narrative. This chapter features my colleague and supervisor Jane and I working together in Vanuatu, and our discussions as I develop a writing methodology for my research. In a sense, this chapter is a writing story, making transparent some of the processes and decisions I make in representing my research findings based on interviews and journal writing. These methods of narrative and autoethnographic crafting are applied throughout this book.

Chapter Four – Dreaming yourself anew: Choreographic strategies in women's solo contemporary dance – is focused around feminist choreographic strategies. Initially in this chapter, I discuss in depth the opportunities a phenomenological approach to dance research offers for examining lived experience and particularly dance making. Using a feminist and phenomenological approach, I represent the dance-making experiences of other solo contemporary artists – Raewyn, Jan, Susanne, Bronwyn and Ali – and discuss our specific solo dances. In the context of the discussion, we explore feminist choreographic practices in our work, leading me to articulate alternative modalities of feminine movement.

The focus of Chapter Five – Knowing differently, living creatively: Embodied ways of knowing – enables me to discuss different ways of knowing in detail and how these ways of knowing support living creatively. I initially focus on the growth of creative practice as research and what this offers to dance practitioners shifting into research and, conversely, to researchers undertaking embodied research. Again, I draw on the experiences of other solo contemporary dance artists, extending the discussion shared in the previous chapter about our specific solo dances to encompass our experiences of embodied knowing. The chapter is contextualized as I prepare to fly to Edinburgh to present these ideas at an arts conference. My travelling prompts me to reflect on and assert the continuing relevance of local, specific and embodied research. Travelling away from home again reminds me about my gendered identity and triggers reflection on my cultural identity. These experiences also prompt me to consider how reflecting on gender, identity and culture is integrated within teaching and learning with dance students.

Taking up the challenge to explore embodied, gendered and cultural identity with dance students is the focus of Chapter Six – Standing strong: Pedagogical approaches to affirming identity. As a dance lecturer I reflect on my teaching approaches in the dance studio as

I consider the challenges of tertiary dance education. I encourage my class of third-year undergraduate students to reflect on their identities through writing and sharing their own narratives, as they create short solo dances for assessment. My journal reflections and teaching notes are woven together with the students' own words from assessments and further reflections undertaken with me. This chapter is set, naturally, in the dance studio and campus environment in which I work everyday.

Chapter Seven – Improvising: Dance and everyday life – is a narrative playfully representing how I crafted a research proposal and investigated performance improvisation within my academic institution. Workshops with practitioner Kristian Larsen and our structured discussions around texts and dance studio activities form the basis of this chapter. We explore the use of improvisational scores, freedom, choice and coincidence in improvisation. Consideration of freedom and choice stimulated me to reflect on the choices and freedoms I have in performing in my everyday life.

Identity in everyday life is the theme of Chapter Eight – Performing identity: Tattoos, dreadlocks and feminism in everyday life. Reflexivity as an academic and my ongoing dance practice causes me to pause and take notice when I am confronted with curious questions about my tattoos and dreadlocks. While my tattoos and dreadlocks may cause anxiety for others unable to 'read' me easily, both are embodied manifestations of my own reclamation of personal and cultural identity and my attempt to affirm my feminist, political subjectivity. Situated in Aotearoa as I am, I affirm in this chapter that I am a *Pākehā* (New Zealander of predominantly European heritage) woman of my era.

In the final 'Chapter Nine – Imaginings: Reaching for a vision' – I draw together the themes explored within these pages, reaching for a vision, imagining the future for my family, my community and myself. I include writing about my recent experiences in choreographing and performing *Dancing Through Paradise*.

* * *

I hope that I am able to engage you, as the reader, through using narratives that stimulate kinaesthetic response and empathy with my experiences as a dance maker and a woman of Aotearoa. Through engagement in these narratives, I trust that you will also be encouraged to reflect and critically consider the value of your own lived experiences, your possible subsequent research and related political commitments. Ultimately, it is my intention to inspire you to affirm the value of your embodied ways of knowing as a basis from which to undertake creative action in the world.

Finally, this book represents my recommitment to the personal, to the embodied, to the specific and to the local, even in the midst of postmodernism and seemingly inevitable globalization. Consequently, as I hope this chapter has already demonstrated, I have leapt away from the style of many theoretical texts that abstractly expound upon the proliferating theories of embodiment, culture, nature, politics and knowledge. Instead I find firm footing in the specifics of my lived experiences. Theorizing and academic rigour is nevertheless present, underlying and integrated within my narratives and allowing my writing to stand not as autobiography or fiction, but with a confidence born out of feminist practice, qualitative narrative inquiry and autoethnography.

Notes

1. I adopt a practice of using indigenous *te reo Māori* (Māori language) names in my writing. I use the name *Aotearoa* (usually interpreted as 'land of the long white cloud') to refer to all our islands grouped together, rather than using the Dutch explorer Able Tasman's name 'New Zealand'. I do occasionally use the term 'New Zealanders', referring to all residents of Aotearoa, and regularly use the phrase *ngā iwi Māori* to refer to the different Māori tribes of Aotearoa. However, I prefer to use the individual's choice of reference to their cultural identities, such as *Tainui* (a specific Māori tribe), *Pākehā* (New Zealanders predominantly of European heritage – see endnotes in Chapter Two), Chinese-, Samoan-New Zealander, etc. I choose to call myself Pākehā and I explore issues relating to Pākehā identity and culture throughout this book.
2. Autoethnography is 'writing about the personal and its relationship to culture. It is an autobiographical genre of writing and research that displays multiple layers of consciousness' (Ellis 2004: 37). In Chapter Three I provide a fuller discussion of narrative and autoethnography.
3. Various creation stories of Māori tribes suggest that the demi-god Māui hauled the North Island of New Zealand out of the sea while fishing. Hence, the North Island is often called *Te Ika ā Māui* (the fish of *Māui*).
4. Limbs Dance Company existed from 1979 to 1991. They made a significant impact by introducing theatrical performance dance to the wider public through national touring and received critical acclaim as a modern/contemporary company who also toured internationally (Barbour and Whyte 1998; Jahn-Werner 2008).
5. I adopt a feminist practice of including the first names of authors the first time they arise in each of my chapters. This is a deliberate feminist strategy to draw attention to the prevalence and vitality of women researchers in the areas in which I work. I deliberately choose to cite feminist writers.
6. I note that I obtained ethical approval from The University of Waikato Faculty of Education Ethics Committee to undertake all of the formal research represented in this book. Each formal research participant who is a 'character' in the book has agreed to be identified by her/his real name and has had the opportunity to read chapters in which s/he features and to request editing where relevant. Where possible, I have chosen to include actual quotations by these research participants. However, some of the narrative scenes and descriptions of unfolding events have been changed. Again, each research participant has given consent for me to represent her/him as I have. I describe the process of creating narratives based on interview material and my researcher's journal entries in detail in Chapter Three. I use and further develop these practices throughout the following chapters. In Chapter Seven, I provide an excerpt of a research application for funding and include a letter of invitation to research participant and friend Kristian Larsen. This is an example of one aspect of my consideration of ethical practices.

    A further comment, however, concerns my writing that includes other real characters, such as my family members, friends and close colleagues. As I discuss above, I have carefully considered relational ethics (Ellis 2007), and in some cases, I have chosen a pseudonym for a real person, or have chosen not to use her/his name when this was a more appropriate option. I have also created fictional characters in some narratives where this was a better choice.

Chapter 2

Becoming: Feminist Choreography and Dance Research

With a sigh I rub my eyes, trying to focus on the laptop computer in front of me. I reach for my mug on the desk – cold green tea – but I swallow it down anyway. Stretching to lengthen my aching back, I catch a glimpse of the clock on top of the piano: 11.55 pm. I better finish my notes soon or I will be too tired tomorrow. As I return to my computer, I re-read my last sentences:

> My interest is in having my dance be me – I recognize that I am a body of knowledge and it is me dancing – sharing my body of knowledge. This is my basic strategy of address. I try to reflect the multiple ways I am, as a feminist in a postmodern world, and as a contemporary dancer, by offering many ways of sharing my knowledge through dance and narrative.

I have been editing and reviewing my notes again, feeling that it is particularly important for me to be well prepared for my guest lecture to dance students at another tertiary institution tomorrow.[1] It has taken me some time to feel confident about my own dance-making processes being the topic of discussion. As I mull over the words I have written, I wonder how the students will respond to my thoughts. I have heard other dancers say that dance cannot be philosophical. But I am 'impatient with that oft-repeated notion that dance can't be about philosophical issues, that it is ill-suited to this kind of inquiry, that its proper providence is the emotional and sensuous' (Dempster cited in Gardner and Dempster 1990: 47). I decide to use this quote from Elizabeth Dempster to initiate some discussion with the students about this issue. I wonder if they will agree that dance performance is a potential opportunity for political and philosophical comment, as well as emotional and sensuous expression. Yawning, I save my file of lecture notes, check on my sleeping son and stumble gratefully into bed.

In the morning I wake to the alarm clock beeping insistently. Struggling out of bed, I set my lecture notes to print from my laptop and claim the bathroom. More awake after a shower, I quickly read through my notes before morning preparations take over, rehearsing my comments and considering possible student responses to my questions.

Guest lecture notes

Feminism and contemporary dance

I would like to begin talking about my dance work by outlining some of the important philosophical influences on my life: feminism, postmodernism and contemporary dance. My interests and agendas, choreographic processes and strategies of address, all originate from these three influences.[2]

As a feminist, I am interested in critiquing dominant Western knowledge. As Rosemary Du Plessis and Lynne Alice comment, 'feminist scholarship is founded on the contestation of what counts as knowledge and what knowledge counts' (1998: xviii). I am aware that much of Western knowledge is based on the reasoning of white Western men and does not necessarily relate to my experiences as a woman in Aotearoa. As a feminist, I am particularly interested in critiquing Western understandings of what it is to be a woman. According to feminist thought, women have been stereotyped in very specific ways. This 'stereotypical femininity' is the collection of attributes that we associate with being female in Western cultures (MacDonald 1995). These attributes have been collectively reduced from the living qualities of real women to a distorted and one-dimensional 'ideal' (MacDonald 1995). In many Western cultures, the slim, white, small, shapely, youthful, weak, emotional, irrational, obedient and passive woman represents the ideal woman (Bordo 1989; MacDonald 1995; Wolf 1991). Over time, this ideal has translated into a social theory of what it is to be a woman, through the productive effects of patriarchal institutions, practices and media (Barbour and Thorburn 2002). Women learn to conform in order to be socially acceptable and desirable, becoming mediums themselves for reproducing these stereotypes (Bordo 1989; Gamble 1999; MacDonald 1995). So this stereotype has become productive in creating and conditioning individual women, and despite being a social construction and an idealization, stereotypical femininity has often become understood as natural for women. Stereotypical femininity, in this sense, is a form of oppression and it continues to undermine feminist action (Wolf 1991).

Susan Bordo (1988) argues that the pursuit of slender femininity through fitness training (or dance) represents a further form of tyranny – the 'tyranny of slenderness' – rather than the empowerment that gyms (or dance studios) may advocate. Thus, any victory a woman might have in achieving a slender ideal feminine body is considered hollow to feminists, as it can be seen as simply complying with dominant stereotypes constantly portrayed by the media. In order to challenge 'the beauty myth' – to challenge stereotypes and redefine power relations – feminists argue that women need to be aware of and resistant to oppression in its many forms, including stereotypical femininity. Perhaps by being resistant, individual women might potentially be able to re-create themselves as women.

The dancer as a cultural stereotype of femininity

Some feminists argue that the female dancer epitomizes the cultural stereotype of femininity. Feminist dance writer Carol Brown (1999: 13) writes, 'The dancing body as a regulatory type is upright (straight), lean, compact, youthful, able-bodied, and feminine.' Through demands from the physical rigour of dance training – the 'tyranny of slenderness' – and the influence of femininity as portrayed in the media – the 'beauty myth' – the dancer might easily become the image of and reinforce stereotypical femininity. The stereotypical ideal feminine woman in Western cultures is therefore potentially realized in the woman dancer.

I have experienced the conditioning power of stereotypical femininity. Personally, I am aware of the delicate line I dance between standing as an exemplar of stereotypical femininity and acting as a politically responsible feminist. It creates a paradoxical situation for me, and is one of the issues I continue to explore in my research. Through reading feminist theories, I have come to think of stereotypical femininity as something I can resist. While I will be, to some extent, culturally constructed, there are possibilities for me to re-create myself. In dance making, I can investigate stereotypical representations of femininity and female identity. Through dance performance I can draw attention to the ways that I am 'both shaped by and resistant to cultural representations' (Albright 1997: xiii–xiv). As Ann Daly (1993) comments, lived experience in contemporary dance can be a site for feminist investigation. I find that reading feminist writers provides me with alternative understandings that I can embody in the dance studio to explore re-creating myself as a woman.

For example, Judith Butler argues that gender is a performance, 'a repeated stylization of the body' (1990: 33). I value her idea that femininity is constructed – a set of repeated acts by women that accumulate over time to give the appearance of a kind of natural femininity. Mostly this idea is appealing because, in understanding femininity as a performance, Butler (1990) opens up the possibility for deliberate failures or resistant acts in the performance of stereotypical femininity. Perhaps a woman could choose to perform differently, to be a resistant performer, rather than simply being a site of cultural production. While I am, to some extent, culturally and socially constructed, and of course I am very specifically embodied, there are still some possibilities for me to re-create myself. And I see potential for such re-creation in dance making. I find this perspective empowering.

I also experience the ongoing 'somatophobia'[3] of Western knowledge (Grosz 1994), which privileges mind and knowledge over body and experience. As a dancer, I attempt to understand my world through embodied exploration, but I have often felt like what I 'know' as a dancer does not count. Sometimes my experiences as a woman dancer can be understood in relation to the political situation, allowing me to articulate a 'politics of the personal'. I realize that it is not only what we have in common as women and as dancers but also what we each know from our different lived experience which is important.

Does this make sense to you? I am trying to say that who I am makes a difference to my dance and to what knowledge is relevant and important to me. Being feminist results in my desire to validate my dancing experiences and my alternative knowledge. In particular, feminism leads me to critique and challenge stereotypical femininity in dance. I will talk more about my feminism later, in relation to my specific choreographic decisions.

I would like to speak briefly about postmodernism and what it means to me as a feminist. I imagine you have discussed postmodern dance in your dance studies classes, but what about postmodernism in general? Postmodernists (in this general theoretical sense) are also concerned to critique Western knowledge, contending that it is not possible to 'discover' ultimate, universal theories and truths that apply to all contexts and all people (Fraser and Nicholson 1990). Instead, what counts as truth and knowledge varies in different cultural, social, political and historical contexts. Truth and knowledge are not 'discoverable' from the world, but instead constructed by people in each unique context. Just as truth and knowledge are not constant and universal, individuals are not constant, fixed, unified subjects. Instead, postmodernists see themselves as multiple, shifting, changing and developing depending on their context (McRobbie 1997). In terms of postmodernism, as well as feminism, it is important for me to consider my life and my dancing in relation to my specific context and to acknowledge my fluid and multiple selves.

We dancers are situated within specific social, historical, political, environmental and cultural contexts, and we create within and in response to these contexts. Like each of you, the contemporary dance and performing arts communities here in Aotearoa are my context (Jahn-Werner 2008). I agree with Sally Gardner and Elizabeth Dempster that 'Movement is still for me a most productive and challenging means of thinking about and reflecting upon the world' (1990: 43). As contemporary dancers particularly, I believe that we can work with a specific intention to foreground our dancing bodies, bodies that are responsive to our world. As Ann Cooper Albright (1997) argues, such a responsive dancing body

> engages with and challenges static representations of gender, race, sexuality, and physical ability, all the while acknowledging how deeply these ideologies influence our daily experience […]. Much contemporary dance takes up and plays with these questions of movement and meaning, giving us some brilliant examples of how physical bodies are both shaped by and resistant to cultural representations of identity. (Albright 1997: xiii–xiv)

When I dance I work with the intention of situating myself as a feminist and being responsive to my context, aware of and aiming to interrogate culturally static representations of female and dancer identity. I do see my dance making as a potential context for contemporary feminist critique and action.

* * *

As I think through these comments my son Tahukiterangi is beginning to wake up. '*Mama*' I hear him call. '*Kei konei au*' (here I am), I call back as I walk to his bedroom. I shift my attention to dressing him and getting breakfast. Finishing my toast, I glimpse the dining room clock – 8 am – time to get going. Eventually ready with backpack and lunch, Tahukiterangi watches as I cram my *kete* (woven flax bag) with notes, books and DVDs and make a final check through my freshly printed pages. We pack our bags into the car and drive to *Kohanga Reo* (te reo Māori immersion early childhood education) where Tahukiterangi will spend his day.

As I drive through the Waikato region, I worry about whether the dance students will be familiar enough with feminisms and postmodernism to understand me. Reminding myself to be succinct in presenting these ideas, I acknowledge that while feminism is crucial for me in dance, the students will have a range of perspectives and may not make the same links I do. I do not want to lose them with academic terminology either. I remember from my years of dance training how hard it was just to concentrate when dealing with the ongoing fatigue and emotional pressure of dancing. I consider asking the students to engage in discussion of one of my solo performances, hoping I can offer an interesting and relevant guest lecture. I will give them a task to identify some of my choreographic strategies of address or means of communication in a DVD copy of my early solo *This Is After All the Edited Life* (Barbour 2001c). Knowing that these students have read Susan Foster's (1986) work on strategies of address, I think this task will be relevant to them.

The sun is shining and the air crisp – one of the clear days of autumn that I love. I turn up my car stereo, humming along as I drive. I pass the two-hour journey remembering how I had begun developing my choreography for *This Is After All the Edited Life*. When I began to choreograph that particular solo, I copied a poem by New Zealand poet Lauris Edmond into my creative journal.

> […] the glossed camellia leaves
> stood still, poised as though to be
> the more exquisitely excluded
> along with the pale petals we did not
> notice as intently we leaned and talked
>
> each word brighter-bodied for
> the shadow of the ones we did not say
> – this is after all the edited life
> to cut, to prune, select, is my profession
> – I did not know such practice
>
> could command a lazy room of polished leaves
> and sun […].

> Excerpt from *Camellias I: Femme de lettres*. (Edmond 1986: 49)

These lines of poetry still speak to me of my choreographic practices and my writing practices in research. Both seem to be a constant and careful process of editing and selection, reshaping and rearranging aspects of my experience. I like the way the editing/choreographic process allows for chosen aspects to be 'brighter-bodied'. Edmond's poem resonates with my feminist interests in the politics of the personal and in valuing my individual experiences. I love her awareness of her own constructive acts as a poet and her reflexive interruption into writing. After I first discovered this poem, I was inspired to name that solo dance *This Is After All the Edited Life* and to explore two themes that were central to my life at that time: finding a home and journeys.

Remembering back to the year before I decided to begin doctoral research in dance, I recall my journeys travelling through the South Pacific and across Canada. This 'overseas experience' was full of adventure and excitement – a kind of 'rite of passage' that many of my peers undertook too (Bell 2002). One of my strongest experiences in travelling across the world at that time had been becoming more aware of what the place 'home' meant to me. I had created pages of lists, sketches and short stories in my creative journal, identifying sounds, smells and experiences that suggested 'home' for me. The cry of the *Ruru* (Morepork owl) in the night; surf or waterfalls in the distance; rain on a tin roof and wind in the trees; the smell of the bush, *Ponga* (silver ferns) and river water; daffodils and honeysuckle and jasmine; warm, bare wooden boards under my feet; dusty signs on gravel country roads; the caress of cool, deep, river water; a bush-clad high rugged skyline.

When I returned home to Aotearoa and to Waikato to undertake my doctoral study, I was faced with re-adjusting to a university context and to academic writing. In a sense, I was trying to find a philosophical home for myself in my research as well as a literal place to live. I really missed the constant new experiences and the variety of challenges that journeying offered me. As much as I could, I continued travelling throughout Aotearoa, and I recall that reading a wide range of academic material also helped me feel as though I was still 'travelling'. More and more journal notes and stories emerged as I tried to make sense of my experiences and theories, writing on planes, in cafes, at the beach and in the bush. At that time I began to see my choreographic and my research processes as a journey. And I deliberately took all of those experiences into the dance studio with me.

I found that the choreographic process allowed me to bring these personal experiences, themes and academic theories together to explore new relationships, juxtapositions and connections between them through movement. As Elizabeth Dempster writes, 'The process allows me to bring together in a kind of laboratory, un-alike, incompatible ideas, activities, objects, so that they are held in temporary, sometimes strained relationship. And through this intensification connections which were at first only dimly sensed are revealed. These dances are […] a process of discovery' (cited in Gardner and Dempster 1990: 46).

I brought my experiences of home into the studio, through CD sound tracks of water and birds, a collection of large stones from the beach and other things I carried around in my kete – green tea and honey, academic books, my creative journal, maps, extra clothes and keys. Using these sounds and props I improvised movement material in the dance studio. The large, round, dense stones that I had 'borrowed' from the beach interested me. They sat in a cluster in the dance studio, like an expectant audience to my choreographic process. I experimented with carrying them, holding them close to my body, feeling their weight and texture on my belly. The smaller ones I could cradle like *taonga* (precious treasures) but the heavier ones dragged on my arms, feeling like a burden I struggled to contend with. Placing them on the floor, I explored the possibilities for rolling, dragging and moving them. I discovered I could swirl my body around and over the stones, moving them slowly as the tide did. Standing on them reminded me of where they came from – the wild site of waves and land meeting on the West Coast of Aotearoa. Moving the largest dense stone taxed my strength entirely. It felt almost immovable, like an anchor stone, and when I sat on it to catch my breath it became a welcome resting place and point of reflection. Improvising and freely associating as I moved, I carried the smallest stone around with me like a worry stone; I built a structure like I was trying to build theory; I piled the stones up, creating a cairn, a traditional way of marking a point to assist with navigation. Suddenly the stones became navigation stars too – the Southern Cross in the night sky – and then stepping stones, a path. My themes of home and journey began to weave together for me revealing new connections and possibilities.

Movement material flowed through this process; pointing gestures to indicate directions, stretching to the points of the compass, a hitchhiking thumb extended in hope of a ride to somewhere else, a hand raised in question or outstretched feeling my way in the dark from one place to another. I lengthened and extended my limbs, reaching out from my anchor stone to my environment and to the stars beyond.

As movement material evolved I crafted sequences, playing with dynamic, momentum and choreographic techniques of repetition, retrograde and splicing. And I worked with imagery. Across a line of stepping stones I created a short journey, my memory of picking my way along the shoreline, the wind tugging at my hair and clothes, the smell of salty sea water in my nostrils and cold water splashing up my legs, overriding the studio space. My ears filled with the rhythm of the waves, my eyes adjusted to the distance of the horizon and my breathing deepened. A deep sense of peace from this particular visualization infused my working process.

It came to me at some point during this process of dance making that my theme of journey was something of a metaphor for my life, for my research process as well as for solo dance making. But I knew that 'metaphor' is a literary term, 'a device by which we are told that something is, or is like, something that it clearly is not, or is not exactly like' (Burroway 1996: 264). Although a good metaphor might work somewhat as Elizabeth Dempster (cited in Gardner and Dempster 1990) describes in the choreographic process, a movement is not a word and movements cannot be related exactly as words can. Janet Burroway comments that a good metaphor should 'surprise us with the unlikeliness of the two things compared while at the same time convincing us of the aptness or truth of the likeness' (1996: 264). Something rather metaphorical seemed to be happening for me in my dancing, but the more I speculated, the more it seemed to me that movement metaphors were very difficult to convey. Sometimes movements could operate as signs, pointing to ideas or intentions, like my hitchhiker's thumb could point to my desire to catch a ride with someone. I was

Photograph 2: In *Fluid Echoes Dance* (Barbour et al. 2007). Photograph by Cheri Waititi.

tempted even to imagine that my hitchhiker's thumb could stand in place as a symbol of my desire to catch a lift. But symbols are supposedly transferable across contexts (Burroway 1996) and I doubted that this movement within my dance would be clearly understood as a symbol of my desire to catch a lift, much less my theme of journey.

I imagined whether I could take this movement – my hitchhiker's thumb – and show that it was like another movement, pointing away with my other hand, for example, and thus create a movement metaphor. As I pondered these possibilities, I could see the words, 'she looked at me like a reluctant hitchhiker', but again I was unsure whether the movement could convey such a metaphor clearly. However, it was fun to experiment.

As I worked to structure my movement material, I continued to explore how I might share my experiences – the sense of peace that had come for me, paradoxically through the juxtaposition of the themes of home and journey. In order to let my dance stand as a metaphor for my own life and research journeys, I realized that I would have to layer signs and symbols with the movement material and framing of the choreography. Aiming to communicate, I began the careful selection and editing process for my solo dance.

* * *

I slow the car to negotiate traffic through Ngāruawāhia, my trip to Auckland today taking precedence over my memories of dance and research journeys. Travelling this busy road, I note the changes in the landscape as autumn begins to take hold. Leaves of all shades adorn the trees and collect in the gutters, swirling as I drive by. Reflecting on the hours I spent in the dance studio experimenting with movement, props and images makes me realize what a great opportunity this is to discuss my solo dance making. I decide to ask the students if they can relate to my feminism and note how they respond to my dancing body as they watch the video of my solo dance. Still driving north through the Waikato landscape, I begin to think through the comments I will make about the specific influences of feminism on my choreographic practices.

Re-creating myself in dance – resisting stereotypical femininity

Being a feminist dancer in a predominantly Western culture here in Aotearoa, I am aware that women's bodies are regularly displayed as objects for consumption, within advertising, fashion, pornography and entertainment. The images of women offered for consumption present stereotypical femininity as the ideal. Consequently, when a woman stands up in social contexts, she puts herself in a position where she is likely to be objectified, to be consumed by an expectant audience. I am aware that people are adept at reading the features of body weight and muscle tone, skin colour, height, hairstyle, manner of dress and make-up, and making instantaneous judgements about the social acceptability and worth of a woman. (You might like to recall your immediate impressions of me when I first came into this seminar room.)

A dance performance gives people permission to look at me at length and to measure me against these dominant images of femininity. If I measure up, then I might be reinforcing stereotypical femininity and I might be accepted and understood in relation to how well I conform. If I do not measure up, I may simply be ignored. Not only do I find myself in this paradoxical situation by standing up in social contexts but as a dancer, perhaps this situation is worsened.

Carol Brown (1999) discusses her concerns about the dancer as a cultural stereotype. Along with being lean, compact, able-bodied, youthful and feminine, it seems to me that being heterosexual and being Pākehā⁴ could be added to the list. I can see that I could be read as a fitting much of this stereotype of a feminine dancer. And consequently, I might be ignored and/or my feminist interest in resisting and re-creating stereotypical femininity simply overlooked. Despite sometimes seducing myself into believing that dance audiences are savvy to gender performances and are interested in my dancing communication, I suspect this might only be a comforting illusion.

Nevertheless, as a feminist it is important for me not to unconsciously reproduce stereotypical femininity and feminine dance in my solo work. Carol Brown's insightful comments inform my studio practice. She argued that

> this body is only a stereotype if it continues to reproduce the tired gestures of a classical inheritance […]. In practical terms, dancers need to be aware of how their bodies, often unwittingly, reinforce certain bodily ideals, and begin to undo some of the assumptions made about them, through what they hopefully do best: movement invention. (Brown 1999: 16)

So, when I was making *This Is After All the Edited Life*, I inspected my own movement for stereotypical feminine gestures, movement qualities and actions. Some examples of these kinds of movements include a typical one-leg balance with the other high in the air (a classical ballet *arabesque*), or movements performed with a gentle, graceful, soft quality with eyes averted from the audience. I kept some movement that seemed feminine, allowing myself to 'perform woman' and then deconstructed this performance. I did this by contrasting and splicing feminine movements with deliberately non-gendered and gestural movements, and by using direct, clear and articulate movement quality. For example, I contrasted a somewhat seductive look and movement, with my finger upheld as though cautioning. I added in atypical elements, like the recognizable hitchhiker's thumb or a shoulder shrug, and I pointed at and verbally addressed my audience. Looking directly at my audience, I challenged them to see me as a person looking back, not a passive body to be objectified and 'consumed'. And I attempted to undo what I set up, again and again, developing (at least for myself) an experience of performing a different femininity.

The framing of choreography is also very important to the overall effectiveness of dance, as you know from your reading of Susan Foster's work (1986). So when developing costuming with a designer, we constructed costumes that included both feminine and masculine items.

We created a feminine costume that I deconstructed and reassembled on stage, then used as a projection screen and then as a bed sheet. And we replaced this with an oversized man's shirt and trousers, and then again with a combination of both. I had a sense of re-creating myself and of being multiply female, rather than only stereotypically feminine. But I felt that to some extent I would continue to reinforce stereotypical femininity despite these (somewhat obvious) efforts to deconstruct it through clothing changes. Ultimately, I wanted to foreground my experience, not merely my body and clothing, and to communicate my ideas. So I needed some other strategies of address.

Kinaesthetic strategies

Dance educator Susan Stinson (1995) offers an understanding of kinaesthetic strategies that I find useful in choreographing. She argues that it is through the kinaesthetic sense that we come to learn more about ourselves, our relationships to others and the world. Sondra Fraleigh also expresses her sense that dancers are intelligent bodies and that 'thinking arises through material physical sources' (2000: 57; also see Gardner 1999; Sheets-Johnstone 1999). The kinaesthetic sense is particularly influential in this bodily intelligence or thinking through corporeality. In addition, it is the kinaesthetic sense that helps us to understand movement, 'to go inside the dance, to feel ourselves as participants in it, not just as onlookers' (Stinson 1995: 43). In my dancing I wanted to find movements that other people would understand because they were familiar to them from their own experience, or at least recognizable – movements that would evoke a particular response, memory, emotion or experience. Experimenting with developing gestures in the studio yielded movement that I thought might enhance a sort of kinaesthetic recognition or empathy with my experience (Foster 1995). Sitting upright on the floor with my head down, legs loosely apart in front of me, I rubbed my eyes like a sleepy child. I hoped to share the way I struggled for clarity in understanding, rubbing my eyes as though somehow clearer vision would resolve things. And then, still sitting I raised my arm straight above my head, stretching it insistently, attempting to get attention. I hoped to express my desire to communicate with others, to try to understand the world around me and to share my own experiences. I lay curled on my side with eyes closed, shifting position irritably and then rolling over as though in a disturbed sleep. Standing while pointing in one direction and looking in another direction, I wanted to share my confusion about where I fitted in the world. I lugged those heavy stones around during performance, the weight dragging on my body and becoming a burden to bear. Standing on a stone looking down, I extended my toes over the edge tentatively as though testing the waters. Through kinaesthetic strategies of address I hoped that perhaps my movement experiences might resonate for others, allowing me to share them. Then I might step away from unavoidably representing myself as simply a feminine object and, perhaps, communicate intelligibly.

Through the actual process of moving, bringing feminist theory and experience together and re-creating myself in response, I came to new understandings of femininity. Relating my theoretical interests to my experiences and dancing the new relationships, I came to understand and re-create my femininity differently. I also began to wonder if I could write about my performance experiences. I experimented in my creative journal with how I might represent my embodied understandings from dancing my solo.

This is after all the edited life

Still ... breath flowing smoothly in and out ... weight and tension releasing as I lie on my side. The sound of waves rolling against the shore in the distance. Drifting images and memories and a sleepy awareness. A gentle wave-like sense of suspension, dreaming of sun, the beach and water.

And then, far off, thunder ... registering in my unconscious. Rolling over, settling, finding release, and then thunder again, disturbing my rest. Disconcerting, coming closer, intruding... Fragments of voices, and a lingering question, infiltrating my calm sleep and shifting my awareness. I linger on the point of sleeping and waking, inhabiting that released state in which strange connections arise between memories, plans, dreams, instinct and reason. Fragments of emotion and frustration awakening in my bones. Disturbance overtaking my released state. Struggling between sleep and clarity. An old memory ... instinct rather than reason comes to my rescue (Woolf 1929).

The sound warps, taking over the gentleness of the waves and a deep bass sound kicks in, resounding in my centre. It pushes me into movement, twisting, tying myself in knots and attempting to untangle myself. I'm forced from sleep into a state of uncomfortable awareness. I roll to crouch, twist up and then turn to collapse into sleep. And then twisting to sitting again, listening to voices in my memories, searching to define my own truth, and frustrated by the contradictions. I desire to share my struggle and I open my awareness to the audience. My arms lock my torso, restricting my breath and then lift to unwind so I can breathe deeply, and then my struggle continues as I travel across the wooden floor. I stagger as though carrying a heavy burden of care, worry, responsibility, expectation, and loss. Contradiction overwhelms me, hindering my movement as I search for a resolution to the tension between the dominant stories I'd been told since childhood about what it was to be a woman, and the flickering instincts I nurture privately. Trying to let my tension release as I cross and uncross my arms and slowly I find more and more chances to breathe deep. I unload my heavy burden to the floor and step back from it as though to see it for what it is. Feminism has helped me to see this burden and to realize it is time to unload it. Finally succeeding as my lungs expand and I draw a full breath at last. I step back and then turn away to the audience, vulnerable, but able to breathe. At last I leave behind my burden and walk gently across the space.

With gentleness but clear intention, I lift a large round stone. The weight drags on my arms but I carry the stone to place on top of a bigger stone. With continued care I build a cairn from stones on the stage, a marker, a monument to laying down my burden. My cairn is a private reminder of my choice to lay down the dominant stories from my childhood and to walk a different direction as a woman. Engrossed in my task, but again an old memory, sound, voices, infiltrate my ritual and I leave my cairn and open out into movement.

My eyes draw me out into the space, desiring to communicate with the watching audience and to explore my differently contoured world. Fluidly moving, finding joy in unwinding and loosening my limbs and muscles, as I explore space. Meditatively I let my arms swing gently and I turn, as though in slow motion. I thread my arms through each other, reach out, suspend and fall into the floor, roll over my shoulder and twist onto my feet again. I respond in movement to gravity, embodying my intention explore space, dynamic, freedom and release. Enjoying moving outside the expected feminine movement patterns, I feel empowered. I dance through release to a state of being centred and calm. And having reached that state, I turn to the audience, seat myself on the stones, and speak directly to the people watching me.

I tell a story of how it is to research in dance, what it means to me to be feminist, and how I embody both. I can see people smiling back at me, responding to me, sometimes looking uncomfortable, or interested, or unsure. I stand and mark out the stage space with my eye, measuring distance and alignment. With deliberation again, I move the pile of stones individually, orienting myself in the world this time, creating a symbolic Southern Cross star pattern on the stage floor. And then I place myself in relation to the Southern Cross, locating myself on stage, in Aotearoa in the Southern Hemisphere, and I dance.

I open my heart and my lungs to space. I feel. I reach my limbs as though compass points from my centre, extending my imagination out to the audience, beyond the performance venue to my family and friends, deep into the flesh and blood of the land, and across the seas to my ancestors. I heal myself as I dance, allowing my own breath, sense of flow and movement dynamic to emerge. From where I stand I send my imagination out. I resolve my embodiment in the here and now of performance, in relation to others and to the world. I stand tall and I dream myself anew.

Once again I deliberately place the stones on the stage, creating a path to walk down. Walking down my own path, I hear 'I see feminism today as the activity aimed at articulating the questions of individual, embodied, gendered identity' (Braidotti 1994: 30).

> *Here I sweat a truth*
> *a conscious skin, bone, muscle map*
> *it could be enough to heal*
>
> *here I sing an emotion*
> *a melody of light, honey, tissue, blood*
> *it could be enough to dream*
> *here I shadow a truth*
> *like blur in a look*
> *it could be enough to feel*

here I stream an emotion
just a bridge between you and I
it could be enough to linger
at the threshold
but I'll shape my own path thank you[5]

Finally I arrive in Auckland, park the car under a shady tree and walk to the dance department. Now sitting in a circle of chairs in the seminar room, I look around at the faces of these dance students. I see fatigue that I remember from my dance training days, but also passion and interest.

Smiling at me, my dance colleague says, 'Well, it is my pleasure to welcome Karen to speak in class today. As some of you may know already, she is a dance lecturer at the University of Waikato and I've asked her to talk about her experiences in researching women's solo dance. Welcome Karen, it's nice to have you here.'

I suddenly feel nervous, but I smile and breathe deeply. And then I begin.

* * *

Just as suddenly my talk is over. Breathing a sigh of relief that I did stay up late last night doing extra preparation, I relax back in my chair smiling at the students. After a short stretch and break from sitting, my colleague encourages her students to consider questions to ask me. I appreciate the first obvious question from one student.

'How did you get started in contemporary dance?'

This question makes me smile as I realize I can tell them my little story about seeing Limbs Dance Company perform in the local community theatre when I was a child.

'I sat transfixed as the dancers transformed before my eyes. I still remember clearly being inspired by their movement and stage personalities.'

Enjoying the students' recognition as I describe historic dance works, I relate how I had known as a young girl that I wanted to be a dancer.

'So going to that Limbs performance,' I explain, 'was the beginning of my life as a dancer and led me to full-time dance training, professional work and to the dance research I am doing now. However, I did study philosophy and psychology first because my parents wanted me to get a "good" education and because dance was not available at tertiary level then. So I came to full-time dance training later than many of you.'

Some of the students comment on how they too had struggled to convince their parents that they should continue dancing and that studying dance was a legitimate area of tertiary education. My colleague confirms to her class that when I was studying dance, more of the students were adult students than is normal in classes now, and she reminds them that there are many more options in dance education for them today. Looking at the faces of these young students, I agree, noticing that many of them appear to have come straight from high school.

Raising her hand tentatively, an immaculately groomed, thin, young woman asks the next question: 'But you trained as a professional dancer. How come you aren't performing in a company now?'

I hesitate before answering this question, acknowledging to myself again that an assumption still pervades our industry that to be a successful dancer is to dance full-time in a professional company. I wonder if this young woman will be one of the few select New Zealand dancers who achieve this goal.

Taking a deep breath I reply, 'I think there are many ways to be successful in dance, but yes, I would have liked to have been a full time dancer in a company, at least for a while. But without many company opportunities available to me, I took on the challenges of fundraising, producing, creating and performing dance with a group of peers.'

Hoping to share my alternative path in dance with the students, I continue: 'Eventually I returned to further study and my dance research always includes performing and choreographing, what we call creative practice as research. I have found that this is a way for me to be a dancer, researcher and teacher while having a stable income to support my family. I encourage all of you to be open to different possibilities in terms of how you can be a successful dancer. There are good careers to be had in teaching dance in secondary schools, as well as in private studios, or working with dancers and non-dancers in community and health settings, or in arts administration, or in combining part-time dance with other work that will provide you with an income when you can't get fulltime company work.' As I suggest this, I realize that the immediacy of the next dance class and performance assessment for this training programme will likely overshadow any more discussion of the future.

My colleague uses my pause to prompt her students: 'Okay dancers, I think we have time for one more question before our class finishes today. Does anyone have a last question, perhaps relating to the theoretical ideas Karen discussed or what you noticed when watching her solo dance video?'

Some of the students are looking tired and beginning to lose interest I think. But one determined woman speaks up, eyes flashing and pen ready in her hand for note taking.

'Do you really think you can be resistant to stereotypical femininity in dancing?'

'Good question', I reply smiling at her and knowing that we are not the only ones who consider this question (see Markula 2006). My thoughts fly all over the place as I weave together previous experiences and new understandings to make sense in this moment. As I speak I try to pick out salient points, mindful that they are ready for a break.

'In some ways, perhaps you can answer your own question, having seen my solo on DVD. Do you think I offered an alternative performance of gender? Each of you in this class might have different answers, as might audience members. In one performance an audience member yelled back "what is it Karen?" when I was doing that movement stretching my arm up insistently like I was wanting to answer a question or tell people about an idea. It seemed that person related directly to my movements. What do you think after watching the solo?' I ask.

'Well, I did get some of those kinaesthetic strategies – you know tossing and turning in your sleep – I've experienced that too and I felt that kind of disturbed feeling as I watched you. And I felt the contrast between your kind-of twisted up movements that didn't seem very "feminine" but I could imagine how they felt, and the opening movements near the end where you seemed stronger and somehow bigger and more confident dancing. That looked like a dance sequence I would enjoy dancing. So I did feel something as I watched you dancing that I could relate to, though I don't know really if non-dancers would have got that as being resistant' she finishes. Some of the other students nod with her comments.

Smiling encouragingly, I offer this curious young woman a more specific answer. 'One thing I do know for myself is that when I am choreographing and actually inspecting my movement to remove or replace the most obvious feminine movements and qualities with alternatives, I do experience the process as resistant. I feel empowered, active and engaged personally in this process. This sense of empowerment comes from thinking about femininity as a performance that I can choose to succeed at or deliberately fail at – that choice is freedom for me. In everyday life, perhaps we might want to succeed at being feminine sometimes, and maybe sometimes in dancing other choreographers may require us to be feminine. But in my own work I can at least choose to try be resistant to it. Maybe some audience members only see my woman's body: they either reject or accept me as feminine rather than seeing something different in how I move and represent myself on stage. But I believe some people do engage in the feminist and philosophical content of dance work. More often these audience members are other women and this gives me encouragement to continue. I feel as though I am being resistant, I know I stimulate other women to consider different ideas through dance, and I think that this is success.'

Drawing my comments to a close, the students respond with applause when I finish. My colleague thanks me and releases the students to their break and their next commitments. As we chat briefly over coffee I realize that I have been able to connect my experiences in a new way today, through storying my life for the students. Sharing this with my colleague, we reflect on the ways in which being educators and academics enrich our own lives in dance.

* * *

Later, in the cool of the autumn afternoon as I drive home to my son in Waikato, I wonder if my storytelling, academic theorizing and solo will stay with the students as they move into the rush of final performance assessments. I still remember what dance training was like and the way in which small details like critical comments from a teacher about my choreography, or choices over costuming or lighting a performance, tended to overwhelm the importance of everything else. Now as a dance academic, my teaching and writing opportunities provide a context to reflect and to story, or re-story, my life and to help me make sense of my experiences. Like dancing, writing has become a passion for me, and I see both as different but complementary ways of knowing.

Notes

1. My acknowledgements to Raewyn Whyte for giving me permission to write about guest lecturing in her Dance Studies class some years ago.

2. Some of this chapter was published in J. Bolwell, (ed.), (August 2001). *Tirairaka. Dance in New Zealand* (pp. 5–11). Wellington, New Zealand: Wellington College of Education, called 'Journeys in dance-making and research'. Another portion of this chapter comes from a conference paper called 'Writing about lived experiences in women's solo dance making' published in P. Markula, (ed.), (2001), *DANZ Research Forum Proceedings*, (pp. 1–9). Hamilton, New Zealand: The University of Waikato.

3. 'Somatophobia' is a word Elizabeth Grosz (1994) coined to refer to the Western enlightenment fear of the body that still pervades much of the English language and Western philosophy.

4. Pākehā is a te reo Māori word used to describe New Zealanders of predominantly European heritage (Ngata Dictionary 2007). Historically, Pākehā have been literally 'white' (paler skinned than Māori), as well as socially and politically 'white' (originating from the United Kingdom and intent on colonization and spreading Western civilization). However, colour terms such as 'white' are no longer stable 'markers' of identity in Aotearoa. Use of the word Pākehā has taken on different meanings in relation to the foundational document, *Te Tiriti o Waitangi* (The Treaty of Waitangi) and biculturalism, as I discuss throughout this book. (For further discussion, see Chapters Five and Eight). Aotearoa, the home of indigenous Māori peoples, was colonized by European settlers but many resisted assimilation and today continue to assert indigenous rights as *tangata whenua* (people of the land, native people). My son is both Māori and Pākehā, although he usually identifies himself specifically, as is customary, in relation to his *iwi* and *hapu* (Māori tribe and extended family (Ngata Dictionary 2007)) (Bell 2004).

5. After writing this poem, I worked with composer Charlotte 90° to transform the words into the soundtrack for my solo *This Is After All The Edited Life*.

Chapter 3

Dancing Across the Page: Representing Research Through Narrative

'Time to destination: 40 minutes' flashes on the television screen over the rows of grey seats and passengers' heads. This 737 plane has almost completed its arc across the blue Pacific Ocean from the islands of New Zealand. In a few more minutes I will be there, arriving into the sun and warmth of Vanuatu. I awkwardly re-cross my legs and wriggle my toes in my shoes, wishing again that I had requested an aisle seat. I will just finish this chapter before we land.[1] My colleague Toni Bruce's words draw me back into my reading:

> The challenges of postmodernism to traditional ways of 'doing' research have been felt throughout the social sciences and humanities. In combination with feminism, cultural studies, constructivism, and other interpretive approaches, postmodernism has changed the way many researchers look at their work. However, it is only recently that researchers have begun to consider the implications of postmodernism for how they 'write' their research. (Bruce 1998: 3)

Toni's comments resonate strongly for me as I read them today and remind me of insights I have gained about writing. I remember vowing to myself that I would not waste precious time on diligently crafting more academic, third person and disembodied texts. Perhaps it was my feminism, or being a dancer, but after I finished my master's thesis, I vowed 'no more writing like that!'

An avid reader from a young age, I have been particularly interested in women's writing, art and music. Perhaps because both of my parents were teachers, they instilled in me a desire for social justice and a respect for different people and cultures, both through our family conversations and by their example. These formative experiences and my broad reading led me to express my reflections on social justice and culture from a broadly feminist perspective, even as a young woman. However, it was not until my mid-twenties when I was training in dance that I began deliberately reading feminist theories.

Sensing I needed more of a challenge than undergraduate readings, my dance studies teacher had invited me to explore her bookcase. I borrowed a pile of books, including Judith Butler's (1990) *Gender Trouble: Feminism and the Subversion of Identity*, Chris Weedon's (1987) *Feminist Practice And Poststructuralist Theory* and Peggy Phelan's (1993) *Unmarked: The Politics of Performance*. I was thrilled with the invitation from my teacher, although in retrospect I realize my choices did not provide an entirely easy or logical place to start with feminist theory. Nevertheless, that is where I began, and on finishing my dance training I continued to read feminist writings, gaining multiple understandings and knowledge that for the first time I related to personally. These feminist knowledges and ways of knowing inspired me as a dancer too, being part of my motivation for establishing a women's professional performance group called Curve Dance Collective[2] when I graduated from dance training.

When I began my doctoral study at The University of Waikato, I became part of the Department of Sport and Leisure Studies.[3] Perhaps this was an odd place for a dancer to undertake research, but I shared with my new colleagues and research supervisors a passion for understanding moving bodies from a socio-cultural perspective. Questions about how to represent moving bodies and movement experience were foremost in our minds, regardless of whether our passion was sport, leisure, outdoor recreation or dance (Denison and Markula 2003). Sitting in on a graduate paper that focused on ways of representing research with Jim Denison, a new world of narrative inquiry and autoethnography opened up to me. In classes we discussed the dual crises of representation and legitimization – the recognition that written language could never fully represent or convey lived experience, and that research and writing were a subjective construction that could not be legitimated by objective, universal standards (Denzin and Lincoln 2000). I related directly to these crises, having lost faith in the third-person so-called 'scientific' writing during my master's thesis, and turning to more personal and contextual expressions. Within these graduate classes, we read contemporary ethnography and autoethnography, and discussed writers who attempted to express lived movement experiences through rich and vital texts and who developed 'new' research methodologies.[4]

When I undertook library searches for dance publications, however, I discovered that few dance researchers were writing in autoethnographic and narrative forms (or at least, few were using these terms to describe their methods at that time). There were a few wonderful writers who shared my interest in embodiment and were part of what Deidre Sklar (2000) identified as a kinaesthetic trajectory in ethnographic dance studies. While I found some inspiration in ethnographic dance studies, I was also quite cautious about more traditional dance anthropology, noting the long history of Western colonization enacted through anthropology in general (Smith 1999). Within the dance literature I connected most closely with Susan Stinson's research and reflection on her own movement experiences (1995). Stinson describes 'knowing in her bones' in poetic vignette form:

As a person whose professional home has been dance for many years and whose personal home has been my body, I experience thought as something that occurs throughout my body, not just above my neck. Until I know something on this level – in my bones so to speak – the knowledge is not my own, but is rather like those facts one memorises which seem to fall out of the brain the day after an exam. (Stinson 1995: 46)

Stinson argues that her lived dance experiences contribute to her development of representational forms of writing, like the example above. When thinking about how to represent her own and other dancers' experiences in words, Stinson advises telling a richly descriptive story of lived experience. She comments, 'I look for words that do more than communicate abstract ideas. I want to use sensory-rich images in hopes that a reader can feel the words and not just see them on the page' (Stinson 1995: 52). Stinson concludes that through cultivating the kinaesthetic sense and using evocative kinaesthetic words in stories, the dancer may more appropriately represent dance and research experiences, and potentially offer the reader a better understanding of embodied ways of knowing.

Another inspirational writer is phenomenological dance researcher Sondra Fraleigh, who states that she 'wanted to weave the intuitive voice of the dancer into a descriptive aesthetics, slipping from the first-person experiential voice to analytical third-person theory, as phenomenology does' (1987: 54). Through inclusion of short personal vignettes about her own learning experiences, and segments of writing from her dance students, Fraleigh validates embodied experiences and demonstrates her appreciation of dance as a way of knowing. She includes poems that speak directly to me about the experience of a dancer and academic moving about the world. Fraleigh's poems 'convey a portrait or reveal something about the culture they represent' (Fraleigh 2004: 6)

I too am actively involved in the project of seeking a deeper understanding of movement itself as a way of knowing, and the work of Susan Stinson and Sondra Fraleigh helps me represent my own movement experiences through narrative. As a Pākehā and feminist in Aotearoa, I feel that my positioning needs to be transparent in my research (Smith 1999). I conclude that the best I can do ethically is to research my own experiences and those of my own community and peers, and to share my findings through kinaesthetically rich narratives.[5] (In this sense, I reject an 'etic' anthropological approach and embrace an 'emic' approach in which I highlight my status as an 'insider' dance researcher (Kealiinohomoku 1983)). I value my embodied knowing and I believe that as a dancer I can contribute to new knowledge about dance. As Allegra Fuller Snyder (2006) suggests, I can also use my embodied ways of knowing to contribute to knowledge generation in the wider world – embodying the environmental activist slogan 'think global act local'.

Desiring alternative forms of expression, I explored beyond the dance literature, relating closely to the strong history of established feminist work in autobiography, personal narrative and storytelling. I also discovered and remain aware of Frances Mascia-Lees, Patricia Sharpe and Colleen Cohen's (1989) feminist caution:

At this profoundly self-reflexive moment in anthropology – a moment of questioning traditional modes of representation in the discipline – practitioners would do better to use feminist theory as a model than to draw on postmodern trends in epistemology and literary criticism with which they have thus far claimed allegiance. (Mascia-Lees et al. 1989: 7)

I love the 'healthy resistance' of these feminists, in part because it supports my instinct that (at least to some extent) postmodernism had been a means for white men to appropriate

Photograph 3: Karen in *Fluid Echoes Dance* (Barbour et al. 2007). Photograph by Cheri Waititi.

some of the self-reflexive and creative practices that feminists and indigenous researchers have long engaged in. In contemporary theorizing and practice, the postmodern forms of anthropology that aligned with feminist creative practices were called 'new ethnography' and writing personal experience stories was called 'autoethnography'. Despite my concerns about using terminology from one academic discipline in another, I do like the term autoethnography, and I use it interchangeably with 'personal narrative' (as discussed in Chapter One).

*   *   *

But back to the question at hand: how can I write the dance research I have undertaken with a group of women from my own dance community? Squished though I am on this plane, I keep turning this question over and over. Provocative discussions with my very postmodern supervisors, reading narrative writing and undertaking qualitative feminist research into lived experiences in women's solo dance making have led me to this moment. Here I am, flying across the South Pacific for two weeks of intensive writing with Jane, one of my supervisors. And, oh so conveniently, the setting for my writing is the main island of Vanuatu where Jane is currently working as a volunteer. I anticipate disciplined writing because I am determined to go home with a chapter draft. I am also desperate to be a good feminist researcher, to account for the conditions of my knowledge production and to offer 'unalienated' knowledge, as Liz Stanley (1990) puts it. So I feel that it is important for me to clearly locate my research representations in the lived experiences of the women I interviewed in my dance research.

But I am still unsure about specifically how I might represent their voices. I have screeds of notes in my journals both from interviewing these five dancing women and from my own dance making during my doctoral research. I also have observations written after attending their performances and, of course, interview transcripts. What sort of research text should I construct from all of this rich material? I have found ways to represent my own lived experiences through personal narratives, but how might I represent the voices of others? Somehow I feel that their stories should be revealed in an 'organic' way, rather than being quoted from the interviews and then inserted into a third person text as illustrations of my theorizing.

Reflexivity

A collective shifting of the passengers around me prompts me to peer out the oval window. Far below, breaking the glittering blue of the ocean, are small green islands rising surprisingly confidently out of the water, white sandy edges sculpted by meeting tides. Like tiny links in a chain that connect us throughout the South Pacific … I ponder how such small links can be found in the vastness of the ocean. Rather like being a researcher I suppose, making links between ideas in the vastness of human experience. Now what was it that Carol Brown writes? I riffle through my papers, accidentally nudging my neighbour.

After apologies and small talk with my fellow passenger, I locate Brown's sentence copied into my journal: 'By avoiding the "objectivist" stance, prized amongst androcentric methods of research, and entering her own subjectivity into the research equation, the feminist recognizes how her cultural beliefs shape the orientation and outcomes of her research' (Brown 1994: 202).

So, my embodied subjectivity as a feminist researcher and as a contemporary dance maker must be present in what I write when I write about other dancers too. I need to locate myself in my own particular socio-cultural context, and make my links and relationships to the other women evident in what and how I write. Clearly, I am playing an interpretive role in my research, even in the choices I will make as to how exactly I represent all of our voices in my writing. I hope that if I can offer a multitude of experiences of dance making, including the other women's voices alongside my own, then perhaps I can invite the possibility of other ways of knowing.

From my reading of research in ethnographic, feminist and sociological writings about movement, I know that there are some very interesting examples of other writers who are reflexive and overtly acknowledge their role in constructing narratives based on research. This is the work of feminist contemporary ethnography that I most enjoy, and I consider Laurel Richardson an exemplary writer. I am inspired by her well-crafted stories and by her passionate discussions about research methodology. As the plane begins to descend, I scan one of Richardson's papers quickly.

> The ethnographic life is not separable from the self. Who we are and what we can be – what we can study, how we can write about that which we study – is tied to how a knowledge system disciplines itself and its members, its methods for claiming authority over both the subject matter and its members. Our task is to find the concrete practices through which we can construct ourselves as ethical subjects engaged in ethical ethnography – inspiring to read and to write. (Richardson 2000a: 16)

Richardson's work (1997, 1998a, 2000a, 2000b, 2005), and other eloquent prompts from qualitative researchers like Carolyn Ellis (1999, 2000, 2004, 2007, 2008; Ellis and Bochner 2000, 2006), stimulated many rich and new representations of research, such as can be seen in the inspiring work of Stacy Holman Jones (1999, 2002, 2010a), Soyini Madison (2007), Carol Rambo Ronai (1998; Rambo 2005, 2006) and Tami Spry (2000, 2001, 2006, 2010), to mention a few. I tuck my papers into my bag, putting aside these questions about writing as the plane begins to descend.

As soon as the nervous moment of touchdown is over, my fellow passengers clamber for luggage and peer out the windows. Bag of papers and travel documents clutched in my hands, I duck under the arch of the exit door at last, savouring the hot breath of the island and the first touch of the tropical breeze. Stepping down onto the tarmac and scanning the people behind the gates, I quickly pick out my friend and colleague Jane's fair hair amongst the dark-haired women waiting for returning family and the sun hats of tourists.

'Straight through' gestures the Vanuatu Customs Officer, and then Jane and I are embracing, laughing at our good fortune to be here and not at home in the cold southerly winds of winter in Aotearoa. We happily exchange travel experiences as we collect my luggage, and after changing into *lava-lava* (sarongs) at her home, we head straight to the water for a swim.

Representing findings from interview transcripts

Later the following day, I am settled comfortably on the *whāriki* (woven mat) in Jane's living room, pondering my next move in this slowly unfolding research experience. I have already conscientiously edited the interview transcripts, removing 'ums' and diversions, as we veered away from and back towards topics on my interview guide. I have sent the transcripts out to each of the women to invite them to participate in editing. And now I have highlighted in bright yellow what seem to me to be salient points relating to each of my research questions.

Struck by some excerpts I have come to know well, I realize that I love the actual word choices and passion evident in many of these comments. The words of my friend, previous teacher and research participant Raewyn Thorburn, immediately invoke visceral memories of my dance training.

I've probably talked to you before about the colonization of the body by technique, and by choreographers. When I began training in modern dance, jazz and ballet, my dance voice was reshuffled and at times torturously categorized to the norms of those codified techniques. My natural sense of weight and momentum in space was pruned, coerced or restricted into patriarchal criteria of how the body worked. Also, the presence of self-expression or one's own creativity was ignored and even denied. It's a different viewpoint not using technique and virtuoso dance now in my own dancing. I am allowing myself to take full ownership of my movement again. Now dance comes from all the things that influence me. I'm allowing a natural process or impulse – the impulse to allow movement to be alive, active, to let it 'speak', to listen nerve and bone to it. That's the place that the work comes from. It's an integrated place. It's very alive and fertile and there's an immediacy of action. It's like you commit yourself to your own aesthetic and to your own body: it's that simple and that demanding.

Re-reading Raewyn's words, I wonder how necessary or ethical it is for me to edit this section of her interview transcript. There is no need for me to offer an interpretation here; Raewyn's own reflection makes her experiences intelligible. Shulamit Reinharz commented that 'Rather than giving phenomena conventional pigeonholes, we should pay attention to the particular descriptions women use. We should hear the richness of speech, and allow our writing to be similarly complex' (1992: 40). Allowing Raewyn's words to stand as she spoke them also means that she can remain active in the co-construction of the understandings developed.[6] But, of course, the way in which I situate Raewyn's comments could further contextualize her statements. I am sure that feminist Germaine Greer writes something about bodily experience of political oppression … again flicking through pages in my journal I find the quote: 'The personal is still the political. The millennial feminist has to be aware that oppression exerts itself in and through her most intimate relationships, beginning with the most intimate, her relationship with her body' (Greer 1999: 424). In dance, it seems to me that this oppression exerts itself through some of the processes of movement training and then in our subsequent choices when we create movement motifs and choose choreographic structures.

Narrative options

Perhaps I could write a short vignette set during the interview with Raewyn. I could describe the scene as we sat at her dining room table, Dictaphone between us, cats prowling for attention. I have some journal notes about how the interview went and I know Raewyn well enough to describe her to a reader – her elegantly composed body and sleek bobbed hair framing a keen intelligent face. Maybe I could mention reading Germaine Greer's book and use this as a link to some theorizing of women's experiences.

I also have journal notes from watching Raewyn's performances of *Sensory Ensemble* (Thorburn 1997), presented in an evening of solo performances by women at a local art gallery. I remember Raewyn warming up in the performance space in front of the audience, recognizing that she had not begun her dance with the usual separation that performers make between 'performing' and 'living'. Instead she just continued seamlessly from one into the other, in this way, resisting audience expectations of the 'dancer'. As Raewyn warmed up, she described her feelings and sensations to the audience. She spoke confidently as she moved, dressed in simple loose black pants and a top, and she was clearly both engaged in moving and responsive to her audience. I was fascinated as I saw in her performance a depth of experience and maturity in her knowledge of movement. I did not see her struggle to achieve 'technical dance' movements. I realized that her dancing was at times improvisational and responsive to her moment-by-moment interests, and at other times deliberately chosen to allow her enjoyment in her own choices.

At one point during the performance, I was genuinely surprised as Raewyn donned an apron and began peeling potatoes. I was moved to giggles as I watched her experiment with peeling potatoes while lying on the floor, and I understood her attempt to think about household tasks as a dance. Sitting in front of her computer, Raewyn parodied the typical uncomfortable hunching and then straightening positions as she attempted to type, and eventually typed for us to see, the words 'perhaps all my movement is dancing' on the screen. Raewyn was using everyday, pedestrian and gestural movement in her dancing, and I experienced an enhanced sense of kinaesthetic empathy as an audience member, recognizing her experiences and relating to them personally. As Raewyn shifted into 'dancing' again, I saw her move with release and ease and obvious pleasure in the sensations of her body. I could feel myself relaxing and breathing more deeply as I watched, empathetically experiencing her dance on a kinaesthetic level.

By weaving together these journal notes, my recollections of interviewing Raewyn and her words from the interview transcript, I could create a narrative vignette. I know that narrative vignettes allow researchers to give richer ethnographic portrayals of lived experiences and to enhance a sense of authenticity (Humphreys 2005). Vignettes also allow researchers to demonstrate their own self-reflexivity. Theoretical discussion and commentary can be embedded within the specific events and experiences described so as to provide a believable context. Doing so helps to address concerns about research 'reliability'. Validity in narrative representations of research means that the researcher seeks verisimilitude: that is, the writer seeks to evoke 'in readers a feeling that the experience described is lifelike, believable, and possible' (Ellis and Bochner 2000: 751). According to Carolyn Ellis and Art Bochner, the validity of research might also be judged in relation to 'whether it helps readers communicate with others different from themselves, or offer a way to improve the lives of participants and readers or even your own' (2000: 751).

So writing a vignette is one option I might explore to share Raewyn's comments about her dancing experiences in an evocative way. Turning back to the interview transcripts in front of me, I read her words again. Hmmm ... did not Jan Bolwell comment about some sort of internal investigation and expressing in richer ways? Maybe I need a series of vignettes for each of the individual interviews, with accompanying descriptions of their solo work drawn from my journal notes? Or what about a collective story even? I have read collective stories that meld together participants' voices with other sources, like newspaper and magazine articles, novels and discussions (Bruce 1998, 2003). In these stories the voices of different women were combined into and expressed through the actions of believable fictional characters. While this would allow me to include our actual words, I wonder if it is relevant for me to combine our individual stories into one collective story. I think there is richness in our differences that I need to honour.

Of course, others before me have experimented with and created a wide range of narrative expressions of lived experience, appreciating too that writing can be a way of knowing (Denison and Rinehart 2000; Ellis, 2004; Markula 1998, 2005; Markula and Denison 2000, 2005; Richardson 1998a). Covering diverse research topics, I have read literary novels and essays, poetry, performance texts and performative texts that explore fragmented text and bricolage, personal experience narratives, autobiography, autoethnography and research stories of many types.[7] Sharing personal lived experiences and being self-reflexive are extolled as virtues of the narrative researcher, just as they are also characteristics of feminist researchers, phenomenologists and ethnographers.

Crafting a specific narrative

Still turning over the multitude of possibilities for writing my research later in the week, I confess my difficulties to Jane over lunch. As she passes me fruit and plates to set on the table outside, Jane responds with a reminder that writers need 'to understand ourselves reflexively as persons writing from particular positions at specific times' and further that writing 'frees us from trying to write a single text in which everything is said at once to everyone' (Richardson 2000a: 9). Jane draws on Laurel Richardson's words, commenting that in the end 'there is no such thing as "getting it right", only "getting it" differently contoured and nuanced' (2000a: 10).

Pouring cold pineapple juice into tall glasses, Jane suggests I consider what I would do if I was choreographing.

'Just imagine that you are making a group dance for these women and for you to dance in. How might you begin?' she prompts as we both sit down at the table. I take a long drink of juice as I consider Jane's question.

'Well,' I begin hesitantly, 'perhaps I would create a duet between two who shared a similar experience. Maybe I'd have sections within the choreography that involved trio and solo too. Maybe a solo danced by someone who expressed clearly a central theme.' A sense of excitement begins to grow in me. I can imagine that there could be sections where all six of us dancers could move together, as well as time for each to express a personal perspective. However, these ideas are for dancing and might not be the same when I write. I need to ponder this idea more.

Jane is smiling at me across the table. 'Why don't you consider a choreographer's approach? Because you might find the answer to your writing questions through thinking as a dance artist.'

We eat under the veranda, sharing avocado with fresh French bread, melon and juice and I find myself relaxing in the heat.

'So what are you going to do this afternoon? You must take time out from writing to enjoy Port Vila. Why not walk up for a swim in the cascade pools?'

Our talk turns from various fun options for my afternoon to Jane's morning progress at work. There is certainly an irony in my being here writing feminist dance research while Jane works to improve policy and social recognition of women's legal status and rights in Vanuatu.

Jane says, 'The progress is slow, rather like the pace of island life. And these women's rights policies are regarded as rather far down the priority list by the men in charge.' Nevertheless, Jane soon catches the little bus back to resume her work and I am left to my musings. Trickles of sweat run down my back as I stand to clear up the table after our lunch. Definitely time for a swim.

* * *

Lush, low and wide, leafy plants open out to the afternoon sun, brushing my legs as I walk along the worn path and begin the small hill climb to the cascade pools. I stop where the overflowing pools widen and allow bathing, joining three young women also seeking respite from the heat. Exchanging small talk, we giggle at each other's different stories of how we escaped from the day's tasks.

'Yes, I am supposed to be working too,' I laugh with them. And then, relaxing in the cool water, another idea dawns on me. What if I created a longer group story that somehow allowed each of us dancers the opportunity to speak as ourselves? Our comments could form a conversation, organized like duets and solos and group dances within this story – a kind of written dance. I could be a character too, as dancer and researcher equally, alongside Raewyn and Jan, and the other women and research participants Bronwyn Judge, Susanne Bentley and Ali East! I could create a fictional context for our comments, imagining that we had actually spent a day together all discussing our solo dance-making experiences. Perhaps I could create a duet using Jan's comments as responses to Raewyn's comments, within a fictional discussion. I wonder what my other supervisors would think about this idea. After all, they argue that ethnographic fiction involves

> a sense of freedom to invent and play; the measure of success, too, lies as much in the telling – characterization, plot, diction – as it does in the message – coherence, relevance, impact. Ethnographic fictions direct us to think and feel narratively, where reality is not what it is, but what we make it into. (Denison and Markula 2003: 113)

Much later that evening, and with renewed enthusiasm, I once again trawl through my pages of transcripts, this time searching for quotations by one dancer that make sense as responses to another. I seize upon two pages, carefully ripping them into smaller bits. Placing these small strips of text on the mat around me, I ponder the relationships. It feels almost like choreographing, finding chunks that actually seem to fit together and resonate for me as though they were parts of a whole. It is not until I hear the first overly optimistic rooster heralding the dawn that I stop, hastily tidying my papers, and collapse into bed. I hope Jane will not despair of me when I tell her I had to rip up my transcripts.

Late the next morning, I read with amusement Jane's small note that simply says, 'Trust your feminist instincts, and remember that you can do things differently! I'll see you this evening.'

I leap straight back into my work, pausing only to make fresh peppermint tea. Having decided to create a group narrative, I can see that I have a number of challenges to resolve. I want to link together exact individual quotations now, so that they appear as a conversation. I also want to include discussion and analysis of our experiences within the frame of the fictional narrative. I know that I need to maintain validity in my narrative and that I can do this by enhancing verisimilitude – I need to write so that the conversations seem believable (Ellis and Bochner 2000).

I set to work on my computer this time, finding Raewyn's quotation and another one from Jan. I try describing Raewyn, picturing her elegantly composed on a sofa, and words flow from my fingertips onto the screen. I imagine the scene as it might have played out, incorporating my own voice to add another layer of interpretation and explanation.

Reading from my laptop screen, I consider what I have so far. After the quotation by Raewyn about how she now takes full ownership of her movement and again quoting the women's words directly from interview transcripts, I have written:

I notice that Jan seems to be relating closely to what Raewyn was saying about taking ownership of her movement, nodding and listening intently. Sitting comfortably in her chair, one ankle crossed over her knee and speaking in a deep resonant voice, Jan describes to us how her loss of interest in traditional dance classes as a mature dancer led her to take up yoga. Jan tells us:

When I was younger I was in my body in a sort of unconscious way. I remember the physical challenge, the sheer joy of conquering something physically, rather than the thought of movement exemplifying some feeling or thought. Dance was so presentational, so external. You know, all those things of 'Have I got my leg in the right place?' But I think there comes a point if you are going to sustain an artistic life, where you have to go beyond the physical. The process of yoga made me become more introspective about my moving, in a way that dance had never done. So I started to have much more of an internal investigation that has definitely informed my choreographic processes. I don't think so much of the outward form. I'm more concerned about how I am expressing from the inside. I am finding new ways of expressing myself that are richer. The intellectual, emotional, philosophical processes that underpin my movement are the more important things: dance imbued with meaning.

For me, although the process of yoga training could also be regarded as colonizing, it certainly has encouraged self-reflection and personal growth for me, rather like Jan describes above. The ways that Jan describes herself as having internal investigations, expressing from the inside, and discovering 'dance imbued with meaning' resonate for me with understandings of dance as thinking in movement (Sheets-Johnstone 1999). Jan describes how dance has moved from being an external and presentational activity to personal movement and investigation of her lived experiences: an embodied way of knowing. Embodied ways of knowing: this is really at the heart of my research.

With this recognition arising from my writing processes, I sense too that this method of crafting my research narrative might work. At least I now have a computer file of quotations to replace the ripped-up interview transcripts. And these quotations are linked together, establishing relationships between the dancers' various experiences and my own. I can see how I can weave our voices together with my feminist readings to construct an understanding of embodied ways of knowing.

Jane's footsteps signal her arrival home after work and she finds me elated, despite 'pins and needles' in my legs.

'Jane, I think I have it: I think I know how to write my research in a way that honours our lived experiences!'

'Excellent' she replies enthusiastically, dropping her basket on the bench and opening the fridge.

'I'll pour the wine and you can talk through your ideas.'

Notes

1. An earlier version of this chapter called 'Dancing across the page: Representing research findings from interviews and journal entries' was presented to and appeared in the conference proceedings for the *Congress on Research in Dance 38th Annual Conference: Continuing dance culture dialogues – Southwest borders and beyond*, 2–5 November 2006. Tempe, Arizona, USA.
2. Curve Dance Collective – 'Creating space for women in dance', presented a debut season in 1997 and four subsequent seasons. Curve is not currently active.
3. Graduate programmes in dance studies have only recently become available in Aotearoa in some tertiary institutions. I was the first person to complete doctoral research in dance in Aotearoa and I returned to The University of Waikato to do so because the one potential supervisor with dance knowledge, Dr Pirkko Markula, encouraged me to begin a PhD and to apply for a Doctoral Assistant position. To date, the University of Waikato does not offer full degree programmes in dance, although I teach dance papers at undergraduate level, and graduate level dance research continues. At the time of writing this book, I have supervised a number of master's students and my first doctoral student has just completed.
4. See Denzin and Lincoln (2000); Markula (2003); Richardson (2000a, 2005).
5. Researching my own and my peers' experiences was the focus on my doctoral research 'Embodied ways of knowing. Women's solo contemporary dance in Aotearoa New Zealand' which I completed in 2002.
6. Each of the research participants, as Raewyn's quote demonstrates admirably, was articulate and actively engaged in co-constructing meaning. I chose to include lengthy quotations from the interview transcripts throughout my narratives to support and honour their generosity.
7. For examples of these types of writings see Bruce (2003); Fraleigh (2004); Gannon (2005); Humphreys (2005); Jutel (2006); Markham (2005); Markula 2003; Markula and Denison (2000, 2005); Pinney (2005); Pringle (2001); Richardson (2000a, 2005); Rinehart (2003); Stinson (1995); and Tsang (2000). I have already mentioned the work of Jones (1999, 2002); Rambo (2005, 2006), Ronai (1998), and Spry (2000, 2001, 2006, 2010).

Chapter 4

Dreaming Yourself Anew: Choreographic Strategies in Women's Solo Contemporary Dance

The welcome winter sun streams in my office window. Clasping my hands and stretching my arms over my head, I gaze outside. From the seventh floor today I can see far West into the distance, unusual for this time of year, picking out both the familiar contours of Mount Pirongia and the outline of Mount Karioi against the horizon. Below me is the familiar city of Hamilton and the university campus. While the campus appears quiet from this height, closer inspection reveals students walking the rhythms of campus life to and from buildings. The cold southwesterly wind will likely blow in some rain this afternoon, making this a good day for writing indoors.[1]

My desk in front of me is littered with books and papers.[1] Rough dog-eared corners and faded highlighter pen notes distinguish some papers from others. When first reading these papers for my doctoral research, I had drawn lines under and around words and added numerous comments of my own. A well-marked article by Kristine Kellor (1999) stands out. I recognized my own experiences in her resistant words. I too had 'soul wrenching struggles to synthesise and theorise' in the flesh (Kellor 1999: 25). This was how Kellor describes her experiences in attempting to reconcile her 'storied' body with the academic 'knowledge' she gained at University. This morning I dug out Kellor's article again as I realized that I still relate to these comments, researching and teaching at University with a body of dance and life experience.

I recall much earlier days of studying philosophy before I trained as a dancer, and how I had learned about the dual ontology of Western knowledge, particularly reading from Plato and Descartes of the 'virtuous' and 'necessary' separation between mind and body. At that time I had leapt into readings on philosophy of the mind, not questioning whether there was a philosophy of the body. With my Pākehā classmates, I had engaged in amusing thought experiments regarding the possible relationships between body and mind, but I did not relate this to my own experiences as a woman and as a dancer. I had not known how to value experiential learning or lived experience. I had enrolled at university to gain 'knowledge' and I elevated rational thinking over experience as 'the' way to learn. I thought that my body was an object that gave my mind a place in the world. I was unable to articulate my experientially based and embodied alternative understandings, and my master's thesis was written in the typical disembodied style of philosophical and academic texts of the time.

It was later, reading feminist theorists, that I came to appreciate that the underlying ontological dualisms I read in philosophy not only included mind/body, but also knowledge/experience, object/subject, culture/nature, reason/emotion, thought/sensation, public/private and universal/particular. Eventually I recognized that the basic rules of this system aligned the first of each pair together and the second of each pair together (Code 1991; Grosz 1994; Hartsock 1983; Warren 1988). The result of this alignment was that, as Nancy Hartsock explains, 'these dualisms are overlaid by gender; only the first of each pair is associated with the male' (1983: 297). Consequently, I came to appreciate the feminist argument that western 'knowledge' was based on dualisms in which being rational, thoughtful, objective, cultural and public were all aligned with being male and masculine. Being female and feminine aligned with the body, emotion, sensation, subjectivity, the natural and the private. I also saw that this western system of dualisms has been, and continues to be, oppressive for women and has resulted in an acceptance of reasoning as the only way to 'knowledge', privileging of mind and exclusion of body, and a stereotypical and oppressive construction of women/femininity. The feminists I read were concerned with critiquing and changing these oppressive systems.

I realized that I need to be resistant to the practices in my learning and knowing that separate my mind and body. As Kristine Kellor describes herself, I too feel a 'passionate and deeply embodied desire and commitment to find ways to intervene' in the dominant ways of knowing and in 'knowledge' itself (1999: 28). I want to discuss and understand my experiences as a woman and as a dancer. I want to share my embodied experiences in an attempt to acknowledge, contextualize and theorize them. I can no longer divorce my knowing from my embodiment as a woman. I cannot be a 'philosopher', conducting disembodied thought experiments about possible understandings of mind or 'knowledge'. My desire to 'know' in such a way that recognizes and values my womanly and dancing experiences persists in my work as a dancing academic.

Within the multitude of feminist perspectives I explore, I am particularly interested in how feminists have developed phenomenological notions of 'lived experience' and of the 'lived body'.[2] I shifted away from thinking about the body as a text and as language as a metaphor for everything (as expressed in a range of post-structural and postmodern positions), and towards privileging experience and 'embodiment'. I can see that feminist research is able to offer reconstructions in the form of alternative ways of knowing, of embodiment and of femininity. Rather than attempting to create feminist knowledge as a replacement for dominant western knowledge, my interest is in offering feminist perspectives to contribute to the range of accepted 'knowledge'. It seems to me that alternative perspectives that can contribute to new knowledge arise in the experiences of individual women like myself, within specific contexts and communities. For me as a feminist, such perspectives are not ultimate 'truths' about all women, but instead must be recognized as an individual woman's alternative perspective. It was for these reasons that I decided that a way for me to contribute to 'knowledge' in my doctoral research would be to explore women's re-creations of ways of knowing, embodiment and femininity, within our specific dance contexts and communities. To guide me in my research I drew on feminist writers who offer a critique of Western knowledge, and who understand ways of knowing, embodiment and femininity differently from the previously accepted history of Western knowledge.

Opening my tattered spare copy of my doctoral thesis, eyes flicking over the familiar contents page, I locate my writing on phenomenology. Revisiting my discussion of phenomenology and particularly Iris Marion Young's work (1980, 1998a, 1998b) seems the best place to begin today. I woke with more clarity this morning than the previous few days, perhaps due to the cold southwesterly chill in the air, and I realize that Young's 1980 work 'Throwing like a girl' continues to provide useful foundations for 're-thinking' moving in the world, not only in dance, but in life in general. So it seems timely to me to pick up my thesis discussion of her work. Settling into my chair and scanning pages, I review my own earlier writing on phenomenology, considering what I might include as I prepare this book chapter.

Feminist phenomenology: Lived experience and body

Phenomenologist Iris Marion Young (1980) draws on understandings from Maurice Merleau-Ponty (1962, 1964) and feminist Simone de Beauvoir (1972) to develop an understanding of women's lived bodily experience. She wishes to articulate the specifics of women's movement experiences, something feminists had noted that Merleau-Ponty did not acknowledge (Grosz, 1994). Young focuses on movement aimed at achieving specific tasks, such as throwing a ball, and outlined the basic modalities of feminine body comportment (1980). She argues that a common experience of many Western women involves being both a subject for herself and object to herself. This kind of experience meant that women often tended to mediate their actions by imagining how they appeared as objects to others, at the same time that they also experienced their actions as intentional subjects (Weiss 1999; Young 1980). This experience resulted in a kind of discontinuity between a woman's intention as a subject undertaking a task and her action as an object that she saw in the world from an 'external' perspective.

According to Young (1980), a woman's feminine bodily experience was: 'intentionally inhibited' (by her perception of her own inability to achieve the task undertaken); 'ambiguously transcendent' (in that she concentrated action in one part of the body while the rest remained uninvolved); and had a 'discontinuous unity' (because she broke the connection between intention and action, between possibility and actual bodily achievement. In short, she hesitated). Young concludes her comments by stating that 'An essential part of the situation of being a woman is that of living with the ever-present possibility that one will be gazed upon as a mere body, as shape and flesh that presents itself as the potential object of another subject's intentions and manipulations, rather than as a living manifestation of action and intention' (1998a: 270). It seems to me that Young's work set precedent for feminist study of women's movement experiences separately from men's (1980, 1998a, 1998b) and, personally, her work became a basis on which I undertook research into women's dance making experiences.

Maxine Sheets-Johnstone (1999) also contributed a great deal to understanding of bodily knowing and the experience of movement as knowledge. She develops Merleau-Ponty's (1962, 1964) and Young's (1980) phenomenological work significantly, arguing for the primacy of movement over the primacy of perception. She comments that perception results from movement and so movement is 'the originating ground of our sense-makings' (Sheets-Johnstone 1999: 161). Sheets-Johnstone (1999) argues that humans learn about themselves and others initially through moving, by attending to bodily sensations of movement, rather than by looking and seeing what is moving. Movement is experienced through the kinaesthetic sense, which provides the individual with information about space, time, movement and objects, and their relationship to these things, as they change in the moment (Stinson 1995). Consequently, an individual is able to develop an understanding of what constitutes herself, and others, and to develop concepts to understand the world (Sheets-Johnstone 1999). The kinaesthetic sense is fundamental to our ability to move knowledgeably in the world (Sheets-Johnstone 1999). Sheets-Johnstone continues, 'creaturely movement is the very condition of all forms of creaturely perception; and creaturely movement, being itself a creature-perceived phenomenon, is in and of itself a source of knowledge' (1999: 132). In this sense, movement experience is profoundly and fundamentally significant in epistemology. Therefore, movement experience must provide individuals with knowledge, though not knowledge as narrowly defined as dominant Western 'knowledge' has been. It follows from the work of Sheets-Johnstone (1999) that experience is also a valid a method of gaining knowledge, alongside rational knowing.

* * *

Pausing to highlight the paragraphs of my text I have just read, I am reminded yet again of the poignancy of feminist phenomenological writing. Iris Young (1980, 1998b) and Maxine Sheets-Johnstone (1999) remain inspiring researchers whose work I re-visit regularly and whose words offer new challenges each time I engage with them. Their articulations led me to consider contemporary embodiment.

However, as I read these theoretical sections of my doctoral thesis, my writing does seem rather ponderous and disembodied. Reflecting, with the hindsight of the years since I completed this research, I wish I had had the courage to write much more of my thesis in a grounded, autoethnographic style. At that time I did not have the confidence to step further away from what a thesis literature review was 'supposed' to look like. I felt that needed to demonstrate that I could write academic texts first and then I could contrast that style with my choice to write subsequent chapters more creatively.

Scanning through the remaining pages of this section, I realize I could re-write this material now … stating that feminists who critiqued mind/body dualism and the body-subject of Merleau-Ponty (1962, 1964) desired, like I do, to shift the 'body' to centre stage in discussions about subjectivity and knowing. Like Elizabeth Grosz (1994), I too adopt the approach of phenomenology and the notion of the lived body. How could I ever fully understand subjectivity and knowing by considering the body merely as something to be cured or dissected?[3] As I have discussed earlier, Grosz argues that 'philosophy has established itself on a profound somatophobia' (1994: 5), and she instead aims, as do other feminists, to develop an

Photograph 4: In *You Know How I Feel* (Barbour and Mitchley 2005a). Photograph by Robert Fear.

alternative figuration of bodily subjectivity.[4] Bodies have 'all the explanatory power of minds', and considering 'bodies' rather than 'minds' also immediately reminds me of differences in gender and other markings like race and age (Grosz 1994: vii). My own differences have to do both with the corporeal aspects of me as an individual and with the 'manner in which culture marks bodies and creates specific conditions in which they live and re-create themselves' (Gatens 1995: 71). My body provides a sense of continuity as the intersection of biological, social and linguistic understandings (Braidotti 1994). I am neither completely biologically nor socio-culturally determined, but 'always already situated in an intersubjective (and thereby already cultural), spatiotemporal, fleshy (and thereby already natural) world' (Bigwood 1991: 66). My body is continually in the process of being shaped by social practices and is, at the same time, the means by which I am able to express my resistance to socio-cultural and bodily norms. I can creatively adopt positions in the world and function interactively (Bigwood 1991; Grosz 1994). Extending this point, Moira Gatens suggests, 'By drawing attention to the context in which bodies move and re-create themselves, we also draw attention to the complex dialectic between bodies and their environments' (1995: 69).

When I undertake detailed analysis of my body in my choreographic practice, I can identify the effects of both cultural construction and corporeality. I may be culturally constructed to some extent, but my embodied options are nevertheless limited by both the individual social history of my body and my corporeality (Diprose 1994/1995). According to this line of argument then, my lived body is always in a process of becoming, is always an experience in the making, rather than existing as a fixed entity (Albright 1997; Grosz 1994; Weiss 1999). As such, my woman's lived body is unstable and open to change, potentially resisting both socio-cultural and biological definitions (Albright 1997; Grosz 1994).

I continue re-tracing the development of my understandings through my thesis pages, shifting uncomfortably in my chair as I struggle with the traditional presentation of ideas I chose for my doctoral writing. Knowing that I can re-write my disembodied 'literature review' style of writing into a more creative and embodied form now eases my discomfort somewhat. I persist in my reading to refresh my memory.

Feminist understandings of embodiment

Many feminists appreciate the argument that embodiment is the existential condition of being a person (see Braidotti 1994; Grosz 1994; O'Loughlin 1995; Weiss 1999). An articulation of embodiment can draw attention to the specificity of individuals (O'Loughlin 1995), and to their particular differences in gender, race, age, ability, sexuality, history and experience. Embodiment has been understood as a subject's existence at the point of overlap between the physical and the cultural. Rosi Braidotti expresses embodiment as follows: 'The body, or the embodiment, of the subject is to be understood as neither a biological or a sociological category, but rather as a point of overlapping between the physical, the symbolic, and the sociological' (1994: 4). Embodiment neither refers exclusively to nor privileges natural/corporeal or cultural/social understandings, resulting in an experientially grounded view of an embodied person. According to Williams and Bendelow, 'meaning inheres in our bodily behaviours and its gestural significance rather than being the product of some prior disembodied "Cogito"'(1998: 8). This view requires the recognition that to be a person, you are necessarily only able to exist and to know anything, as a result of being embodied.

However, to some extent even describing 'embodiment' as a point of overlap requires an understanding of biological and cultural categories in an opposing relationship. There is a tendency to re-inscribe some sort of body/mind or cultural/biological distinction, even when trying to theorise embodment as an overlap or relationship.

From my perspective, embodiment includes recognition of individual difference and incorporates many things as one. I use the term 'embodiment' holistically to avoid the tendency to re-inscribe this biological/cultural distinction. I developed my articulation of embodiment as simultaneously and holistically cultural, biological, spiritual, artistic, intellectual and emotional, with recognition of difference in terms of race, gender, sexuality, ability, history, experience and environment.

* * *

Seeking relief from my academic writing and sitting position, I move to lie on my back on the floor and reflect on re-reading my pages of phenomenological writing. I can accept that a range of writing styles is required in my multiple roles as dancer, writer, researcher, teacher and mother. However, as I breathe deeply I reaffirm to myself that writing with an engaging, embodied voice is equally as important as experiencing embodiment in my dance research. I do acknowledge dance making as a lived experience in which I am immediately and reflexively aware of my world (Van Manen 1997). Through dance I can embody, express and reflectively articulate my lived experience. Having re-visited phenomenological and feminist research, I am also clear that focussing on the nature of women's lived dance-making experiences continues to be a valuable research agenda (Daly 1993).

Research into lived experience is 'a process of deepening and extending the quality of our coming to know; a process of changing the way we understand the phenomena of our experience' (Brew 1998: 39). Undertaking research to explore my own and other dancers' lived experiences allows me to investigate the experiential 'process' of dance making rather than focussing on critiquing the dance 'product'. I believe that in dance making I have the opportunity to dream myself anew or to re-create myself as a woman, despite the way in which female identity has been stereotypically constructed in Western societies, and perhaps typified in dance. I remain interested to develop my own choreographic strategies and to explore those used by other women, to foster an experience of re-creating femininity and feminine identity. This was the focus of my doctoral research and I have not yet tired of this project. It is not hard to recall my research experiences, discussing dance making with enthusiasm and delight in the opportunity to talk with women dancers I admire and respect.

Solo dancers talk (part one): Feminism and choreography

Discussion flows as we sit in this warm room overlooking the river, sipping herbal tea and talking openly of our solo dance experiences.[5] We have this day together, lounging on the comfortable sofas and large easy chairs. I look around at my friends and colleagues:[6] Jan – a confident leader and educator in dance, strong and resilient despite living with cancer; Raewyn – a soft-spoken, empathetic teacher, always ready to engage in a sophisticated discussion about patriarchy or femininity or anything else; Ali East – opinionated but quick to laugh at herself and at life, and keen to debate education, art and politics; Susanne Bentley – thoughtful and quiet as she considers her opinions about dance and choreography, and at times infectiously bubbly; and Bronwyn Judge – alert, engaged and intensely committed to her own investigations in dance and history. Their words and laughter fill the room. And myself, well, I am prone to ask many questions as a researcher and to listen with admiration, at times voicing my dance experiences in earnest.

Already, we agree that we share an appreciation of feminism and enthusiasm for solo dance making. We also share understandings, or more accurately, experiences, of embodiment from our dancing. Talk of what it is to be a woman and our understandings of stereotypical femininity in dance arises naturally as the day's discussion unfolds.

Stereotypical femininity and re-creating femininity

With concerns about stereotypical femininity fresh in my mind from research and creating my own solo dance, I want to ask the women about what they see as characteristics of femininity. I begin by commenting that I do not consider femininity itself to be problematic, but that the way in which the stereotype reduces the wide range of characteristics and qualities we women embody to a one-dimensional ideal concerns me greatly (MacDonald 1995). I personally have experienced the stereotype of femininity as both productive in conditioning me and as unproductively oppressive. I am interested in exploring our understandings of this stereotype, including personality characteristics, movement and body ideals, and considering how this impacts on our dance making. Developing this understanding helps me think about re-creating femininity, and I am interested to hear whether the other women consciously re-create themselves through dance making.

Raewyn responds quickly and speaks about how she sees 'that the predominant view of the feminine is weak, unfocused, doesn't know what she wants, needs to be rescued, is helpless, over emotional, irrational'. Her sarcastic comment that she is just 'thrilled' about this view prompts knowing laughter from the other women. Raewyn goes on to describe, with much relish, how she re-created femininity for herself (Barbour and Thorburn 2002). 'I rewrite "weak" as inner strength and intrinsic knowing, which to me is a high state of mental awareness or facility; "unfocused" as multi-layered, multi dimensional focus – take the multi-tasking, or the ability of a woman to have an overview and to see the larger picture or the consequences of things. So this focus has breadth as well as specifics. "Needs rescuing" as able to self manage. Women are working and earning money, as well as doing the majority of the housework, as well as maintaining emotional well being of the family unit. So they don't need rescuing. "Doesn't know what she wants" as being based on a non-feminine criteria, with the male viewpoint not knowing a female's. Or even more revealing: an inability to realize there is another viewpoint; shockingly the assumption that the masculine way is the only way. A male criterion is not necessarily suitable for a woman. She may be disempowered because she is not permitted a voice. She may appear "over-emotional", according to male criteria, but again perhaps her emotional response is a result of not being acknowledged within patriarchal contexts. So that when she is disempowered or is not able to exercise her rights or her voice, then she will get emotional. And if she could have her voice then she wouldn't need to do that.'

As Raewyn speaks I realize the alternative perspective she has on femininity. Rather than denying those characteristics that are considered to be stereotypically feminine, she is embracing and valuing them as legitimate responses. Understanding her own 'grief' over the denial of femininity, Raewyn has been able to analyse, move on and allow feminism to empower her personally. Raewyn's comments prompt a lot of thought and our discussion flows on.

Flicking aside her long silver hair, Ali leans forward to offer a different perspective: 'When I think about femininity I think also about the difference between femininity and masculinity. And I think I have mostly been particularly androgynous in almost everything I have created. I'm not being rebellious against femininity because I love it. I'm pleased that I am a woman and don't have the problems that men have in expressing those things that you were talking about Raewyn. I think that women don't mind admitting that we don't know something, that we are still always happy to learn and wanting to learn. We are much more willing to be equal with other women and other people. We strive for equality. I think these are things that may almost be able to be generalizations about women, but I might be wrong about that. It seems to me that they are particularly womanly kinds of aspects.'

There are nods of agreement from around the room. Thinking about the ideal body image and movement associated with femininity in dance. I comment, 'I am aware of the delicate line I dance between standing as an example of stereotypical femininity and acting as a responsible feminist. I've been inspired by a comment by Carol Brown (1999) that dancers need to be aware of how they may reinforce feminine bodily ideals unconsciously, and instead could try to undo these ideals through movement. As I developed my work I began to have more and more confidence in working with kinaesthetic strategies so that my audience could empathize with my experiences, rather than working in a deliberately resistant manner. I felt like I was managing to re-create femininity for myself and to express this through my dance making.'

I ask the group for responses to this idea that dance making can be a way to re-create femininity and to re-create ourselves as women. Sitting cross-legged on the floor beside me, Susanne responds, choosing her words carefully as she describes how she worked to avoid 'feminine' movement in her solo dance called *Someone Else's Weirdo* (Bentley 2000). 'I don't personally like dresses and I don't like being feminine. I don't particularly like flowery movement or "feminine movement". I prefer quite strong or harsh movement or to change or corrupt or adapt that which might be perceived as "beautiful". I don't want to say that every time that I make a dance, I change or corrupt or adapt. But at this particular time for my solo *Someone Else's Weirdo*" it was relevant.'

Re-crossing her legs as she reflects, Susanne resumes her comments, describing a particular experience to us. 'One day when I was coming home on the bus from the *Lord of the Rings* set, I saw an advert on top of the Embassy Theatre. I looked up and read "everyone is someone else's weirdo" and I started thinking about this concept. I thought about what I found weird. People have perceptions of who you are based on what you wear and what you look like. I thought about the way I felt in the dress (my solo costume was a restricting grey dress) and how I wanted to be seen. A dress is not what I would normally wear, and because it restricts my movement it provided lots of interesting ways of moving. I thought about being a mannequin, and I had lots of pretty movements, like the ideal women in 1950s advertising poses, which I wanted to try and corrupt a bit. Because of my height I'm aware that I can be perceived as kind of weak or young. I feel that I can wear a dress and feel okay about it with no hair, whereas if I had hair I couldn't wear a dress because I'd be too pretty and because of my height especially, I'd be too girlie. I guess shaving my head gave me a bit of confidence to be staunch, to feel stronger in myself, and kind of stand up to people. I made movements that were "wiping off" or "saying no" to people's expectations of me and "brushing off" social conformity.'

Susanne speaks about how she had deliberately tried to challenge and change, corrupt and adapt those movements that she considered feminine, particularly poses of the ideal woman. I think she was using some resistant choreographic strategies, and I sense her resistance is based on an underlying feminism. Susanne had also chosen to alter her appearance by shaving her head, so that she would not fit the ideal image. Discussion about height, weight and the idealized body image of women dancers follows Susanne's comments,[7] and I am reminded of Carol Brown's (1999) statements about the dancer standing as a cultural stereotype of femininity. I share her statement with the other women: 'The dancing body as a regulatory type is upright (straight), lean, compact, youthful, able-bodied, and feminine' (Brown 1999: 13). We discuss more specifically the issue of the ideal dancer and body image.

Jan comments on the relationship between the young, slim, toned, petite feminine body image and the dancer. 'There is a big issue with body image for dancers. Why shouldn't large-hipped and large breasted women be out there and look absolutely amazing, as they do in many cultures? You know it's regarded as something, as a real attribute, in other contexts. We don't regard women with good-sized hips and breasts in Western dance as having attributes, do we?'

Sitting opposite me on the couch, Bronwyn uncurls and stretches. I am curious to hear her thoughts and she adds to Jan's comments with a story. 'Last week I went to a belly dance club, and the woman teacher, who is my age, had this enormous belly! And it was just big and out there and naked, and she rolled it around and it looked wonderful … wow! I thought, that's not our stereotype. That is ageist too, because dancers are supposed to be young. But it depends what dance form you do, like you say Jan. There is that whole perception when you are dancing of what you should look like, and how your body naturally moves does affect the type of dance you perform. You have to find something that really suits and I think in modern dance, that is what people do. They choose the form and movement. That is why we have such diversity in modern and contemporary dance, because once you have your style and your movement, you have dance that suits your body.'

I speculate to myself that, perhaps, we became involved in contemporary dance because both 'success' and the desired range of movement were not tied so much to ideal body image.

Bronwyn's comments inspire a debate about the value of dance technique training for each of us as women. Raewyn describes dance technique training, particularly ballet training, as 'colonizing' the dancer's body. I consider how some techniques impose a set of strict and often dysfunctional rules and behaviours on movement, such as over-rotation of the legs at the hip and hyperextension of the back. Technique training can also limit or curtail possibilities for expression and creativity in movement, as certain types of 'feminine movement' are valued over others. It seems to me that this is especially an issue for women already limited by patriarchal social contexts. Raewyn's view of technique training as a colonizing process is one I think we all can empathize with to some extent, from our experiences. Our awareness as dancers of the oppressive effects of stereotypical femininity goes beyond thinking about our bodies – perhaps we can also see the effects of dance technique training on our movement experiences and choices as choreographers. I see Raewyn's commitment to choosing movement based on embodiment and expression of her feminine principles as her attempt to resist and subvert oppression in dance.

Wanting to hear more from Raewyn about movement, I ask her about choreographic strategies and whether she thinks her choices of movement in choreography are subversive. She replies, 'There are definitely times when I consciously subvert, that's for sure, such as directly interacting with the audience thereby breaking the usual separation of performer and audience. Talking to the audience is a way to subvert the separation that conventionally exists. Also, the norm is being "together", ready to be seen when you step onto the stage. I'm rather working with coming on stage and taking my warming up process into the first few minutes of the dance. So I'm subverting or deconstructing that norm of how the performer presents herself.'

Listening to Raewyn I think about my own attempts to resist or subvert audience expectations of myself as a dancer based on my understandings of postmodern choreographic strategies (Rainer 1974). Susanne and I both interact with our audiences by talking, too. My experience has been that the traditional audience/performer relationship does break down (at least a little), and a more personal and intimate connection can develop.

Ali brings our discussion back to the issue of the dancer and women's body image. 'I've been much more interested in the essence of the movement and the image of and shape of it, than whether it was a man or woman dancing it. I love the female body, I love the way it moves, I love its sexuality, and I love its gracefulness. My women dancers have always been required to be particularly strong and gymnastic and lift men. It has never bothered me to try to make women all feminine or men all masculine, in anything I've done. I haven't got a tiny female body, you know … I've been raised in a farming area as you were Karen, and my legs were built for running up and down hills and chasing sheep and whatever.'

As our conversation develops further Raewyn picks up on Bronwyn's comments about ageism. She suggests that the youthful ideal also dictates what movement is appropriately feminine, laughing as she says, 'When you look at the kind of stereotypes of how a 50-year-old woman is supposed to behave – oh my god! Yes, she doesn't skip, she's very sedate, and she does not wiggle her hips, at least in the white middle class. She does not speak loudly. And yet when I think of my post-menopausal women friends we are stroppy – continual paradoxes of opposites.'

Gales of laughter erupt from Jan and Ali at Raewyn's words. Susanne and Bronwyn are giggling too, perhaps imagining, as I am, themselves later in life, or perhaps knowing other mature women who confound stereotypes.

Continuing her comments as our laughter subsides, Raewyn argues more seriously: 'There are assumptions about type of body, type of movement, context, aesthetic content. Because of these assumptions about body and what's worth watching, people think that older woman wouldn't have anything worthwhile to say. But there is something else that is valuable in terms of depth of personality and depth of embodiment that can imbue a performance with something stunning and people are not used to looking for that in a dance performance. There is an assumed age limitation in the dance world. My generation is starting to challenge that assumption.'

Nods of agreement follow from us all listening to Raewyn's insight. 'I'm not wanting to be coerced by these external norms, but allow myself to live and express myself fully, freely and openly. Bringing all of these things about being a woman of my age and being feminine back to my solo, basically I have said "no – I am a woman, I am going to live as a woman, and I'm not going to live by male criteria." I realized that most of my life my body has been the most reliable source of information for me as a person. So that in the embodiment of my experience, or my body's response to me and what has happened in my life, my body has been the most affirming and accurate source of knowing who I am, and what my life contains. So that is what has led me to say "yes" to my processes on stage and my choices around physicality that I have been making in the last years. But you know, I was having to deconstruct various assumptions about the performing person, as well as put myself out as a statement, so it felt like I was doing a double job and it was very exhausting. Psychologically and psychically, it was a hard job.'

Raewyn's confidence in embodiment as a site of knowledge, and as a way of knowing, has allowed her to explore her own processes and validate her personal experiences in dance making. I see that the other women are also contemplating Raewyn's comments about femininity and ageing and the 'virtuosic' body. Jan speaks now about her recent solo dance work (Bolwell 2000a).

'I was sort of catapulted into considering femininity, really, as a result of losing a part of my body – my breasts – that is so clearly identified with being female. So it forced me to deal with that at a very personal level. But it also then led me to reflect on it in a sort of societal way. My solo dance *Off My Chest* attempts to look at the female body, particularly breasts and how that is a sexual symbol and how we regard that. And so I was trying to make sense of that myself I suppose, in coming to terms with the fact that I am breast-less, and how I feel about that. Having thought about that on a personal level, I guess in terms of the dance it made me then reflect on it in a wider way. Its very liberating being breast-less because I feel freed from the constraints of femininity. I have made a political decision about how I deal with this issue. And I think having done that the path is just there. Part of this is always me saying, if I can do this in a public way I am learning to live with the reality of what's happened to my body … so I am reconstructing myself for myself you know, but I think also, in the process, hopefully, I might also be doing something for other women.'

As Jan speaks, images from her solo performances *Off My Chest* return to me. I remember how she first appeared on stage, posed on a chaise, adopting positions like the reclining female nude in the paintings of history. She wore a green hospital cape, gloves in latex and a matching dress, and behind her stood a small white screen on metal legs. Jan sat up slowly from her pose to face me in the audience, dignified, poised, confident, though perhaps resigned too I thought. But suddenly she rushed forward, hands pressed against her chest and agonizingly walked her fingers across her chest, searching. Then seeming to panic, she ran upstage and stopped to stare at the screen on which images had been projected. I realized in horror that the projected images were slides of cancerous cells. Stabbing, slashing, sawing movements of her arms alternated with movements where Jan seemed to be protecting her chest, and in the violence of her movements I saw Jan's depiction of mastectomy. Collapsing, Jan curled up protectively, reflecting her grief and pain. Coming eventually to standing, Jan slowly removed her green hospital cape. To my surprise, under her cape Jan was wearing a large set of false breasts that sat over her dress. As I watched with amusement, Jan manipulated her false breasts, squeezing them, dropping and catching their weight. She tried unsuccessfully to tuck them away and I could see Jan enjoyed this new acquaintance with breasts, finding humour in the painful reality of her experience. She then removed her false breasts, and with athletic commitment, turned and dropped to pose in the manner of an ancient Greek statue. In powerful, athletic movements, Jan travelled across the stage, striding, reaching, extending, leaping and arching. Later I watched intrigued as Jan rescued one of the false prosthetic breasts, cradled it and wound it around her head, nestled it into her shoulder to rock it and placed it on her sternum. I could see how Jan demonstrated her resolution with mastectomy through returning the prosthesis to her chest, though not to its appropriate position. In the final moments, Jan deliberately placed the prosthesis on the head of the chaise, and seated herself a distance away from it, indicating to me her sense of resolution. The lights went down.

Remembering Jan's performance and listening to her comments now reminds me again that the personal really is bound up in the political for feminists. And while I am concerned about re-creating myself and dealing with femininity for political reasons, I have not been prompted by the same traumatic experiences as Jan. I appreciate the courage Jan has to reveal and share. It seems clear again to me that Jan values her personal experiences and through dance making can explore them in embodied ways of knowing. Our conversation moves into a more casual discussion about our changing relationships to body image.

Choreographic strategies

Reflecting quietly as the conversation continues around me, I consider my own experiences in dance making. I have developed some basic choreographic strategies as a feminist to express my embodied ways of knowing in my own solos.[8] My choreographic strategies were to use gestural, pedestrian or everyday movement designed to enhance kinaesthetic empathy with the dancer; to subvert or resist audience expectations of the dancer; to challenge and change stereotypical feminine movement or movement qualities; and to make embodied expressions of my lived experiences. I combined these choreographic strategies with theatrical devices to enhance my lived experience themes of 'home' and 'journey' in *This Is After All the Edited Life* (Barbour 2001c). It seemed to me that I was able to be resistant and create my own alternative femininity using my choreographic strategies. When I reflect on the other women's comments, I can see that while we share some strategies, there are other unique strategies they developed.

Susanne's strategies to 'change, corrupt or adapt' pretty movements and poses, and to include 'strong or harsh movement' is similar to my strategy to challenge and change stereotypical feminine movement or movement qualities. Jan chose to emulate and contrast images of feminine nudes from historical art, reclining on her chaise lounge and then subverting her own seductive image with her direct gaze and gestural movement. Both women used costume, a restricting grey dress for Susanne and a green hospital cape and dress for Jan, to contrast and highlight their movement and enhance their themes of either being a 'weirdo' or dealing with trauma. Raewyn's discussion of stereotypical movement for mature women provided much amusement as I imagined her trying to be sedate instead of the playful, mindful and intelligent performer I saw in her performance of *Sensual Ensemble* (Thorburn 1997). What interested me especially in Raewyn's comments was the way in which she valued and reclaimed feminine characteristics, such as having a sensory, intuitive body focus rather than a rational, abstract focus in her dancing.

For those who used improvisation in their solos, particularly in Susanne's dance where she gave herself permission to do whatever interested her at the time,[9] I can see acceptance of the stereotypically feminine characteristic of 'irrationality'. Alongside this is a focus on private lived experiences in dance rather creating a 'product' or external object to be consumed. In these choreographic strategies I can see links to the work of postmodern dance choreographers. Both Susanne and I also worked with specific movements that challenged and changed the stereotypically feminine movements of the dancer.

I enjoyed Susanne and Raewyn's attempts to express openly and freely through improvisation and childlike movement, allowing them to challenge and change through movement as well as to integrate gestural, pedestrian and everyday movement to enhance kinaesthetic empathy. Both were thinking in movement (Sheets-Johnstone 1999). Watching Susanne emphatically 'brushing off' expectations in *Someone Else's Weirdo* (Bentley 2000) and Raewyn peeling potatoes and hunching up typing at her computer in *Sensual Ensemble* (Thorburn 1997), I responded kinaesthetically to their experiences. In privileging kinaesthetic experience, the focus shifted away from our female bodies, as our postmodern predecessors had done (Rainer 1966, 1974). Raewyn's comment that she wanted 'to explore commonplace real experiences that are likely for the audience to have done, to offer the likelihood of a visceral response in the audience, and engage them in the process' reflected her commitment to enhancing kinaesthetic empathy.

I was amused to recall how my own expectations were subverted and resisted in Susanne and Raewyn's dancing when both spoke to me in the audience.[10] Their direct speech interrupted my expectation as an audience member that I could sit back unnoticed by them to passively observe their performance. In both Susanne and Raewyn's solos, and in Ali's performance of *How Being Still Is Still Moving* (East 1996), moments of improvisation allowed them to resist expectations that the dancer should outwardly be 'in control', prepared and rehearsed when she dances, and ready to perform when she steps on stage. I was curious about what these women would do next as they did not simply fulfil my expectations and provide me with a choreographic 'product'. Instead I realized that I was witness to and part of their processes as dancers. Again they were thinking in movement, thinking in action within improvisation and thinking about action in choreographed sections of their solo dances. I felt that I could connect with them more personally because of this and I was aware they were responding to me in the audience. In creating my solo *This Is After All the Edited Life*, I had also wanted to offer and share my alternative re-created femininity. I experienced a sense of empowerment as I offered embodied expressions of my lived experience, and as I included movement designed to stimulate a kinaesthetic response to my experiences.

To me, Jan's work (Bolwell 2000a, 2000b) is a superb example of an embodied expression of her lived experiences with breast cancer, and of course of her commitment to the politics of the personal (Warren 1996). Jan's comment that she was dealing with personal issues and also being a conduit for bigger political issues shows how the feminist notion of the personal as the political had become embodied for her.

Also dealing with political issues of an environmental kind, Ali was able to express her lived experience in an embodied way in *How Being Still Is Still Moving*. Having been in the audience for Ali's solo performance, I remember the introspective quality of her movement and how uncharacteristic it seemed for dance, from my perspective at the time. Created in three main sections, Ali's solo began with still, meditative poses, gestural movements suggesting splashing water over her face and movement inspired by birds. Rather than considering her movement as feminine, Ali described to us how she 'enters the psyche' and emulates the movement of rocks, sea, birds, driftwood and insects. While obviously she was still a woman performing, Ali shifted the focus of attention away from her moving body onto her experience of relationship with her environment. Ali's performance drew attention to her quality of movement, and through use of clear gestures such as bird-like movements with her arms, Ali seemed to 'transform' herself from a woman into a creature or an inanimate object. As an audience member, I was able to experience something of Ali's alternative understandings and her lived experiences in environmental politics. Ali's solo then moved into a lively, improvised dance incorporating movement from the hula dance of Rarotonga. Ali worked with two musicians from Rarotonga, who played a rousing ukulele duet for this second section of dance, reflecting traditional Pacific life based around the sea. The final section of Ali's dance brought together those themes as a video projection of her dancing at the beach showing movement alongside the driftwood, sand, water, birds and rock that clearly inspired her choreography. The video, like Ali's choreography, had long still moments focusing on textures of water, wood and sand. Ali continued to dance on stage as the video played, incorporating quick changes in gaze, moments of stillness, an internal focus and moments of travelling through the space with deliberate intention and commitment. The final lasting image was of Ali running down the beach into the distance, as though she continued to dance beyond my ability to see her. While she was challenging and changing stereotypically feminine movement and movement qualities, Ali was also offering her alternative femininity and sharing her lived experiences in relationship with her environment.

In our own ways, we were all focused on sharing our lived experiences, 'walking the talk' and embodying the political and the personal in our dance making. Each of our dances was an embodied expression of our lived experiences as women. The ways in which we each attempted to re-create femininity are very different from those strategies I read about in general feminist literature. I recall the interest feminist writers had in the female body and body image as sites of re-creations of femininity, remembering the self-controlling practices of women to change their bodies through exercise regimes, dieting, eating disorders and surgery (Bordo 1988; Greer 1999; Macdonald 1995; Markula 1995; Wolf 1991). Even though we were acutely aware of the influences of the stereotype of femininity on dance, understanding that the dancer might even be seen as the epitome of stereotypical femininity (Brown 1999), we were remarkably accepting the uniqueness of our own bodies. Rather than attempting radical changes to our bodies, we sought personal re-creations of femininity through developing alternative choreographic processes and movement, through valuing our experiences and ways of knowing, in changing attitudes about ourselves, and in creating contrasts between our individual bodies and our attitudes as performers.

Our re-creations of femininity might be seen as alternative 'performances of femininity' (Butler 1990), at times utilizing parody and resistance. But our re-creations were, perhaps more importantly, part of our embodied ways of knowing ourselves as women, rather than simply 'performances' that begin and end in a specific dance. Our dances were a focus for exploring and re-creating femininity throughout our lives. They were embodied ways of knowing.

Noticing that everyone has been engrossed in other conversations while I have been musing privately, I re-focus on the discussion at hand. Shifting to sit next to Raewyn, I comment to her briefly about my attempts to understand our dancing experiences.

Raewyn's response reflects her own intentions to reconstruct herself in her solo dance making, and her understanding of feminism. 'It's a feminist statement, just being myself, rather than some other sort of extraordinary person, or having an altered persona. But being this 50-year old woman just standing up there doing stuff, is definitely a change compared with the norm.'

The conversations around me naturally draw to a close, and I suggest that it might be time for another break. Lots of stretching and yawning and enthusiasm for coffee follow my suggestion.

Susanne and I open packets of biscuits and fill coffee mugs, catching up on news from friends overseas while the others enjoy the crisp air on the veranda. My cat's attention-seeking antics provide a welcome distraction from the intensity of the conversation, as do the paddlers training on the river below my house.

Alternative modalities of feminine movement

During our coffee break, I recall seeing each of the solo dances and begin to piece together an alternative analysis of the modalities of feminine movement to that which Young (1998b) offers. In our discussions I noticed that our intentional movement did not seem to obviously fit the instrumental (and masculine) model of action by having identifiable plans, singular intention and control (Young 1998b). Instead, our dancing reflected our individual ways of re-creating femininity. It seems to me that I can consider Young's question 'What might a phenomenology of action look like which started from the mundane fact that many of us, especially women, often do several things at once?' (1998b: 289). Our dance making was thinking in movement (Sheets-Johnstone 1999), and included unplanned, improvised movement and movement with multiple intentions and without recognizable 'control', in the sense of following a repeatable pattern.

Raewyn, Susanne and Ali included improvised movement for specific feminist choreographic purposes, and this unplanned movement allowed them to be responsive to information and feedback from the audience, and to develop a different relationship with the audience. They were able to think in action and had the freedom to compose dance on the spot without mediation (Sheets-Johnstone 1999). Improvised movement encouraged freedom to play and respond to personal interests moment to moment, to move outside the constraints and expectations of feminine movement, taking the opportunity to be childlike and to value intuition and sensation. This was an empowering, life-giving and self-sustaining process. Hence, rather than only valuing movement with identifiable plans and structure, they privileged improvisation and play in dance.

In many cases there was more than one intention to the movement we performed in our solos. Movements had multiple intentions to communicate, to satisfy us personally in an embodied manner, to be life-giving, to establish alternative relationships with our audiences, and to resist and construct differently our experiences of being women. Any moment of improvisation within the dance performance fostered a loss of control, in that no movement was planned from moment to moment. As Sheets-Johnstone (1999) puts it, there was no level of premeditative decision-making in improvised dancing, and we could respond immediately to the specific information in the moment.

Derived from our work, an alternative understanding of the modalities of feminine movement acknowledges the attempts we made to 'dance an expanded feminized norm', as Ann Albright (1997) describes it. Qualities such as improvisation and play, responsiveness to the moment-to-moment performing context, and receptivity to and integration of multiple sources of information might be more relevant to understanding feminine movement. Receptivity means that I can be both thinking *about* movement through choreography and thinking *in* movement in improvisation to demonstrate being a mindful body (Sheets-Johnstone 1999) or 'phenomenal' dancer (Preston-Dunlop 1998). What this means, for example, is that I can fully embody specific movements I have rehearsed, as well as be expressive and reflective about how these movements feel in the moment of dancing, as well as further develop these movements while dancing as I respond to changing feedback from the audience. Improvisation in performance also necessitated moment-to-moment embodied responsiveness as these multiple influences were integrated, understood and subsequently fed into the next moment in the ongoing lived experience of dancing. As Maxine Sheets-Johnstone (1999) expresses it, dance improvisation is a clear example of thinking in movement.

Based on our lived experiences, I think that movement in women's solo contemporary dance making might be understood as receptive to multiple influences, integrated and understood through embodiment, and responsive in multiple ways, including both choreographed and improvisational expressions. This understanding of alternative feminine movement relates to our individual choreographic strategies and ways of re-creating femininity. The re-created understandings of femininity and feminine movement that we have developed reflect our embodied ways of knowing. Such empowering practices in dance making allowed us all to re-create ourselves, at least for a time. I was able to 'dream myself anew', or to imagine, explore and create in my solo dance moments of embodying my dream.

Ali spoke of being able to reveal her connectedness with the world, and to 'exhibit a person at her most whole and beautiful' within her solo dance. Jan experienced the opportunity to connect the threads of her life, and Susanne found that re-creating herself in dance allowed her to express her relationship to the world and to interpret her life. For Raewyn, she was able to experience 'a greater sense of meaning, pleasure and fulfilment' in her life as she matured, and moved differently.

Our re-creations of femininity might be seen as alternative 'performances of femininity' (Butler 1990), but these performances were, perhaps more importantly, a focus for exploring and re-creating ourselves throughout our lives. They were embodied ways of knowing ourselves as women (Barbour 2002).

*   *   *

I feel a bit stuffy in my office, the heat of the winter sun having thoroughly warmed the room. I rise to standing, spreading my toes on the carpet, reaching my arms up and feeling my spine elongate. Delicious sensations … but I crave fresh air. I abandon my reading and messy office, grab the keys and rush down the stairs and out the doors into the cool late morning. The day is still clear and I think I smell a hint of spring as I stride along the path towards the café. It has been a productive morning too, considering the development of phenomenological research by feminist and dance researchers that led to this welcome shift beyond somatophobia. Happily from my perspective, dance and movement researchers are now able to develop understandings that account for the integral nature of lived movement experience and body in knowledge. And significantly, more of us are writing in alternative texts.

Phenomenological and dance research methods have enabled me to develop a methodology that provided not only further understanding of dance experience, but also of the nature of embodied knowing. Movement is of such integral and central importance in understanding ourselves, our relationships with others and our relationships with our world. Having been on a winding path through different academic fields of study in my life thus far, I really am excited that my research investigating lived movement experience can contribute to knowledge. I hope to stimulate interest in new possibilities for researching and sharing lived movement experiences in other researchers too. Perhaps other researchers engaged in creative practice might find phenomenological methods helpful. In particular, I am inspired when I see researchers allow their theoretical and embodied understandings to be revealed through rich narratives of lived movement experience.[11]

Notes

1. Some sections of this chapter were presented to and appeared in the conference proceedings for the *World Dance Alliance/ Congress of Research on Dance International Conference* (August 2004) Taipei, Taiwan. Some other sections of this chapter were published in my 2005 article 'Beyond somatophobia. Phenomenology and movement research in dance', *Junctures. Journal of Thematic Dialogue*, 5, pp. 35–51.

2. Phenomenologists study 'lived experience', the explication of phenomena and the description of the experiential meanings as lived by individuals (Van Manen 1997). According to Sondra Fraleigh, the 'lived body' is a non-dualistic understanding of the conscious, intentional and unified body, soul and mind in action (1987: 4).

3. In the limited consideration of the body in the history of Western thought there has been a tendency to focus on the unhealthy or sick body, or the corpse – a body to be cured or dissected (Grosz 1994; Nettleton and Watson 1998).

4. The feminists I discuss represent a range of feminist perspectives and each offers a slightly different understanding of body. I borrow and adapt understandings where relevant, drawing from Carol Bigwood (1991), Rosi Braidotti (1994), Moira Gatens (1995), Elizabeth Grosz (1994) and Iris Young (1998a, 1998b).

5. This narrative section of writing comes from my doctoral thesis findings chapter. Unlike the earlier sections of writing taken from my literature review, I was confident to write more creatively in representing findings. I note that I wrote this scene as set in the apartment I lived in as a student, but that the whole scene is a narrative construction, as I have discussed in Chapter Three.

6. I chose to undertake my doctoral research work with five women whose work I found personally inspiring because of their commitment to reflecting lived experience, and who I thought might be willing to engage in discussion. I included myself as the sixth participant. We are all Pākehā women, sharing at least some cultural values and participating in the same wider community of dancers. Alison East has grown children and is a dance and improvisation lecturer at the University of Otago in Dunedin. Bronwyn Judge is a dance teacher and mother living in rural Otago. Jan Bolwell is a dance educator, writer, policy advisor and performer based in Wellington. Raewyn Thorburn is a Skinner Releasing Technique teacher and body worker living in Coromandel and has grown children. Susanne Bentley is a freelance contemporary dancer, improviser and teacher living and performing in Belgium. I am a mother to our young son living in Hamilton and working as a dance lecturer and researcher.

7. In response to reviewing her original comments in this chapter, Susanne reflects, 'hypocritically, I was constantly a gym member, obsessed with my body since being a teenager.'

8. My theorizing of choreographic strategies is derived from my choreographic research. As such, it should not be considered an exhaustive or prescriptive list of choreographic strategies.

9. In response to reviewing her original comments in this chapter, Susanne now adds, 'I placed myself in a physical experiential moment – embodying that young character – in contrast to the highly controlled/subverted/strong movement earlier. The realization that I didn't have to set everything was a revelation. I did it because I could – it was my solo. I remember thinking in the moment of extended stillness in the middle of my solo – "I'm going to hold this as long as I can and you just have to watch me – ha ha." It made it interesting for me to pop that in, out of the blue, and now I realize it was a fantastic choreographic tool to intensify everything that came afterwards – a 'suspense/ expectation moment.''

10. I write from the perspective of dancer/choreographer in theorizing choreographic strategies and practices. It is beyond the scope of this chapter to comment as to the success of these strategies in my own work from an audience perspective. However, I do recall and include some of my own responses as an audience member to the other women's solo dances here.

11. Such narratives can avoid the need to slip between third- and first-person research representations, as I did in my doctoral thesis and have discussed in this chapter.

Chapter 5

Knowing Differently, Living Creatively: Embodied Ways of Knowing

Television news tonight is dominated by updates on bombings in London. We learn that tight security procedures will be taken at Heathrow Airport and that passengers can expect some delays. I leave tomorrow for a conference in Edinburgh and I imagine that the delays and dramas will most likely be over by the time I arrive. My sister is travelling with me as far as London for her own research work and we discuss travel plans. She is staying with me tonight, and we reassure each other, estimating that we should be safe because we are flying via Heathrow and they now have extra security measures in place. The latest website update for travellers states that we cannot even carry papers with us on the flight: only passports, boarding passes and medication required during the flight are permitted. We are both bothered by this, having planned to read and work on the long flights ahead.

I check through my suitcase again, making sure that I do not have any restricted items with me and wonder what it will be like to travel for over 24 hours without personal items and hand luggage. This is my first conference trip to the United Kingdom and I am extremely excited about presenting at an arts conference, attending dance performances during the Edinburgh Festival and travelling around Scotland. I have three weeks away over the teaching break for this trip: considering my 'ecological footprint' and the cost of flying around the world, I crammed in as many research and holiday activities as I could. And I am thrilled to be travelling away from our winter again.

Carefully moving aside my folded clothing, I locate my conference papers and the CD containing my presentation material in my suitcase. Below these papers is a copy of the *Lonely Planet* guidebook for Scotland, safely tucked away for now but ready for quick reference when I reach the other side of the world. I guess I should read through my presentation now. Typically I rehearse my presentation during flights.

My sister seems to be packed already I notice, and taking advantage of her organization, I ask her if I can practice presenting my conference paper to her.

Luckily for me she agrees, putting aside the paper she was absorbed in. Happily I explain that the aim of my conference presentation is to articulate and make clear the case for embodied ways of knowing in research.

'I hope I get good feedback,' I continue. 'At this arts conference, I probably won't be the only one sharing embodied research – there should be theatre practitioners and musicians and visual artists there too.' I know that scholars are increasingly engaging in embodied research and that the nature of qualitative research is expanding to encompass and validate arts research.

Beginning to read aloud from my script, I am immediately conscious that I am not including narrative or video material within this presentation. This bothers me somewhat and I wonder if there might at least be room for me to include a very short movement improvisation during my presentation. I will have to deal with this when I see the room I am scheduled to present in. I put these speculations aside as I recognize that my conference presentation, although scripted, will also allow me to improvise, even if only through how I 'perform' my delivery of words. I let the rhythm of my words take centre stage now.

Embodied engagement in arts research: Introductory comments

In this presentation[1] I argue that embodied engagement is crucial for creative practice as research and for research in general. I am grounded in dance research myself, but I share my comments imagining that there will be value for you, as researchers engaged in your own forms of creative practice. It is through rigorous and reflective practice that theoretical knowledge and lived experiences can be embodied, made meaningful, and thus contribute to the generation of new understandings. I contend that this embodied knowledge is then available for subsequent expression and aesthetic communication via a wide range of mediums and interdisciplinary practices. Following these comments, I will then offer guidelines for undertaking embodied research, before concluding by emphasising the continuing relevance of performing arts in expressing individual human embodied experience in an increasingly virtual and global world.

So, I will begin by discussing creative arts practice and academic research, then discuss and present an understanding of embodiment, before moving to articulate an epistemological strategy which I call embodied ways of knowing. I relate my discussion throughout to current literature on embodiment, creativity, experiential learning and creative arts practice as research.

Artists have the potential to significantly contribute to the generation of new understandings, not only of artistic practice, but also to knowledge and to society in general. For those of us engaged in research in the arts, there has been a welcome shift towards the legitimation of artistic practice in education.[2] This shift has provided room for the creation of new research methodologies and forms of research representation through which we can share our knowledge and findings with a wider social audience (Barrett and Bolt 2007; Denzin and Lincoln 2000). Particularly in performing arts, this shift has been propelled by the growing acceptance of experiential and alternative ways of knowing (Bannon 2004; Dewey 1934; Eisner 1998, 2002b; Pakes 2009) and a move away from 'somatophobia' or fear of the body as a site of knowledge (Grosz 1994). Specific research projects have explored the nature of practice as research in performance: research that explores relationships between theory and practice (Barrett and Bolt 2007; Piccini 2005). (I note first, though, that my discussion of embodied engagement in arts research refers primarily to 'performance', by which I mean live performances of theatre, dance, music and multi-disciplinary performing arts by specific artists, as distinct from performative written texts.) It is my contention that one way artists might contribute to new knowledge is through embodied engagement in arts research.

Creative and academic processes

Within the academy there is a growing acceptance of research processes involving practical performance outcomes, as well as film, video and audiotape outcomes (Barrett and Bolt 2007; Piccini 2002; Tertiary Education Commission 2004). To assist academic institutions in validating artistic practice as research in performance, traditional and familiar academic research processes have been aligned with creative arts processes. This step formalizes 'institutional acceptance of performance practices and processes as arenas in which knowledge might be opened' (Piccini 2002: 6). This move has also helped guide artists into academic research, with reference to generic and simple creative process models proposed by music, devised theatre and dance educators.[3] These creative process models can be placed alongside standard qualitative research processes as I outline below in Figure 1.

Creative Process (Balkin 1990; Bannon 2004)	Choreographic Process (Ashley 2002; Coe 1999; Janesick 2000; Schrader 2005)	Academic Research Process
Preparation	Research/ Setting the Scene	Literature Review
Incubation	Vision/ Ideas / Themes	Perspective/ Question
	Experiment/ Improvise/ Explore	Design/ Methodology Methods
Illumination/ Insight	Choreograph/ Select/ Score	Data/ Evidence/ Findings
	Rehearse/ Refine	
		Discussion/ Conclusions
Verification/ Elaboration	Performance	Research Outputs
	Audience Feedback/ Reflections	

Figure 1: Creative and academic processes.

As illustrated in Figure 1, the creative processes involved in preparation and research for an artistic work align with academic literature review, that is, the preliminary exploration of a subject area. Incubation of creative ideas and themes, and subsequent experimentation, exploration and improvisation, relates to the development of a research perspective and question, and the design of relevant methodology. Moments of creative illumination or insight that occur when choreographing or scoring an artistic work also occur in research when specific methods are put into action during the data or evidence collection, and during the subsequent discussion and analysis of findings. And the verification or elaboration stage in a creative work of rehearsal, performance and feedback aligns with the research processes of discussing the conclusions and implications. (These creative and academic processes are generalized of course. More specific processes that individual artists and researchers use can be identified, and new creative and academic processes will continue to evolve as different challenges arise.)

As a dancer, I have long been engaged in creative choreographic processes. A crucial part of my change from artistic practitioner to dance researcher has been in engaging in academic research processes alongside my choreographic processes, and in articulating how it is that I come to know. I appreciate that my epistemological strategies as choreographer are different from traditional ways of knowing. I realize that I come to know through other ways, as well as the traditional methods for establishing propositional knowledge (knowing that) and procedural knowledge (knowing how) (Butterworth and Wildschut 2009; Pakes 2009; Risner 2000). There is much that I know as a dancer that is tacit (that is, knowledge in action), that I am unable to translate directly into words and that is better expressed through movement. However, as a researcher I appreciate that I can still contribute to new knowledge based on my epistemological strategies – what I describe as embodied ways of knowing. Consequently, I place embodiment at the centre of my research; this is an agenda that I share with a number of feminist writers.[4]

Embodiment is a holistic experience, different from 'body' experience (which remains differentiated from the 'mind' and is typically based on a Cartesian dualistic understanding of body and mind). I argue that embodiment encompasses an individual person's biological (somatic), intellectual, emotional, social, gendered, artistic and spiritual experience, within their cultural, historical and geographical location. Embodiment is not a random or arbitrary set of genetic material – it recognizes the material conditions of race, gender, sexuality, ability, history and culture. Embodiment therefore indicates a holistic experiencing individual. Most importantly, embodiment can also be understood through movement, an embodied activity.

Movement and knowing

A number of theorists have offered partial understandings of moving, or bodily intelligence. Examples include Howard Gardner's notion of bodily kinaesthetic intelligence (1999) and Merleau-Ponty's 'body-subject' (1962, 1964). But it is the work of phenomenologist Maxine

Sheets-Johnstone (1999) that resonates most strongly with me. She identifies movement as 'the originating ground of our sense-makings' (Sheets-Johnstone 1999: 161). In short, she argues that movement is a source of knowledge and that movement experience is of profound epistemological significance (Sheets-Johnstone 1999).

Notwithstanding the views of Sheets-Johnstone (1999), which are more complex than I am able to discuss in this presentation, I am convinced that more needs to be said about the epistemological significance of movement. Building on the research by Mary Belenky et al. (1986) into women's ways of knowing, I have explored new possibilities for articulating the epistemological significance of movement.

Belenky et al. (1986; Goldberger et al. 1996) identify five epistemological strategies from their research with women: silence, received knowing, subjective knowing, procedural knowing and constructed knowing. While I note that these strategies should not be regarded as universal, fixed, exhaustive or necessarily exclusive to women, they provided me with a useful starting point in my research. Here I focus on the strategy of constructed knowing because it resonates with feminist agendas and postmodern research, in the sense that those who attempt to integrate their own and other voices understand 'that even the most ordinary human being is engaged in the construction of knowledge' (Belenky et al. 1986: 133). Belenky et al. suggested that some individuals construct knowledge in order to 'reclaim the self by attempting to integrate knowledge they felt intuitively was important with knowledge they had learned from others' (1986: 143). Such individuals are characterized by self-reflectiveness and self-awareness, a high tolerance for ambiguity, awareness of the inevitability of conflict, attempts to deal with the rich complexity of life as a whole and the desire to share their knowledge in their own way. Belenky et al.'s (1986) strategy of constructed knowing provided me with new ways of thinking about knowing, but not about how movement could specifically be utilized as a strategy.

Noting that there was no focus in this research as to how embodiment might more specifically be involved in knowing, I set out to articulate embodied ways of knowing. This understanding derived from research undertaken through my own solo contemporary dance making, and discussion with other solo dance makers.

Furthermore ...

* * *

My sister interrupts my reading, 'Sorry, I think I drifted off a bit there. Have you got a visual presentation to go with your talk, because that was quite a lot of stuff on epistemology to take in?'

'Yes. Are you following the stuff on ways of knowing?' I ask.

'Well mostly, because I've read your work in this area before but this sounds more "academic" than normal. Were you wanting to do that?' She slides comfortably into the couch as I respond, watching me flicking through my pages.

'Is it too much?' I ask.

I reflect on the slides and visual images I have planned to accompany my presentation, wondering if I should add some more images of dancing.

'Well, maybe you could try being a bit more conversational,' she suggests. 'I realize that your audience will be more familiar with these ideas than me, but you always complain when you hear presenters that are monotone speakers and just read from their notes. So keep it more personal and you'll be fine,' she says encouragingly.

I am grateful for her attention and for the reminder about style. I make notes in the margins of my paper about places to emphasize certain words, to pause where relevant to let ideas reverberate and to build the volume as I near important points in my presentation. But as I reflect, I wish I was including the words of my friends and research participants too: their words continue to inspire me to attempt to articulate embodied ways of knowing …

Quickly I unpack my computer from my luggage, power it up and search through my computer files. Maybe I should print out a copy of some of my doctoral research findings to have to refer back to if I want to bring my presentation more alive? Even scrolling through the paragraphs on my screen for what is likely the thousandth time, my eyes are caught by interesting quotations from my research participants, reminding me of our discussions of solo dance making.

Solo dancers talk (part two): Articulating our embodied knowing

Our conversations in this warm room have deepened even further now.[5] Despite our long day of discussion, we all listen intently as Raewyn shares her thoughts with us about how her dancing and knowing come together.

'I realized that my body has been the most affirming and accurate source of knowing who I am. In the embodiment in my work, there has been a much greater sense of the meaning of life for me. A sense of physical pleasure, personal satisfaction, of being more fulfilled and happy in my life, and of being more fully myself. So my body is totally involved in my knowing. So that the knowledge gained, well, as an example, it enabled me to be much more effective in self-sustainable physical processes in my life. I feel I do actually come to a clearer state without the denial of body, without the denial of emotions, without the denial or absence of a sense of spirit.'

I am particularly interested in the way that Raewyn describes her life as becoming more meaningful and self-sustaining through her embodied knowing. Raewyn's solo work, *Sensual Ensemble* (Thorburn 1997), and the understandings she derives from bringing her different knowledge together seem to me to demonstrate the importance of her embodied ways of knowing.

Ali expresses her sense of how dance teaches us about embodiment (East 1996). She speaks slowly, aiming to find non-dualistic terms I think, becoming clearer as she continues to talk.

'I think maybe, in performance improvisation, we might understand a little more when we actually sense everything working together suddenly in the moment. Maybe this notion of wholeness, of embodiment, is more about being in relationship with ourselves and others and the environment, all at once. It's a total kind of awareness, where all your "antennae" are working in those directions. Maybe you understand something that might not even yet have words for you. You understand what integration means, or what that whole idea of mind/body/spirit means. And you can exhibit as a dancer, this fabulous organization in the moment, of intricate movement patterns, emotive expression, spiritual states of being, and qualities of energy. Basically revealing the kind of fantastic brilliance of the human animal at its best. You can articulate that extraordinary intelligence of humans in dancing.'

'Yes, yes', agrees Jan. 'Dancing is intelligence in action, kinaesthetic intelligence!'

I feel like cheering, listening to Ali and Jan speaking. I hear both women trying to articulate and explain embodied ways of knowing that are so clearly relevant to my dancing and my research!

Everyone is smiling at Ali, who immediately starts laughing and we all join in. While I reminisce on Ali's solo dance, the laughter eventually subsides and, seemingly sensing a good moment, Bronwyn shifts our conversations back to embodied ways of knowing. Bronwyn asks if I can clarify further what I mean by dance as an embodied way of knowing. I reply that I feel Ali has just managed to articulate her experience of embodied ways of knowing, but I try to describe what I feel.

'I guess I am still trying to articulate what an embodied way of knowing is Bronwyn. But I do mean knowing and understanding yourself and your world through the process of personally integrating and experiencing different knowledge. This way of knowing and understanding does not leave out your individual embodiment, and the sense of wholeness and integration that comes through moving, but instead focuses knowing through moving, or thinking in movement. I think about embodied ways of knowing in terms of the dancer-like ways of knowing – the things we have been discussing, and other processes that we each individually have been exploring in making dance. Earlier, you described how your solo *Housework* (Judge 1998) gave you a focus that allowed you to interpret, understand and know something new – hence an embodied way of knowing. And you have expressed your embodied knowledge in your solo.'

I realize that I am one of the few people to have seen Bronwyn's video dance *Housework* (Judge 1998), and I attempt to describe it to the other women so that they can appreciate more of Bronwyn's comments.

'Bronwyn's video *Housework* opened with scenes from a flower garden and a beautiful building. I wondered at first whether this building was a museum, but I realized that it was a home of delicate and exotic furniture and ornaments. Within this setting, Bronwyn appeared, dressed in an ensemble costume of harem pants, a leotard and an embroidered Chinese jacket. She danced respectfully within her environment, as though perhaps the furniture was not her own and the objects she handled precious to her. She did not appear to be doing any "house work" of the domestic kind.'

I laugh, sharing with the other women that I realized the title of her solo *Housework* reflected Bronwyn's work as a dancer in her own home.

I describe her dancing from memory, continuing, 'Bronwyn moved in an expressive and intentional manner, her deliberate hand movements, raised arms, turning and stamping reminding me of flamenco and folk dance. I remember that I had a sense of travel and different cultural heritages from her dancing and from the setting. I guessed that Bronwyn was drawing on her family links to Europe, her own travels around the world and her study of other cultural dances. Bronwyn was alone in her solo dance, and yet I understood that she was remembering other people and times as she leafed through old photos of family and dancing. I was more curious about her as the video finished, feeling like a detective as I pieced together a meaning for myself from Bronwyn's solo.'

I know I have just glossed over Bronwyn's engaging work by sharing some of my recollections, but I see that Bronwyn is ready to speak. 'I think it is all art really … something that lets you interpret what you see and hear and feel. Anything that helps you interpret is giving you more knowledge isn't it? In dance making, I find out what is really moving me, what is motivating me. It's teaching me something about myself. Again, referring to *Housework*, I look upon that as a progression, a coming to terms with something, and learning a new perspective about myself, and the world. And sometimes it's about finding my roots. It is an ongoing process that reflects my life, when I am doing my own work and what really interests me. I think this idea of dance as a way of knowing is very valid.'

There are murmurs of agreement with Bronwyn's comments. I agree that dance making is like most art in allowing interpretation. I see differences too, in the way in which dancers, as opposed to painters, understand and communicate in an embodied way, being themselves the art 'object' when they perform their own solo work. Through this discussion I am becoming more able to articulate the integrated, embodied understandings that come for me in the moment of moving. Together we are creating an understanding of embodied ways of knowing in dance making, as we ask for clarification and challenge ourselves to express our lived experiences.

Susanne draws on comments she made earlier in the day about bringing her lived experience into her solo *Someone Else's Weirdo* (Bentley 2000). Susanne considers the idea of dance as an embodied way of knowing in relation to understanding and resolving her personal experiences. 'In the past, making solos has been a way of dealing with whatever is the big issue in my life at the time. And if there is a big issue in my life at the time, dance is a good way of expressing it. It's cathartic, getting it all out, a way of expression. It was another way of expressing my relationship with the world, or how I felt about relationships in the world. My solo *Someone Else's Weirdo* looked at me and my uniqueness. It affirmed my "right" to be weird or silly in public, and stated that being me was okay, if not fantastic!'

Susanne continues, explaining that while her solos have been a way of expressing whatever is going on in her life, she had also been able to delve into her own experiences and understand something new, rather as Bronwyn described it to us. So dance making enabled Susanne to look at herself, her relationship to the world, and to both understand it and to express her knowledge. Creating her solo work had not only been a cathartic release and expression of emotion, but it had also become a liberating, powerful source of knowledge. As she performed she came to further understandings of herself and her world.

As the other women ask Susanne about her solo work, most having seen her performances, I recall one of my clearest memories of her performance – the beginning of her dance. Susanne was in the upstage right corner with her back to the audience. She remained perfectly balanced in a yoga headstand for over a minute, dress falling over her head and only her bottom (in practical purple underpants) and her legs visible. I remember thinking that clearly this dance was not going to be an ordinary one! I also remember watching as Susanne later switched from a movement quality that accentuated the restrictions of her futuristic grey dress to a playful improvisational state where she turned her hands into chatting puppets and somewhat cheekily demanded I witness her not dancing but being a 'weirdo'. I remember her brushing her hands down her body, in seeming frustration, and then extending this movement into a high energetic jump into the air. Susanne's singing and words throughout the dance helped me to understand that she was allowing herself to play and to have the freedom to move as she wished, embracing being 'weird' or different. So I felt satisfied, as I understood how Susanne was challenging us to understand that everyone was 'someone else's weirdo' and I was excited with the way in which Susanne had theatrically integrated all these personal elements to communicate publically with me in the audience.

Aiming to make their experiences relevant to others was something Jan and Susanne both worked towards. Jan had commented that the power of dance was likely to be diminished if it remained purely personal. She mentioned that she had become more introspective about her movement, finding richer ways to express herself more meaningfully in her dance. Perhaps recalling these comments, Jan details her experiences in making *Off My Chest*, offering further understanding of dance as an embodied way of knowing (Bolwell 2000a, 2000b).

'I really do have a strong sense of connecting threads of my life. And some of those threads are physical threads, as well as emotional and intellectual ones. My work has to be concept-rich for me to sustain it. I have learned through study about the process of finding and distilling ideas, and I bring some of that to the way I work in dance. I'm interested in internal movement coherence and phrasing of movement – actively playing and finding new nuances. Concepts inform my creation of movement. And movement feeds back to me in a constant search for clarity and subtlety. It is a cyclical thing. Dancing is intelligence in action, or kinaesthetic intelligence. So I can relate to dance making as an embodied way of knowing.'

To me it seems quite clear that Jan has come to understand, to know more about herself and her experiences with breast cancer and to deal with her experiences through her dance making. I know too, from having read Jan's writing, that she is able to express and share her experiences with others in written words (Bolwell 1998, 2000b). I suggest that dance offers us all opportunities to reflect on, understand and express our experiences, like Jan has.

Ali comments, 'I can see that dance is a way of thinking about life generally. The working processes of dance making help me to understand something about where my movement is coming from and what is going on deep down in the silent place where I live, in my subconscious, if you like. So it is a way of understanding and knowing that. I see life in a particular way, through the eyes of a dancer, and I have acute sensitivity to things and particular knowledge because I am a dancer. And you know knowledge in itself is of no consequence unless it finds a means of expression, and dance is one means of expressing knowledge, isn't it? And you have to express yourself.'

I see the other women nodding at Ali's words. I am trying to weave together the many insights I have had over the course of the day talking with Raewyn, Jan, Ali, Bronwyn and Susanne. There is richness in our individual manner of expression and the depth of knowledge that we each have from our embodied dancing experiences. I realize that for me it is our individual understanding that matters in what we have discussed. Our knowledge is connected to our personal experiences and embodiment.

I comment, 'You know, I have this sense that I am my body of knowledge and I am the site of my research, as a solo dance maker embodying feminist theory. My interest is in having my dance be me – I recognize that I am an embodied knower and in dancing I am sharing my knowledge in my solo dance … does that make any sense?'

I get nods and smiles in reply. While I have struggled to articulate my experiences of embodied ways of knowing, I feel that the other women understand what I mean in some way, and we are becoming clearer and creating more sophisticated understandings together. We each have individual embodied understandings and experiences, yet we all share some interests in making wider social, political and feminist commentary through our dance making. We also come to understand ourselves, and our relationships in the world, in new and rich ways through our embodied ways of knowing.

As I am pondering this further, Ali muses out loud, touching on something that I feel in my cells is at the heart of embodied ways of knowing.

'I'm thinking about myself as a place to store knowledge, a kind of diary or running journal. A place to store knowledge, a place to extract knowledge from, and a place to exhibit knowledge. And that exhibition is revealing the organized integrated mind/body/spirit. Ultimately, that is what a great dancer can reveal, not just for their own sake, but as a kind of "calling". I think that the most we can do for humans, as a contribution toward life and peace on earth, is to reveal ourselves fully in our wholeness. And to try to realize our potential in whatever way we can. Maybe what is most important is this embodiment and wholeness – the exhibition of a person at their most whole and beautiful.'

With Ali's last comments, I cannot stop myself cheering this time! The room fills with smiles and as we bring our discussion to an end, it feels like we are all encouraged from this process of sharing and constructing knowledge together.

* * *

'Hey Karen, are you reading me your paper or what?' my sister's voice brings me immediately back to the present. She is curled up comfortably on the couch now. I make out the title of the upturned paper on the floor beside her – *Documentary and Descriptive Linguistics*

(Himmelmann 1998). My sister is a linguist and agonizes over field methodology as much as I do about writing methodologies.

'Do you think I should read some quotes from my research findings to liven up my presentation?' I ask. 'I really don't want to just read out theory stuff, you know.'

'I'm not sure what you should do – maybe just keep going with what you had planned. It's getting late and we have to catch the early airport shuttle. You will be fine. Stop stressing.'

Noticing my sister's tired voice, I locate my abandoned paper from the now-strewn contents of my suitcase.

'Ready?' I ask.

Embodied engagement in arts research: Embodied ways of knowing

Derived from my own experiences and discussion with other dancing women, I developed an articulation of the epistemological strategy of 'embodied ways of knowing' to integrate my alternative understanding of embodiment. An embodied strategy for knowing acknowledges explicitly the importance and influence of who a person is. Individual differences (including gender) cannot be denied in the pursuit of knowledge or the quest for self, but need to be highlighted. In my outline of an epistemological strategy for embodied knowing below, I integrate research literature on creativity.

Firstly, embodied knowledge is developed from experiencing knowledge as constructed, contextual and embodied. In using an embodied strategy for knowing, we can experience ourselves as already embodying knowledge and also as able to create knowledge. This means that we must value our own experiential ways of knowing, such as dancing or paddling or playing the violin, and that we can work towards reconciling knowledge gained from these experiences with knowledge gained through other strategies, in a personally meaningful way as we live out our lives. In this sense, we individuals, using an embodied way of knowing, attempt to understand knowledge as constructed or created rather than existing as independent truths 'out there in the world' and, more importantly, as embodied, experienced and lived. So, knowledge that seems intuitively important can become integrated and assimilated with knowledge learned from others (Belenky et al. 1986; Stinson 1995), and with a conscious awareness of how to embody them. In this way, knowledge can be woven together with passion, experience and embodied individuality.

Secondly, embodied knowledge arises in the lived experience of combining different ideas through experimentation. Using an embodied strategy for knowing means that we creatively search for and judge potential new combinations and juxtapositions of familiar and perhaps seemingly unrelated knowledge and experiences (Eisner 2002a; Fraser 2004; Gardner and Dempster 1990). Einstein (1952) called this 'combinatory play'. Insight and intelligence are required to accommodate internal representations in relation to experiences in the world (Stinson 1985), and to understand a wide range of sources of existing knowledge from which we might perceive gaps and subsequently create new knowledge (Fraser 2004). Redefining problems, considering recurring themes, recognising patterns and relationships to see things anew are all part of embodied ways of knowing and this requires new questions, new methods of research, new ways of representation and no small measure of flexibility (Eisner 2002a; Fraser 2004). For those of us using an embodied knowledge strategy, living with alternative understandings of the dominant knowledge creates challenges and tensions that we continually have to resolve throughout our lives. As creative people, we will often be required to deal with tensions and to tolerate ambiguity. It may be that resolutions do not necessarily come through rationalisation, or through intuition, but through embodying and actually living out the possibilities. In living out the possibilities, we experience and evaluate knowledge, sometimes discarding knowledge that is not relevant or liveable in our own lives. In this sense, embodied ways of knowing foreground knowing as creatively living in the world.

The potential of embodied ways of knowing as an alternative epistemological strategy corresponds with the recent shift in academia towards accepting alternative ways of knowing, alternative research fields and new qualitative methods (Butterworth and Wildschut 2009; Denzin and Lincoln 2000; Pakes 2009; Piccini 2002, 2005). In New Zealand, my choreographic work has been acknowledged as standing alongside more traditional written research outputs using qualitative or quantitative methods (Tertiary Education Commission 2004). However, developing the rigour and fulfilling the processes necessary for master's, doctoral and ongoing research has necessitated creativity in resolving the tensions immediately apparent in articulating theoretical understandings and methodology through movement,

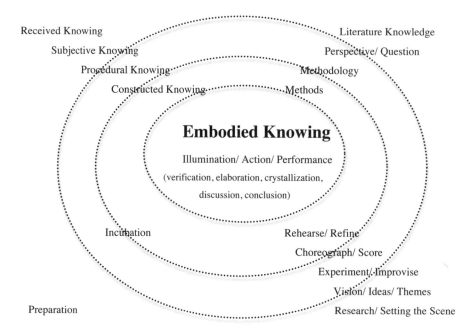

Figure 2. Embodied engagement in arts research.

and in communicating these to examiners and colleagues. From my perspective, embodied ways of knowing are required.

In Figure 2, I have attempted to link together some of the processes of research, creativity and knowing. In attempting to write or map experiences and ideas, I find that I need to move to express embodied knowledge through dancing. But this presents an ongoing tension for an academic researcher (Barbour and Mitchley 2005b; Markula and Denison 2000). As a consequence Figure 2 does not fully capture the richness of embodied research experiences. Nonetheless, it may provide a simple map for others to begin thinking about their own embodied research processes.

* * *

Embodied ways of knowing can be articulated as an epistemological strategy that corresponds with the creative and academic research processes I discussed and outlined in Figure 1. In Figure 2, there are further relationships apparent between the various epistemological strategies and the stages within creative and research processes. In a sense, however, embodied ways of knowing might ripple outwards to encompass all research stages, so that a dance researcher might undertake 'literature review' through engagement in embodied experiences (such as training and focused practice in yoga) and devise choreographic research methods working in the dance studio (based on reflection on patterns of communication and life experiences).

Engaging in embodied research prompted questions as to how I might develop my research skills and creative processes to support research through embodied ways of knowing. I now wish to offer some guidelines I have derived for embodied engagement in arts research. Here I draw on the wider educational research and the context of experiential learning (Kolb and Fry 1975). The experiential learning model outlined by Kolb and Fry (1975) and developed by others (such as Bright 2005, 2010) places the 'concrete experience', or arts practice, within a cycle of ongoing reflection and engagement. Following a concrete experience is a phase of reflection on the experience, then re-evaluation and, finally, conclusion, outcomes and a future action plan that feeds back into arts practice. Many models of creative process in the arts, such as those indicated in Figure 1, also compliment the basic experiential learning cycle.

I make a small note in the margin of my paper: 'short movement improvisation here if there is enough space.' Turning over the pages of my paper, I notice my sister attempt to suppress a yawn and hurriedly I refocus on my words, reading more swiftly now.

Guidelines for embodied engagement in research

Based on my arguments and experiences, and drawing from literature on creativity and experiential learning,[6] I offer seven general guidelines for arts practitioners and researchers to refer to when engaging in embodied ways of knowing. These guidelines, which draw together a wide range of research, are practical and designed to assist arts researchers to

Photograph 5: In *Fluid Echoes Dance* (Barbour et al. 2007). Photograph by Cheri Waititi.

participate in academic scholarship in relevant ways. However, they are also broad guidelines that necessitate creativity on the individual researcher's part to implement.

1. *Acknowledge* that everything is possible and potentially relevant, including movement, intuition and lived experiences.
2. *Engage* in relevant literature and in art-specific learning, practice and collaboration.
3. *Play* through actively experimenting and improvising with new questions and challenges.
4. *Learn* from life, as understandings and resolutions may emerge throughout everyday life as well as within arts practice and/or research.
5. *Look again,* explore through trial and error, recognize, rehearse, redefine, re-create and reflect on themes, patterns, combinations and relationships.
6. *Be flexible* and allow many methods or means of representing yourself as researcher and artist.
7. *Proceed* with courage, passion, commitment and unbending intent to explore tension, paradox, anxiety, conflict, ambiguity and resistance to new knowledge.

The value and implications of these general guidelines will likely be different for each of us as arts researchers, in the context and medium of our artistry. Creativity in applying these guidelines is required of us as arts researchers as we undertake embodied engagement in arts research.

* * *

'Okay, I think I have gone over this enough tonight' I finish, looking apologetically at my sister. With reassuring comments she stumbles off to bed in the spare room. I make a mental note to read and re-read my paper when I am safe at my friend's house in Edinburgh.

After methodically repacking my suitcase, I place my passport and travel documents on the top of the case, ready for the early morning trip to the airport.

* * *

Forty-eight hours later, a dozen or more interminable queues, cancelled flights, unanticipated visits to cousins living in London, lost luggage and exhaustion, I arrive in Edinburgh. I do not have my bags, computer, copy of my conference paper, PowerPoint presentation files or even a change of clothes. The first day at the conference passes in a blur of anxiety as I phone home and cajole a colleague into breaking into my office computer to email me my paper and PowerPoint files. I wash my one set of clothes and leave many urgent messages with the airlines regarding my lost luggage.

For the first time since the bombing of the Greenpeace ship *Rainbow Warrior* in Auckland,[7] the long arms of terrorism touch me personally. What seemed unreal at home is making everyone nervous and suspicious around me, and affects me directly.

It is not until after I dance a small improvisation near the end of my conference presentation that I exhale fully. I had not even been aware I was holding my breath. As I shift to my final PowerPoint slide, I carefully read my additional handwritten notes, editing as I speak. I felt compelled to add to my conference presentation to emphasize my commitment to the politics of the personal, thinking globally and acting locally.

Aspirations (additional notes)

The shift in qualitative research towards an acceptance of new ways of knowing has coincided with the growth of arts research. Arts researchers can and do contribute to the development of new knowledge, not only about the arts, but to broad and general knowledge. It is a good aspiration for any researcher to contribute to knowledge generation. However, more needs to be articulated about how creative processes and research processes align, and the actual guidelines for researchers and academic institutions to support embodied arts research. Indeed, these are my aspirations in this presentation.

I believe that arts researchers should aspire to engage in embodied research to contribute to knowledge generation and also for other broader social and personal aspirations. I believe that engagement in arts research through embodied ways of knowing is particularly relevant to research here and now. In our increasingly virtual and globalized world it seems that humans are becoming more disembodied, more disconnected from local communities and contexts, and more self-destructive. A re-engagement in lived experiences in specific local contexts seems to me to be crucial to counter the sense of loss of personal empowerment that many people, especially artists, feel in the face of globalization and terrorism. Engaging in description, reflection and interpretation of our own and of other's lived experiences can open us as researchers to recognize and appreciate the diversity in human experience.

Through our research we can potentially engage actively with our own and other societies, cultures and environments as artists. Maintaining an awareness of, and respect for, diverse lived experiences can potentially enhance our own capacity to empathize kinaesthetically with others, and may support us in representing our research through the arts in order to enhance the capacity for our audiences to empathize kinaesthetically with others. Embodied engagement in arts research can allow both researchers and audiences to 'walk in another's shoes', at least for a time. As individual researchers, the knowledge we gain through arts research and practice is embodied knowledge that is available to us not only in performance and research, but also in our everyday lives. Such knowledge can be shared with our students, families and communities through our art and through living.

Finally, embodied engagement in arts research can lead to improved personal health and well being through opportunities to be active in local contexts and environments, potentially communicating messages of protest, or support or healing through our arts research and practice. Empowerment through embodied arts practice and research is a vital aspiration. Through embodied engagement in research I feel that we can be empowered to act, and aim to be responsible human beings. We can, as Andrea Olsen (2002) wrote, expand our ability to respond to, and recognize ourselves as contributing to the world around us.

*   *   *

Embodied engagement in culture: Reflections on identity

With my presentation and the conference over and finally re-united with my luggage, I begin to explore Edinburgh city. I walk the Royal Mile and catch buses from one theatre venue to the next, absorbing with enthusiasm as much of the rich feast of dance in the Edinburgh Fringe Festival as I possibly can, and a few small samples of whiskey too. Hiring a car, I venture out of the city, consulting my *Lonely Planet* guidebook to important Scottish sites, as well as tracing the geographical shifts of my ancestors around Scotland.[8]

Although I was born in Aotearoa, I trace my genealogy back to Scotland through my father, and through my mother via Canada and again back to Scotland and Ireland. I visit the buildings and towns my paternal grandparents were born and raised in, and the graves of many ancestors. I am reminded of how much travelling brings into sharp relief my own home and culture. On these journeys I wind through the Highlands in my little car and I feel strangely comfortable: the high skylines, rocky outcroppings and stormy weather remind me of the rugged landscape of my childhood. Driving down the coastline towards the Mull of Kintyre some things seem very familiar, rolling green pastures and dairy farms being common in Waikato where I live now.

However, I am yet to see those faces my Dad said I would recognize as 'people like me'. A man even comes up to me in the street saying, 'You're obviously not from around here? Where are you from?' I am only two generations removed from Scotland and I can recount my genealogy many more generations back. But somehow I do not feel this is my cultural homeland. When I automatically greet the man on the street with '*Kia ora*' (Hello), I realize how far I am from home.

Describing myself culturally as Pākehā, I distinguish myself from those who like to claim the label 'European' or 'New Zealander', and I clarify that I am not indigenous Māori. I accept that both historically and today, not all New Zealanders of predominantly European heritage identify as Pākehā (Liu 2005). It was customary for early immigrants to identify according to their specific European origins (Bell 2004). For example, my paternal grandparents, arriving in New Zealand in the 1950s, identified themselves as Scots New Zealanders. Today, many still choose 'New Zealander' to describe themselves. However, I do not support the argument made by some Pākehā that they are a new, second indigenous people of Aotearoa or 'white natives' (King 1999). Instead I recognize the United Nations' modern understanding of indigenous peoples (2004, 2010). Consequently, as a Pākehā woman, I make no claim to being indigenous and recognize that I have no continuity with pre-colonial societies. I cannot argue that Pākehā have distinct social, economic or political systems (as I share these systems with my

European ancestors and other colonial societies in various parts of the world). I feel that I am, however, aspiring towards biculturalism, engaged in a partnership with ngā iwi Māori as participating indigenous peoples and supporting their needs for protection of their unique cultural identity. As a Pākehā woman I cannot claim I have a distinct language (I speak English. I am learning to speak te reo Māori). Although some Pākehā aspects of culture and beliefs may be distinct from those of our contemporaries in Europe or even other 'New Zealanders', I am still figuring out what these significant differences are. I am a member of the dominant group in Aotearoa, not a minority. I respect ngā iwi Māori, 'resolve to maintain and reproduce their ancestral environments and systems as distinctive peoples and communities' (United Nations 2010: para 3), and I cannot advocate for anything uniquely Pākehā in this regard. In fact, the only point in the United Nations' modern understanding of indigeneity I can justifiably relate to is having a strong link to the local environment and concern about natural resources. However, I do not feel that this is an acceptable basis from which to claim indigeneity and to do so would undermine the claims of ngā iwi Māori. For me, my relationship to this land is a call to action to support environmental conservation, in partnership with Māori practices of *kaitiakitanga* (guardianship).[9]

Instead, I feel that I am part of an emerging Pākehā culture of peoples who share the islands of Aotearoa as home, and who are influenced by ngā iwi Māori, South Pacific and European cultures. I feel some resentment at the expectation that I should uncritically validate previously dominant European cultural understandings when the realities of being Pākehā seem very different to me (Bell 2002; Dann 1991; King 1999). I do not wish to be overwhelmed by colonial guilt or shame, but at the same time I sense I must not engage in the 'historical amnesia' of many New Zealanders about the injustices of colonialization (Bell 2006).

> [...] Māori and Pākehā are joined at the hip, and associating 'Pākehā' with nothing but grievances will not foster the development of a future relationship. Unlike most indigenous people, Māori hold the key to a secure national identity for all New Zealanders. This is a most precious gift to be keeping, and it should be held as a sacred trust. (Liu 2005: 16)

To me, being Pākehā means living together with ngā iwi Māori and recognizing Te Tiriti o Waitangi as the founding document of the peoples of Aotearoa. I chose this label – Pākehā – precisely to acknowledge and draw attention to the fact that my parents could immigrate here and I can live here as *tangata tiriti* (people of the Treaty) (Bell 2006).

Te Tiriti o Waitangi is the treaty that was signed at Waitangi in 1840 between chiefs of Māori tribes and colonizing representatives of the Queen of England. In part because of differences in the English and te reo Māori versions, there has been enormous injustice, loss of land and loss of autonomy for ngā iwi Māori (Orange 1987, 1989). The current disparity between Māori and Pākehā in income, access to education, health and many other socio-cultural aspects is a clear indication that the colonization process, while unsuccessful in assimilating ngā iwi Māori, has been oppressive and long lasting in its impact (King 2003; Ritchie 1992; Smith 1999).

While Te Tiriti initially served as an instrument of colonialization, as a founding document it also provides a means for redress and compensation for past wrongs (King 2003; Orange 1987, 1989; Ritchie 1992). We are now more than 30 years into the process of redress through the Waitangi Tribunal (set up in 1975). Te Tiriti provides the grounds for biculturalism, built on relationships between *tangata whenua* (ngā iwi Māori – the people of the land) and tangata tiriti (the early British colonials who settled here, all other immigrants and Pākehā.) As Jonathan Mane-Wheoki points out

> Although political and cultural biculturalism alike grow out of an historic and often painful relationship between Māori and Pākehā, other cultures join Pākehā on that side of the equation as people who have entered Aotearoa New Zealand as a result of the Crown exercising its prerogative under the Treaty. (2003: 86)

Te Tiriti thus remains a significant document and I think it provides a valuable reference for people in Aotearoa.

So, for me being Pākehā means attempting to live a bicultural life in alignment with the sentiments of the Treaty (Mane-Wheoki 2003; Orange 1987; Ritchie 1992). Te Tiriti has been interpreted as outlining a relationship of partnership, participation and protection with ngā iwi Māori (Robertson and Masters-Awatere 2007; Royal Commission on Social Policy 1988), and these are principles of relationship that I value professionally, politically and personally.

Being Pākehā means working to articulate what it is to be Pākehā because the name does not refer simply to an ethnicity (Fleras and Spoonley 1999; Ritchie 1992). Christine Dann prompts me to reflect further as she argues

> That's what becoming Pākehā is all about – thinking about who you are, how you got to be here, who was affected in the process, and where and how we go from here. Loving implies commitment. If you love this place, these islands in the South Pacific that are your home, then you have to make the commitment to knowing and caring about the land and the people. *All* the land and *all* the people. (Dann 1991: 59–60)

I also endorse the comments of Avril Bell, when she argues that '[…] any project to enhance Pākehā belonging must focus primarily on relationships with Māori (in the past as well as the present), rather than on a relationship to place that ignores Māori existence and prior claims to this place' (Bell 2004: 135; United Nations 2010 A number of scholars, notably historian Michael King (1991, 1999, 2003) and those who follow his arguments, draw on a strong sense of Pākehā relationship to land in order to define Pākehā identity. While stating a sense of relationship to land and place, and poetically expressing this relationship through art is (arguably) easy to do, 'reconciling that with a sense of history is a challenging task' (Jutel 2004: 60).

For myself as a Pākehā woman, the first step in articulating my relationship to Aotearoa, my sense of place and belonging here, is recognizing that there are already tangata whenua and I am here in relationship with tangata whenua as much as with the land. That means that I have to recognize the different understandings of kaitiakitanga and Western notions of ownership. When I reflect on my strong sense of identification with my childhood home, I know that I can only carry my relationship to that land in my heart now, because I no longer have a home or a place to stand there. I neither own nor have rights as a guardian of that land. Accepting these realities are part of my attempt to resolve and articulate Pākehā identity. While I feel I do belong here, my belonging is not necessarily straightforward and uncontentious.

Another aspect of being Pākehā that I see is the obligation to stand against injustice, whether this is articulated through supporting the rights of ngā iwi Māori or protesting against nuclear testing in the South Pacific. Such political commitments for me particularly are expressed as a Pākehā and feminist consciousness. Being a Pākehā feminist means standing against injustice and violence in relationships, families, communities, sport and in environmental or political terrorism.

Being Pākehā also means celebrating and providing spaces for expressions of cultural, gendered, embodied differences in all the communities in Aotearoa. As a member of the broader community of artists and particularly, the dance community, I recognize and support the development of diverse methods of artistic expression. In contemporary dance, I admire and support the teaching, choreography and performances of many culturally different dancers as much as the Pākehā dancers with whom I have undertaken research work. However, I retain my focus as a researcher on writing about Pākehā dancers because, as I explained in Chapter Three, I feel this is an ethical approach consistent with my feminist agendas.

I travelled to Scotland to present a conference paper about embodied engagement in arts research. Necessarily, my embodiment is the means through which I experience the world and my means of artistic expression. My fledgling attempts to articulate embodied ways of knowing, or to demonstrate them in dance, led me to new understandings. My enthusiasm for fostering embodied research contributes to the generation of new understandings and methodologies in creative practice as research.

I know also that the new embodied knowledge I develop as I travel feeds into my deeply felt commitment to expression through narrative and embodied ways of knowing. The continuing relevance of dance and creative practice in expressing my individual human embodied experience, in this increasingly virtual and global world, is even more apparent to me. I am committed to researching my own experiences of embodiment, gender and culture further as part of my commitment to the politics of the personal and the local. As an educator, I realize that I am committed to offering opportunities for my students to engage in knowing differently and in living creative lives through their learning in dance.

Notes

1. Some of this chapter was published as 'Embodied engagement in arts research', *The International Journal of Arts in Society*, 1: 2, pp. 85–91.

2. For examples, see Bannon (2004); Barbour (2007a); Brew (1998); Dewey (1934); Eisner (1998, 2002b); Grove et al. (2005); Ness (2004); Piccini (2005); Tertiary Education Commission (2004).

3. For examples, see Ashley (2002); Balkin (1990); Bannon (2004); Coe (1999); Janesick (2000); Schrader (2005); Van Dijk (2006).

4. I have discussed embodiment earlier in Chapter Four and the continuing discussion in this chapter provides the 'pivot point' for my book. In previous chapters I represent the research and experiential 'grounds' for articulating embodiment and embodied ways of knowing. Subsequent chapters represent research that builds upon my articulation of embodied ways of knowing. Additionally, my discussion of Pākehā cultural identity also provides a 'pivot point' for the unfolding themes relating to culture and identity in this book.

5. This narrative excerpt follows on the narratives in Chapters Three and Four.

6. Drawing on Ashley (2002); Balkin (1990); Brew (1998); Bright (2005); Einstein (1952); Eisner (2002a); Fraser (2004); Green (1996); Kolb and Fry (1975); Schrader (2005).

7. To date, New Zealanders have had few experiences of terrorism at home. The notable exception – the 1985 bombing by French military security service of the Greenpeace ship Rainbow Warrior while it was anchored in Auckland – caused an enormous public outcry and lingers in the memory of many of us (King 2003).

8. While clearly my travelling after my conference and festival experiences does not constitute a 'big OE', I was undertaking a small 'secular pilgrimage' to explore places familiar to me through family stories of our Scottish heritage (Bell 2002). My earlier travels through Canada (referred to in Chapter Two) provided the opportunity to explore places and spend time with my Canadian family. Like many others travelling away from New Zealand in this type of secular pilgrimage, I became much more conscious of my cultural and personal identity as distinct from these origins (Bell 2002).

9. *Kaitiakitanga* is usually understood as the practices of guardianship and/or the roles of a being trustee, custodian or caretaker (Ngata Dictionary 2007; Ritchie 1992).

Chapter 6

Standing Strong: Pedagogical Approaches to Affirming Identity

O pen umbrella clutched in one hand and kete (woven flax basket) of teaching materials in the other, I walk across campus hoping to reach the warmth of the Academy of Performing Arts before the spring rain becomes torrential. Underneath the safety of the umbrella, I consider Sherry Shapiro's (1998: 14–15) inspiring quotation as I move.

This shift from disembodied knowing to embodied knowing calls into question traditional dance pedagogy. The question of knowledge changes the relationship between the teacher and the student. The intent of the learning experience moves from one of learning movement vocabulary for the sake of creating dance to gaining an understanding of the self, others, and the larger world for the possibility of change.

While I keep this quotation foremost in my planning for teaching, it certainly takes some time to unpack and transform dance exercises and activities in order to develop a different pedagogical approach.[1] Today I have some different ideas for my third-year class, a diverse group of Pākehā, Māori and Pacific Island students whom I have been encouraging to participate in different ways of moving and in stimulating discussion.

I catch a glimpse of feet in wet sneakers making a dash for the front entrance ahead of me and recognize Elaine's black track pants. Shaking my dripping umbrella under the shelter of the eaves, I gather my thoughts as I enter the building. Other students follow Elaine and I into the dance studio, each of us relieved by the cheery comfort of our dancing space and the time together. As I sort out my CDs, teaching notes and books, the rest of the third-year students enter and various handshakes, hugs and commiserations about late buses and other challenges pass casually around the room. I notice some settle into their own routines and rituals for beginning class: stretching quietly, joking with others while jogging around the room and others still arriving, turning off cell phones or turning up iPods for that last injection of a favourite Hip Hop track.

While I wait, I muse on previous classes, recalling how we had devoted our discussion time in class to our understandings and experiences of bodily intelligence. As a basic introduction to ways we might discuss bodily intelligence in general, I had invited the students to recall and share one of their earliest dance combinations. We had all enjoyed watching small moments of remembered movement, from both dance and sports that they had learned in childhood. The activity had also reminded me of some movements I thought I had forgotten – the positioning of arms and feet I had learned in my few childhood Scottish Highland dance classes, and the arch in my back with extended arms when completing a gymnastic tumbling routine. Over the past week, I suggested that the students write a short narrative about their childhood dance experiences, particularly in relation to their learning about gender. Today I hoped that the students might have some narratives to share. I wonder what might be revealed about masculinity and femininity from their experiences, especially given that I had offered them each copies of my narrative about my journeys in understanding gender in dance differently.

Body, gender and culture

Glancing at the clock on the wall and scanning the room, I realize it is time to begin class. I press play on the stereo and the gentle sounds of Trinity Roots[2] fill the room. Slowly the focus in the room shifts and the students gather together to sit with me on the floor for this first class of the week. They are beginning to participate in my rituals of practice too, I think with relief.

Turning the music down, I greet them 'Kia ora koutou. (Hello everyone.) How are you all? How are those injuries? Any improvements? Any weekend highlights to share?' I ask. Updates follow from each of the twelve students and then I introduce our discussion topic for the week.

'So, how did you get on with reflecting on your early movement experiences? Remember I asked you to write a short narrative[3] about how you learned about gender and culture?' I get nods from most students and one or two guilty looks. Not too bad a response I think.

'Today I'm hoping that some of you will share your short narratives with us all [...].' I sense a little anxiety about reading aloud from some students as I wait for a response.

Courtney speaks up, her focus clear in her blue eyes. 'Well, I really started thinking about femininity when I read your article but my experiences were a bit different. I have a little bit to share,' she says. Courtney is studying theatre at University and I have enjoyed her contributions and inquisitive nature in dance papers in the past. Perhaps it is theatre training that gives her confidence to share her narrative first.

Courtney reads from a fresh typed sheet of paper, brushing her long white-blonde hair away from her face and sitting upright in preparation. 'My nine year old eyes study the faded photograph of the young ballerina in awe. She looked so feminine, so light and so elegant, stretched up on pointe and dressed in a pale coloured tutu. I was so full of desire to be like the girl in the photo that I felt the hairs on the back of my neck stand up. She looked like me, only older, especially in the eyes. My mother walked into my bedroom, gentle and poised as ever. "Are you looking at those photos again Courtney?" she exclaimed, while leaning over my shoulder to study them with me. "I like them," I replied. "Mum, why did you have to give up ballet? You look so pretty here." "Because I got bored with it," she sighed, having had this conversation with me many times before. "And I wanted to be able to do other things, like be a mum." My mother kissed me on the forehead and left the room again, leaving me alone. I took another look at the photo, then ran to my dress-up box and pulled out an old floaty skirt. I put it on. It was too big but that didn't matter. I stood in front of the mirror and balanced on my tiptoes, imitating my mother in the photo.'

Sitting next to her in our circle on the floor, Holly nods, commenting immediately that she understands that childhood desire to be a ballerina. Nodding too, Desiree speaks to us all, saying that dance has always been about being feminine, about doing the 'right' moves well, although she had never critically thought much about it until now. I smile at Courtney and thank her for sharing her story.

'It is interesting to think about how we learn to "perform gender", as Judith Butler (1990) would say, through dance. I think you've given us a good example of this Courtney. Does anyone else have any thoughts?'

Speaking slowly and thoughtfully, Whetu explains that 'There is frustration for me as to how as a Māori *wahine* (woman) I am meant to begin to fit into these Western stereotypes of femininity – you know – white, slim shapely, obedient, small and youthful. Within my dance experience I want to empower the female energy and promote what we believe the feminine is about … And I think each culture has its own unique understanding of what is considered dance. This is where the challenge begins for me. I am not limited to one culture and I have come to embrace many different cultures without concern of how I am part of all these cultures. I like this quote from Lemi Ponifasio (2002: 54) "The body in this sense is the site of difference. Different peoples have their own history to access. The performance is the unveiling and the uncovering of layers that are continued in this history."'

Nods from the group follow Whetu's comments.

'Kia ora Whetu,' I respond. 'Any thoughts from you others?' I prompt a little more discussion, asking Desiree if she can respond to Whetu's comments. Desiree collects her thoughts, and then replies that femininity and culture have been concerns for her in dance.

'I do experience the expectations of how a woman should look and move in cheerleading … As a dancer and teacher in American Tap and Jazz, I do see the value in learning these techniques. However, I do feel that we place too much importance on those techniques from Europe and America, forgetting and neglecting the dance lineage we have here in Aotearoa … I think I am taking my first steps to live more within dance and move through space in a way that makes sense to me. In my solo dance I want to work with the theme of my experiences of being a *Palagi*[4] (European New Zealander) and *Niuean*[5] New Zealander and my feeling that I don't fit into just one ethnicity.'

'Hey, we should get together sometime and talk Desiree,' I hear Whetu whisper to her. A couple of other students are nodding, perhaps reflecting on their own cultural and personal experiences exploring identity.

'Interesting insights here Desiree and Whetu. I can see you are both beginning to think about how these theoretical notions might influence your dancing.'

Aware that the guys have not contributed much to the discussion yet, I ask them, 'How do you think dancing experiences might teach you about performing masculinity?'

Feeling a little unsure of whether I will get a response to this question I look around the group. Lying on his stomach across the circle from me, Wiremu's head is buried in his crossed arms, long hair tied in a loose knot at the back of his neck and the sleeves of his black sports sweatshirt emblazoned with white stripes.

I am about to check if he is awake, when he lifts his head and says, 'I've got a story about learning *Haka* from my Aunty.[6] I think it is also about learning to be a man.'

At twenty years of age, Wiremu is continually surprising me, even after three years of having him participate in dance papers. Just when I think I have lost his interest with some feminist idea, or a new improvisational activity, Wiremu seems to make a huge lateral leap and lands back in the centre of the discussion or the practice. He rifles through assorted, handwritten notes, props himself up on his elbows and begins to read to us. The other men lean in to catch his words as they spill out.

'"Wiremu stand still. Stop fidgeting around. I want a straight back, chest out, chin up, legs apart. Boy don't you dare look at the ground or else! When you do your actions they better be strong. You are a descendant of a chief, show me that you are. Look at the audience and single one of them out. Stare at them. Show them how good you are. Show them how manly you are. When you *pūkana*,[7] big eyes, tongue out, gritty teeth. And stop smiling! Haka is not about smiling. If you want to smile I'll put you in the front row of the women and give you a *poi*.[8] Do you want that?" So there I was being like my brothers, staunch and proud, with my eyes to the front, chest out, straight back and standing tall.'

Tim is clapping and snickers erupt from some of the other guys in response to Wiremu's story; I guess Tim must relate to Haka training experiences personally. The vivid image of Wiremu's aunty telling him off is enough to send a couple of the girls into giggles. Wiremu is an experienced *Kapa Haka* (form of competitive Māori dance)[9] performer and tutor, regularly demonstrating to his friends his knowledge of *mau rākau* (traditional stick fighting) in class and incorporating the precise footwork and coordination of his training in a contemporary context. Without commenting out loud about this, I reflect on the confidence he must have felt in his classmates to read this story aloud. Also, that joking around is often a strategy that he and some of the other students use to disguise or lighten some of the impact of what seem to me to be important insights.

'*He rawe* (excellent) Wiremu! I think you've given us another good example of how dance socializes us and teaches us how to be a man, or a woman. I've got a clear image of your Auntie threatening to make you dance with the women ... Before we go on to further discussion, does anyone else want to share a narrative? Remember that you can use this as an opportunity to try out your narrative and that you can include it later in your final assignment.'

I look hopefully around the group, my gaze catching Elaine's upright posture and eager face next to me.

I nod and Elaine responds, 'I've got two stories I can read out, but they don't fit together yet. Umm, so ... this first bit maybe relates to my culture and learning to dance female.'

'"All you need to do is have your hands soft and relaxed, then slide your middle finger along the face of your thumb as if you're rolling a pencil. See! You've got it, now just keep going and now move your arms like this." After years of practice and performance I don't recall ever being properly taught by someone how to dance a *Siva Samoa*[10] (Samoan dance), but will always have a memory of teaching someone else how to do it.'

'You asked about learning how to dance feminine?' says Elaine, 'well it is just part of me and my culture I guess. But I can see that if I wasn't Samoan then I wouldn't necessarily think that this dancing was feminine. Maybe I'd move differently as a woman. Anyway, well my second story is about my Hip Hop dance ... and I do remember learning this really clearly ...'

Elaine re-crosses her legs and leans over her journal spread open on the floor in front of her. I notice rough sketches, perhaps movement floor patterns, drawn on the other page from which she reads. My eyes are drawn most to her hands, following the words on the page and gesturing articulately as she speaks.

'Never in my wildest dreams did I ever think I could choreograph a dance piece. Being the youngest, I was exposed to a lot of the 80s Hip Hop music and R&B singers and bands through my older siblings. I would imitate Janet Jackson, who I admired, by attempting to dance her famous "soldier charge" moves on *Miss you much*. While other girls shopped, I spent a lot of my spare time watching video clips where back up dancers would perform with perfect rhythm in seamless synchronized movement making the technical dance moves seem effortless to do. It was when I hit my teenage years I became solely obsessed with learning dance moves ... it was a long process but eventually I was able to perform the moves as if I were one of the back up dancers ... I would always wish that I could one day become a choreographer, but it felt impossible to even create an original dance phrase ...'

'Oh I did that too,' Desiree admits with a giggle.

Excited discussion breaks out amongst the group as they recognize shared experiences. I hear one student comment, 'Do you remember that Janet track? I practiced and practiced and did it in the school talent quest.'

I hear Barry chuckle and comment to Wiremu that copying the moves on music videos was his main form of entertainment with his peers. 'Living in a poor area all you could do with your mates was play sport on the road or have dance competitions,' I hear Barry reflect.

I remember too. Even without television at home when I grew up, I had managed to learn some moves from Michael Jackson's *Thriller* video (Landis 1983) and had watched the film *Flashdance* (Lyne 1983) over and over, much to my father's dismay. While artists of an earlier era influenced me as a teenager, I recognize the huge impact of the Hip Hop and R&B music video genre on us all. It is easy to trace the spread of Hip Hop culture through our dancing (Osumare 2002, 2007).

Around me the excited chatter is drifting off topic, so I interject with a thank you to Elaine for sharing her narrative and encourage her to reflect on how she might bring together her experiences in learning to perform femininity in a Samoan cultural context and in a Hip Hop global context.

After checking to see if any other students want to read their narratives, and receiving limited enthusiasm, I shift our group discussion on.

'Okay, I've given you these different articles and today I suggest we continue more detailed discussion about the issues of masculinity and femininity in dance. How about you take some time now to discuss the relevant article on either masculinity or femininity in groups of three or so, and then we have some general discussion together. In your groups come up with some main points that you want to share with us, remembering of course that you don't have to agree with the writer's ideas. If you don't agree, please try to explain to us why you disagree, okay?'

General nods follow and the students roll across the floor and group together with a degree of comfort unusual in most University-teaching contexts.

I give them time, knowing that there will be some who have not read the readings yet but will engage if one of their classmates initiates discussion. Glancing casually over, I look for the telltale signs of students who have done their readings, finding at least one book in each group with highlighter pen or notes written in the margins. Whew – we should be able to get into some discussion then. I wander around the groups of dancers spread out on the wooden floor, lying or sitting with heads together and beginning to share experiences and responses. The murmur of their voices builds in volume and then eventually subsides. Now is the time.

'So let's move back into a circle people and share some responses to the readings. Guys, what did you make of Matthews' (2004) article on Haka and communicating messages through the body? Do you think he offers some ideas that might help us think about masculinity in haka and maybe in dance more generally?'

Looking at the guys' hesitant expressions, I catch my breath. I have lingering doubts about whether I can, as a Pākehā woman, expect to have discussion about Māori dance and masculinity. These doubts bubble up now. I am about to jump in with my disclaimer – that I am clearly no expert about Māori dance and that I am not trying to teach them about masculinity either, and that I acknowledge that some of them have been immersed in Haka their whole lives, and that maybe it is useful to reflect on some of the embodied assumptions that we each have about gender and movement within our different cultures …

Tim speaks, a little self-consciously but is engaged: 'I really got what Wiremu was saying in his narrative before. I think this article relates a bit. I like that Mathews wrote about *ihi*, *wehi* and *wana*, although it is hard to really understand these things through English words. But I can think about these things even when I'm performing a contemporary dance. You know, how does he say it in English … oh here the quote is where he tries to explain it':

The portrayal and attainment of *ihi* is considered to be the achievement of excellence in performance. *Ihi* is a psychic power that elicits a positive psychic and emotional response from the audience. The response is referred to as *wehi*; a reaction to the power of the performance. *Wana* is the condition created by the combination of the elicitation of *ihi* and the reaction of *wehi* during performance. (Matthews 2004: 10)

'Doing my solo I really want to give an excellent performance and get an emotional response from the people watching and together that helps make wana I suppose. Well that's what I reckon.'

Most of the Māori students in the group are nodding.

'Yeah that's true aye,' one of the others says quietly, perhaps unwilling to commit to a longer comment but listening closely to the discussion.

'Yeah, that's okay but I'm more interested in this other stuff he writes about Haka and movement,' says Wiremu in a characteristically confident voice.

'Maybe it's just because I'm from a different iwi, but this guy reckons that the words are most important in Haka. I think you have to have the movement too.'

He continues, 'You know that feeling, when your body is amped, muscles flexed, staunch, sharp actions, intensity, speed, precision … and your back is straight, head held high and chin parallel with the floor, giving it all. You can't captivate the crowd without having excellent movement. Us men pride ourselves on our staunchness and showing the body and our muscular attributes. No one would believe you, even if your words were good, if you looked like an idiot. "*Kia kōrero te katoa o te tinana*" (the entire body has to speak). That's from Timoti Karetu's book on Haka (1993: 22). So, even if it's not a Haka I'm doing I think I have to be staunch or people won't believe me,' he concludes.

'Yeah, but bro, you can still be a man and do contemporary dance, or else why would you be here in this dance paper?' challenges Whetu.

A few snorts escape from the other men in the group.

'Yeah, yeah. She got me into this contemporary dance but I'm still doing Kapa Haka with the whānau, with my family,' retorts Wiremu with a gesture towards me.

He continues, 'But I reckon my stance and my body type and the way I have been brought up allows me to keep to my Haka, my main style of dance … I guess stepping outside the boundaries is still a bit of a challenge even though this is my third year in dance,' Wiremu reflects and the other students nod with understanding.

'So what do you think Whetu, about performing femininity and also about ihi, wehi and wana?' I ask.

'Yeah, I thought about these things performing Kapa Haka too, but in contemporary dance I also think about them,' she replies. I wonder if the students share some common beliefs about performance, despite their different cultural backgrounds and movement heritages. I decide to prompt more consideration of the idea of cross-cultural understandings with the students.

'So thinking back to Lemi Ponifasio's article (2002) on creating cross-cultural dance in Aotearoa, some of you have seen his choreographic work, or at least photos of his work. I believe his performances are some of the most exciting and cutting-edge "dance performances", often because of the way in which he is able to shift my perspective on culture and politics, my experience of time and space and challenge my assumptions and feelings about who can dance what movements. In classes last year we talked about what "traditional" and "contemporary" dances might be, if you can remember back to those classes, and whether there is really a need to categorize dance like this. Lemi certainly challenges categorization.

There has been a tendency to label Samoan Sasa and Kapa Haka and other cultural dances "traditional dance", and use the word "contemporary" to mean this kind of Western "imported" dance that originated in Europe and America (Kaiwai and Zemke-White 2004; Taouma 2002). But of course, all dance forms evolve from somewhere. We've talked about how these labels are problematic because Western contemporary dance is also cultural and "traditional". And Kapa Haka can be seen as a "new" form of structured concert dance that developed in response to colonial musical influences, rather than being "traditional" in the sense of ritualized *marae*[11] practices (Kaiwai and Zemke-White 2004). So maybe Kapa Haka can't be called "traditional". And we've talked about how Sasa seems to be a distinctly New Zealand form of Samoan dance that now even incorporates Hip Hop movements in the school groups' competitive performances at Polyfest (Polynesian Arts Festival) each year. So anyway, I think we might be able to link these ideas together next week – I'd like you to read Halifu Osumare's article on Hip Hop and the intercultural body please. Just to give you a little preview, Osumare wrote,' and I pick up my copy of her article to quote

> Against the rubric of the imported hip hop vernacular, continuing Polynesian-Asian indigenous styles are also embodied in gesture and posturing, such as martial arts and local Hawaiian gaits. The synthesis of globally proliferating popular culture body styles with local movement predilections that have been present for centuries forms what I call the Intercultural Body. (Osumare 2002: 38)

'As you read, look for what makes most sense to you, what helps you understand your own experiences as a dancer. Most of you are embedded in Hip Hop culture and dance, so this reading might add another layer to your thinking. I do think these readings will really help you as you refine your themes and improvise to develop movement for your new choreographic assignments. Okay, so, five minute break everyone, and then we will begin our dance class.'

The students collect papers together and amble out the door to fill water bottles or change for moving. Tying my outer top around my waist, I force my hair into a knot and load CDs in the stereo. I have just enough time to practice the new exercise I have planned for class before the students assemble again.

Dance class

Two-and-a-half weeks later, I am again rushing across campus to the dance studio, ready for teaching dance class and meeting students for an update on their choreographic progress. After greeting the students I begin class as I close the studio doors and press play on the stereo. The students settle on the floor, lying flat on the wood or with knees bent up in constructive rest position. Quiet surf breaks and ambient music fills the studio and I begin a slow rhythmic walk around the outside of the group, my footfalls on the wood and voice just audible over the stereo.

'Take some time to rest this morning ... allow your breathing to deepen ... let your body weight to drop into the floor ... notice how you feel today.'

A few minutes into this guided relaxation and I can feel the energy of the studio change as the students' breathing deepens and a quiet focus unites the group. My own voice slows and I fold softly down to lying on the floor with the students, encouraging them to move with each out breath, simply responding to their own movement needs. As this activity develops into a warm-up improvisation, I am reminded again of how much I need this relaxation too – how my awareness, even while teaching, can deepen to allow me to ease the tension in my shoulders as I roll into a familiar stretch.

'As you move bring yourself through to sitting ... then continue, perhaps rolling through the space. Let yourself build momentum as you move now. Maybe you can roll higher, coming to standing perhaps. And releasing back into the floor ... and move again up to standing.'

I sense the activity gradually increasing as each person participates as he or she feels appropriate today, a degree of fatigue evident in some students focused on lower-level explorations, and enthusiasm in short bursts of running and sliding obvious in others. I catch a glimpse of Holly, suspended in a small jump before collapsing into the floor to roll and spiral back to her feet. Stretching into a deep lunge myself, I notice Tim exploring balancing, hands sliding along the floor and legs swinging into the air, searching for the perfect positioning of pelvis over shoulders that will allow him to sustain his handstand.

As I find myself in 'downward facing dog' yoga stretch, I notice that the students' movement has also become a little more task- or practice-oriented and I encourage them to remain improvisational for the last minutes of the activity. As this initial activity returns us to lying on the floor, observing again how we feel, the music changes into a rhythmic track and I cue the students into the first of a series of more structured exercises, familiar enough to them that I can move around the room to observe and provide encouragement and feedback to individuals. We move through simple patterns based around human developmental movement, aiming to enhance their awareness of functional integrity and efficiency within their own bodies, while also warming up.

I remind the students of the sequence of the first standing exercise and I encourage them to transfer their learning about releasing muscle tension and finding functional alignment, from the floor where they have been relieved of some of the forces of gravity, into vertical work. The students around me remain focused but as we come to standing, they begin naturally to interact with each other. Suggesting that they now move with a partner, they progress through foot coordination exercises and into light jumping before we all begin travelling across the room. Weaving specific skill practice together with the students' own contributions of favourite movement patterns, we maintain higher heart rates and match the beat of the drumming rhythms of the music from the islands of Rarotonga.

Next I introduce the short new phrase to the students. 'Now here is a short sketch of movement for you to try. Once you feel you have got the basics, make sure you add your interpretations, flavour and style. Take this sketch and make it yours. Use your choreographic tools.'

I watch as the students work, Barry adding Hip Hop gestures and a sharper rhythmic accent, Desiree practicing one section repeatedly to incorporate a double turn and add precision to her arm placement and Holly extending one movement into a jump and spiral roll to the floor. In contrast, Whetu has slowed the movement down and concentrated her focus on centring, her breath visible to me with each movement. Wiremu seems to be relishing the inverted work as I watch him adapt a low cartwheel into a one-handed turning kick.

Elaine looks somewhat frustrated and I pause to enquire if she needs help.

She sighs, and comments quietly, 'From my cultural dancing and learning the proper way of dancing traditional Siva, I just always use my hands and I'm meticulous about details from head to toe. I find this task hard. I just automatically adjusted this movement to the styles in me – Pacific dance styles – I can never shake them off.'

I reassure Elaine that she is still doing the task set and ask if she has read Osumare's article yet. 'Do you remember the way in which Halifu Osumare (2002, 2007) described the intercultural body? How your everyday movement, popular dances like Hip Hop, and cultural dances, can become synthesized, making an embodied social identity that we are not always conscious of? Perhaps this is one way to understand what is happening for you now. What do you think?'

As she nods in response to my questions, I encourage Elaine to keep playing with the movement sketch and I suggest she try to avoid judging herself harshly.

'Eventually you will find what interests you as a choreographer,' I reassure her.

After the students have had more time to work on their task, I invite them to show their full phrases in threes for each other.

'Once each person has shown their phrase, I suggest you all have a short discussion about what makes their interpretation of the phrase unique. See if you can identify some of the specific things that make your classmate's movement different. Then swap roles. Go to it people.'

As the students work together there is scattered laughter, bursts of movement and applause as they dance, observe and discuss.

Bringing the group together into a circle, some share their insights as we finish the structured part of class with a stretch on the floor. As each of us collects layers of clothing from around the room, some preparing to rehearse now, I remind the students of their individual meetings with me to discuss their choreographic progress. I agree to meet Barry for a discussion in twenty minutes or so, and then pick up my kete and walk slowly to order a coffee, reflecting on the morning's class.

Pedagogy

Sipping coffee slowly as I enjoy the spring sunshine, I think again of the inspiring writing of Sherry Shapiro (1998) and my attempts to develop my pedagogical approach. A page is marked in my personal copy of her book, handy in my kete, and I open it to remind myself of the full quotation.

> [...] the body in feminist and postmodern theorizing comes to be seen as the personal material on which inscriptions or particular discourses of the culture have become embedded. To read the body in dance education is to see the values of the culture from whence it comes. In Western traditions, the body in dance is discussed in terms of size, shape, technique, flexibility, and life (that is of the body). It is a biological and physiological object. Contrary to Western traditions, I see the body first as a subject inscribed by cultural meanings and values of our time. The body is a vehicle for understanding oppression, resistance, and liberation. This shift from disembodied knowing to embodied knowing calls into question traditional dance pedagogy. The question of knowledge changes the relationship between the teacher and the student. The intent of the learning experience moves from one of learning movement vocabulary for the sake of creating dance to gaining an understanding of the self, others, and the larger world for the possibility of change. (Shapiro 1998: 14–15)

Having trained as a dancer, I still want to see a certain amount of physical competence and sophistication in the students' movement vocabulary. As a feminist I desire to see the students develop for themselves their own ways of moving and to create their own art works. At times I worry that I do not give them enough repetition and discipline to master useful techniques and skills, such as working as a unified ensemble or to achieve recognizable patterns familiar to dancers internationally. But what is the value of only learning 'chassé pas de bourrée glisse assemble with classically positioned arms' or even 'eagle left eagle right two step drop six step freeze' when ultimately I hope they will come to understand dance more as a site of embodied knowing, rather than solely as a means of demonstrating mastery, regulation and control. I have been trying to balance the development of movement technique with creative and individual movement expression in my classes.

But how much technique do I need to teach when, as Elaine recognized this morning and others have articulated through discussion, they are already encoded with sophisticated movement vocabularies that they value? In fact, what right do I have anyway to expect that adding to such rich existing dance knowledge by making them learn some of the eclectic contemporary dance preferences that make up my own vocabulary is appropriate for these students? These questions trouble me. Flicking through the remaining pages of Shapiro's chapter I read

> Arts education can be a place where students make connections between the personal and the social; develop their perceptual, imaginative, and sensual abilities; find their own voices; validate their feelings and capacity for compassion; and become empowered through affirmation of their ability to be co-creators of their world. (Shapiro 1998: 18)

As I reflect on my teaching, I realize that fostering embodied ways of knowing in the studio is integral to my teaching practice. Supporting the students to recognize their existing embodied knowledge and their potential to create new understandings is important to me

Photograph 6: Patti Mitchley, Karen Barbour, Emma Goldsworthy and Alex Hitchmough in *Dancing Through Paradise* (Barbour 2010). Photograph by Marcia Mitchley.

to integrate within dance activities and assessments. Alongside this focus is a deliberate celebration of the students' embodied, cultural, gendered and other differences (Bolwell 1998; Mane-Wheoki 2003). I see this as reflected in encouragement for students to draw on their varied existing dance knowledge and their cultural heritages as they undertake assessment tasks and engage in new learning. I continually invite the students to reflect on their learning about body, gender and culture, and to share their experiences in discussion, written assessment and in dance. It is important that in celebrating the students' embodied differences I avoid imposing my own knowledge and practices upon them. I believe strongly that exchange and dialogue is a more respectful process for teaching and learning.

My ruminations reveal to me that supporting the development of critical understandings through embodied reflection on notions such as the intercultural body (Osumare 2002) and gender performance (Butler 1990) is particularly productive. However, the development of critical understandings seems to be more meaningful for these students when undertaken as creative, narrative and embodied explorations.

Of course, these specific pedagogical strategies are situated within familiar, general pedagogical approaches, the foundation of which I believe is the development of a student-centred, supportive learning environment. An important part of such a learning environment, from my perspective, is reducing the power relationship between students and teacher – a more general and feminist pedagogical agenda I hold. Using open-ended questions that encourage students to respond in the manner most appropriate for them assists further in keeping the focus on their learning. Reflection plays a significant pedagogical role, in discussions, in movement activities and in artistic and written forms (Coe 2003; Leijen et al. 2008). Reflection allows the students to recognize their learning and to demonstrate their new understandings within the class. Providing individual, respectful verbal and movement feedback, and negotiating both content and assessment are also more general pedagogical strategies I employ (Gibbons 2004; Hamalainen 2004). As I continue researching my own practices, I anticipate further understandings will unfold.

I figure it will be a long process of transforming my teaching, but I suppose at least I am trying to be conscious of the movement I am encoded with, and the teaching and learning methods I use. I hope I am offering my knowledge in such a way that students can be co-creators: this is something at least. And I am, as dance educator Tina Hong suggested, actively trying 'to take due consideration of the multicultural dance heritage of the student population and incorporate their contributions accordingly' (2003: 153).

I feel the familiar circle of this debate come around again as I finish my coffee – Lemi Ponifasio's words ringing in my ears as I walk back to the Academy of Performing Arts to meet Barry. 'The body in this sense is the site of difference. Different peoples have their own history to access' (Ponifasio 2002: 54). There is so much for me to ponder and at times I feel the weight of responsibility of my work as an educator. Negotiating issues of personal and cultural identity is a challenge for me personally, before I even begin to face the dynamics of teaching 12 unique students. A colleague, Tainui educator Bella Te Aku Graham, suggested that 'We need Western academics to challenge and *change* the inherent hegemony of the

Academy leaving us to speak for ourselves' (Graham, 1995: 61 italics in original). Is this my role as a dance educator – to challenge and change the hegemony within dance studios? Am I here to create a space for these students to speak for themselves?

Face to face with students

Reaching the Academy foyer, I turn my attention to Barry. As we sit together at an unoccupied table I wonder what he will have to say in our meeting. 'How are you going Barry? Have you chosen between the two tracks of music for your solo?'

I start our discussion generally, hoping Barry will relax a little before we get into talking about the development of his solo motifs and phrases. I had challenged Barry to work with a less literal approach to creating movement as he had produced a music video style interpretation of a Pop song about heartbreak for the first version of his solo dance. I had been giving him a lot of comments in class about his alignment too, hoping to encourage him to stand taller and move more confidently. So I was expecting a little anxiety from Barry about my 'expectations' of him and concerned that I had pushed too hard.

Barry replies, 'Oh, no not yet, I'm still listening to both music tracks. But I've been thinking about metaphor and what you said about me being too literal.'

Barry speaks quickly, talking immediately about the focus of his solo explorations and I realize that the anxiety I had expected has become excitement about his experiences.

He explains in a rush, 'My first rendition of my solo would have taken more shape if a metaphor was used I think. I had a picture in my mind of being in love and the only movement motifs I came up with were obvious ones and … I ended up using the lyrics to develop my story, instead of creating a personal story with different movement metaphors I could of created. Then rehearsing with you, you said "why not try opening up your chest and spreading your arms?" Then a light bulb turned on in my head. I thought "why not personalize my dance completely to help me perform to my best?" This move of opening my arms and chest has become a major movement motif that I've used in different ways throughout the piece. I think this is a huge improvement on my motif used in the original piece' he finishes, looking expectantly at me.

Barry's enthusiasm is catching, almost hiding the small doubt I feel about whether I have influenced Barry's motif development too much. But I respond positively, agreeing that this new motif could be more evocative, and that when I watched him in rehearsal, even not knowing what he was intending exactly, I had felt some of his vulnerability in the movement myself and had empathized with his expression of emotion.

'Great work Barry. Maybe this solo will allow you to move through your experiences to feeling differently. This is what I mean when I talk about embodied knowing – how we can understand our experiences differently through moving. Where are you at now with completing your solo? Do you know how you will end your dance yet? Do you have a different ending now?' I enquire.

'Well, nearly, it just depends on which track of music I use really.'

After discussing our production timeline leading up to performance, I suggest to Barry that he make his decision about music as soon as possible so that he can complete his choreography, focus on rehearsing and think about his costume too.

Sauntering off to rehearse again, I conclude that Barry is closer to completing his solo.

As Barry disappears into the Dance Studio, Holly walks over to me in the foyer and folds herself into the empty chair, half-eaten apple in hand. I listen eagerly as she describes her last rehearsal morning, munching her apple between sentences. 'I was working away and just felt like I wasn't getting anywhere, you know?' she begins.

I respond sympathetically, knowing exactly how this feels myself.

'I'd restart the sound track and quickly run to the centre of the studio to practice my motifs yet again. As the music started I'd slowly begin, turning and swaying my entire body. The speed and quality of my motifs gradually intensified, contrasting the music in my effort to imitate the wild and ever changing wind. But after that I'd struggle with slow, sustained balancing movements and lose my balance and fall,' she finishes, with a sigh and shaking her hand with the recollection of a fall.

Seeing my concern, she hastens, 'It's all right, I just don't want to keep doing that. I kept thinking to myself – what's wrong with me? Why is this so hard? My preconceived ideas for my motif and this piece just didn't seem to be working. So I was ready to give up and planning to tell you I was stuck. But I decided to try once more. This time however, I thought I'd use improvisation and try responding spontaneously ... As the music started, I took a deep breath and attempted to improvise movement relevant to me. Inspired by my theme and the music, I started slow, moving around on the floor. Gradually I made my way up to standing, continuing to try new movements inspired by the theme ... As the dance progressed, I felt like my creativity bloomed and my personal excitement built as I started to discover ideal movement motifs to express my theme! Anyway, so I think I found it just now – I think I know how to develop my solo!'

Holly jumps up to show me her new movement phrase and we both celebrate her moment of inspiration.

'Well done Holly. You've got through being stuck and used your improvisational skills really effectively. Is there anything I can help with now? You do know what our production timeline is?' I ask.

'Yes, yes, I'm okay. Can I just go back and keep working on this phrase? I feel I need to just keep going.'

'Of course', I reply, chuckling as she races back to the studio, apple core left forgotten on the table in front of me. Throwing the remains of Holly's apple in the rubbish bin I stand to stretch. One more meeting before lunch I think ...

Desiree wanders across the Academy foyer to my table. As we sit down together, she runs her fingers through her loose hair and re-folds the top of her dance pants.

'Nice work today in class', I begin. 'Did you find the activity to create your own version of my sketch phrase helpful?'

'Yes, although it was hard not to just make it into something jazzy,' she confesses. 'This semester I feel I have taken my first steps in working through a process where I feel like I have been challenged to move as an aware and thinking dancer. You know I've been dancing jazz, tap and cheerleading for years. But, always, previously, I thought dancing was purely kinaesthetic.'

I nod, understanding that this shift from dance as achievement of objective form to dance as an experience and an embodied way of knowing is challenging, particularly for dancers trained in 'traditional' dance studios.

Desiree continues, 'However, these theoretical articles with ideas about gender, body and culture that you gave us, and me being more thoughtful about my choices of dance moves, and basing my dance piece on actual themes, I realize that I actually do think as a dancer. In fact I feel that dancing should instead be approached holistically, to not only achieve relevant movement, but to acknowledge it as an emotional, intelligent and physically challenging act. Hey, I should write this down for my assignment.'

'Do write these ideas down Desiree. I can see you're engaging more critically and I imagine that these ideas are influencing your choreography too. Are you still exploring identity in your solo?'

'Actually yes, well, I think so', she says. 'My movement motifs for my solo *Half 'n half* were developed from situations where I have found myself disconnected … not at peace or confident in my own skin. I used my "body intelligence" to illustrate these ideas. For an example, at an Uncle's funeral I was unable to lament his passing in a Niuean hymn as I am unable to speak Niuean and I didn't know the hymn. Everyone else seemed to know. That redundant, empty feeling set my heart thumping faster and faster, eventually releasing when I finally cried … From this feeling in my body I created movement that felt like a heartbeat speeding up and then releasing. Another idea that I used was acknowledging both sides of my heritage, through reaching out to each side of the stage. However, I decided to return to the centre of the stage to show my position as not being just Niuean or just Palagi. But I personally find it difficult to perform emotional issues in front of an audience and I was disappointed when I watched the DVD of my solo because I don't think the audience could tell it was emotional. So I want to keep working on not masking my emotions and not having this glazed-over look.'

Desiree sits quietly, reflecting privately. I suggest gently that she keep working with these themes and remark on her courage to explore these challenges through embodied knowing. After arranging a time to offer Desiree some support while rehearsing the following day, we hug goodbye. I collect my CDs from the Dance Studio where Wiremu and Holly are still rehearsing determinedly.

Emerging from the Academy building I breathe in the spring air. The fresh smell of moist earth permeates my being as I meander back to my office. Musing on Desiree's comments, a sentence from research on cultural identities in education pops helpfully into my awareness: 'the recognition of our cultural and historical situatedness should not set the limits of ethnicity and culture, nor act to undermine the legitimacy of other, equally valid forms of identity' (May 1999: 33). This seems to fit with Lemi Ponifasio's demand that 'cultural identity must not limit the imagination of the body' (2002: 54). Hmm ... something to add in relation to my coffee-inspired personal debates.

Back in my office, I follow up an article on 'culturalisms' in arts education in Aotearoa, pondering the way in which dance students may need support to articulate and express their multiple cultural identities as Pākehā or Palagi, as well as Māori, Samoan or Chinese.

> Studying the ways in which the lived experiences of being Māori, Pacific Islander or Asian in New Zealand are expressed in the arts is relatively straightforward: finding the Pākehā equivalents is more problematic. While Pākehā identity and culture have begun to be systematically studied by sociologists, historians and linguists [...] the arts of the Pākehā have yet to be theorised. When this occurs, as it must, the Pākehā arts will claim their rightful place alongside the Māori, Pacific and the emerging Asian New Zealand arts – separated out to demonstrate the richness and diversity of our cultural scene – as the authentic New Zealand expression they undoubtedly are. (Mane-Wheoki 2003: 89–90)

While I have been thinking about supporting the students and developing more critical pedagogical approaches, I realize the challenge in these words for me personally. Perhaps I should be contributing to 'theorizing' Pākehā dance? Maybe my research into solo contemporary dance can be part of my contribution? I recognize that, throughout all the rich dancing forms of the South Pacific, solo dance performed for personal self-expression is rare. In this sense, perhaps solo contemporary dance is more clearly a Pākehā dance?

The freedom of the imagination of the body (Ponisfasio 2002) and the legitimacy of self-expression in contemporary dance can be translated into classroom activities and, I imagine, into opportunities for students to articulate their own identities through solo dance. I have to critically consider how I undertake such activities to avoid just imposing my own Pākehā beliefs and movement practices on my students. This is the challenge I feel acutely as an educator and I take up as a dance researcher.

Pondering these ideas, I recall the comments Whetu made in her earlier written reflection about the first version of her solo work. She submitted a painting and poem with her written work, demonstrating her integrated perspective of *ngā toi* (the arts) and their function in her own life. She had again drawn on Lemi Ponifasio's (2002) writing about the imagination of the body.

Locating my copy of Whetu's work, I scan through her artistically presented assessment until I find the section and read, 'Each culture has its own unique understanding of what is considered dance due to the context, function, process, structures and aesthetics ... I find satisfaction in the wholeness that I am from being a part of all these cultures. I celebrate these cultures by enhancing my views of what is understood to be dance ... and to find movement that is relevant to me as Māori with all its vast values, *tikanga*,[12] beliefs and historical and present state. I cannot be defined by one culture, I have had the privilege of being exposed to a number of cultures and they have all influenced the person I am today … In accordance with Mead, "Creative talent was expected to be used to enhance the quality of life, to transform the environment and to apply the stamp of culture on it" (2003: 263). Thus I shall proceed by making and pushing boundaries of fear within the Aotearoa dance world. I want to explore the variety in Māori contemporary, contemporary dance and Kapa Haka.'

As I continue reading, a little of the tension I feel about my role as a teacher starts to dissipate. Sometimes I feel like my role is to introduce students to experiences and ideas, and then to simply get out of the way so as to allow them to come to know through their own embodiment. Certainly, as I read Whetu's intelligent and thought-provoking personal conclusions I gain more and more admiration for her ability to explore the challenges of personal and cultural identity and express them through her articulate art works.

Student solos

Sitting in the dark of the lighting booth, ready to press play, eyes searching for the stage manager's cue, my breath is shallow and muscles tense. I have been in this moment so many times as a performer. But tonight I am here watching my students' final assessment performances … and operating the sound system. I get the wave from the stage manager. I sense the lighting operator's hands move beside me and amber lights slowly rise to reveal Elaine standing with her back to us. Moving in the silence, anticipating the soft piano chords, she begins tracing expressive arcs through the empty space with long gestures.

Dressed simply in black pants, a white top, with bare feet and her glossy black hair swinging from a ponytail, Elaine's grace is mesmerizing, feminine but articulate, thoughtful and unique. Fragments of the lyrics – 'let me start all over again' – resonate in my shoulders as the dynamic of her movement catches my breath and I feel as though I open my arms with her, dropping to curl too and undulating while my foot sweeps the surface of the wood. In that indefinable magic of theatre, Elaine's presence transforms the empty space of wooden boards, black curtains and honey coloured-light, wrapping me in a cocoon with the rest of the audience and drawing us all into her experiences. Rather than embellishment, her gestures seem almost to write her experiences visibly through the space as she arches and curls her torso, sinking to the floor and rising to fly in surprising travelling barrel rolls. As she returns to centre, her eyes follow her delicately circling wrists and flowing fingers. The backs of her fingertips brush softly up her neck to lift her chin. I sense the traces of Siva, of contemporary dance and of Hip Hop, and I register that these movement knowledges have somehow become integrated and embodied in an entirely captivating Elaine. Cheers and enthusiastic applause fill the Dance Studio as the lights fade.

With a growing sense of pride I watch the students fill the space and the audience with their personal stories; Barry's intensity of expression, his arms spread wide, head back and heart open as he repeats that evocative motif, contrasting with staccato Hip Hop gestures, head up and confident in his ability to communicate.

Desiree commands the space with a lyrical quality that is infused by her movement backgrounds, and yet, like her own sense of cultural identity, refuses being labelled.

Wiremu rises from the floor to take a familiar stance, hands clasped as though wielding a *rākau* (fighting stick). His fists clench, readiness vibrating through his body but then softening as his footwork shifts from precise steps to sliding and pivoting, his spine mobilizing and one hand dropping to the floor into a cartwheel turn. Culminating with the dynamic build of the music, these strands of mau räkau, Hip Hop gyrations and crouching contemporary floor work somehow weave together into Wiremu, standing before us.

Scarcely drawing a breath, I move through my tasks with the protocols of theatre, attending to sound cues and feeling the programme build with almost tangible momentum. Courtney's solo allows her to indulge in her childhood love of lyrical, ballet-inspired femininity, but is contrasted with her musical-theatre characterization of 'Alice' from 'Alice in Wonderland'. She retains an overtly feminine costume – white silk with long white-blonde hair flowing freely and accentuated eyes drawing my attention to her facial expression. Yet these are conscious choices I know; deliberate gender performances undertaken with an appreciation that the femininity Courtney thought born in her is more a result of her own socialization and her childhood idealization of her ballerina mother. Courtney chooses to present herself as feminine in this dance and yet she meets the eyes of the audience, curiosity and intelligence unsuppressed by her performing femininity.

Tim, well, he appears to hang suspended in the space, intent on exploring the mechanics of movement, surprising the audience with sudden gymnastic rotations, his risk-taking contrasted with the surety of his solid embodiment.

Whetu's performance, accompanied by her father's artistry on a sitar, creates a space in which her embodied cultural heritages and influences weave together with a sense of meditative ritual.

Watching Holly's solo concludes the evening's program, I share the pride I know she feels in revealing the layers of her past history and heritage. Her variations of light, visually aesthetic reaching movements contrasting with swinging and collapsing reflect both her theme and her intercultural body. As she dances I recall Holly's description of how an old *Kuia* (respected female elder) quietly explained that she saw Holly as a contemporary replica of her great grandmother, a Māori performer renown for her charismatic performances. Holly carries this story with her, celebrating her inherited traits and strengths from her ancestors. Passion, commitment and a deeply rooted sense of spirituality resounds in Holly's performance, swelling my chest and inspiring me to rise to join the audience's cheering and applause.

Lined up across the stage, the students stand strong, heads held high, hands clasped, smiles wide. I rush down stairs to hug each of them as they arrive back stage.

Epilogue

In her final narrative assignment Elaine writes, 'After a night out celebrating a captivating and overwhelming performance I lay in bed contemplating what I had accomplished both as a performer and a choreographer. Endless hours of rushed rehearsals, high and low moments of appraisal and frustration, thinking how to come up with an engaging performance before taking the first steps to get there … Loads of thoughts popped up one after the other as I lay motionless on my coloured bedspread. How on earth did I do it? It was then I realized that I had become one of them: a choreographer.'

Notes

1. An earlier version of this chapter called 'Standing Strong: Pedagogical Approaches to Affirming Identity in Dance' was published in C. Stock (ed.), *Dance Dialogues: Conversations across Cultures, Artforms and Practices, Proceedings of the 2008 World Dance Alliance Global Summit*, Brisbane, 13–18 July. Online publication, QUT Creative Industries and Ausdance, http://www.ausdance. org.au following presentation at the conference of the same name.
2. Trinity Roots was a three-piece New Zealand reggae/soul/jazz/dub band very popular during the years in which I taught these undergraduate students (cf. http://trinityroots.co.nz/).
3. The narratives that the students in this chapter share are their own and I have quoted their words at length to honour my pedagogical commitment to providing a space for them to speak about their own identities. I obtained research and ethical approval to ask students to keep and use copies of their written work following the completion of their dance paper. I situate their narratives in the chapter as though the students read them aloud to each other during classes (although I actually draw their narratives from their submitted written work. I also draw comments from the meetings I had with students from their written descriptions of their creative process). I describe the scenes in the dance studio, the meetings I had with students and try to represent their performances based on my teaching plans for classes, reflections and observations. Each student personally received a copy of the material I chose from their written work and the sections of my writing where I describe them personally. Once they had edited and approved this material, I sent the whole chapter to all of them so that they could see how I had positioned their comments and descriptions in relation to each other. I was also particularly concerned to discover whether the narrative had verisimilitude, as they were really the best judges of how 'real' I wrote the narrative. Again edits were made and finally all students approved the chapter. I note I only feature the six students who gave permission for me to use their words and agreed to be indentified by name. So the named characters are real people, with the exception of 'Tim' (a fictional character I created to support the other men).
4. Palagi is a common Polynesian word (a bit like Pākehā) and used to refer to descendents of Europeans living in the South Pacific and in Aotearoa.
5. Niuean refers to an indigenous person from the Pacific islands of Niue.
6. Haka is a generic name for all Māori dance, but is most often used to refer to the forms of dance in which men are the main focus. The most well-known Haka internationally is 'Ka mate ka mate', the Haka often performed by the New Zealand All Black rugby team (Karetu 1993).

7. Facial expressions are important in Haka, particularly pūkana (to widen the eyes), to emphasize the words and theme of the Haka (Karetu 1993; Matthews 2004) and demonstrate excellent performance.

8. A poi is a ball swung on a string, traditionally used for training exercises for the wrists in preparation for fighting and other activities, and now used as a dance in Kapa Haka competitions and performance (Huata 2000).

9. Kapa Haka is a contemporary performance and competitive form of Māori dance involving performers in lines singing, dancing, speaking and manipulating implements and/or weaponry. Kapa Haka is an enormously popular performing practice that has played a significant part in retaining knowledge and expressing cultural ways of knowing for Māori (Kaiwai and Zempke-White 2004).

10. Siva Samoa is a general name for dance from the islands of Samoa (Taouma 2002).

11. A *marae* is the central courtyard area outside the main meetinghouse in a traditional Māori settlement (Ngata Dictionary 2007). Sometimes, marae is used to refer to the whole settlement.

12. Tikanga refers to the particular sets of correct protocols, customs, conventions and guidelines that govern Māori social and cultural practices (Mead 2003; Ngata Dictionary 2007).

Chapter 7

Improvising: Dance and Everyday Life

'The truth is this. We are on an island.'[1] Enveloped in the gentle dark, registering the enticing simplicity of this statement, I lean against the wood of the backstage wall, adrenalin subsiding as I breathe. I am warm from performing and now, happily resting in the wings, waiting with anticipation for the next moment of performance. I slowly pick out a form in the darkness, tinged grey-green in the theatre light, awakening on the floor, revealed as my friend Kristian. Coming to sitting, he abruptly looks directly out at the audience, bird song of the sound score echoing in the quiet of his gaze. Sculpted lines of a shiny grey suit contain his form as he moves in and out of squares of white light, defining the dark, defining what is said and what is not. Short brown hair framing an expression that is engaged, mobile, intelligent. Small muscles around his eyes and mouth effecting twitches and shifts. Gestures deliberate, meaningful, linking logically together, conceptually embodied. Thought articulated through the motion of bones around joints, resulting in a sudden turn, a slide and he is floor-bound again.

I register the pressure of my own weight pressing into the wood, remembering sliding and the welcome sensation of relief from standing against gravity in my own cells. More and more layers of sound fill the theatre space I inhabit with Kristian, the backstage crew and the audience.

Layering gesture upon gesture, streaming thoughts rushing from skin, then a silence, the rustle of fabric and stillness. A pause. Interrupted suddenly by a well-known television theme song from the shared childhood of our generation. Humour drops into the space and suddenly Kristian is comedic, or at least he might be. Or maybe, he is deadly serious … Witnessing his choice to resist imposing a comedic narrative on top of the events of the performance, I understand freedom.

Effortlessly in the moment of improvisation, Kristian's decision-making reveals movements that engage me kinaesthetically, reappearing and manifesting as motifs: an inverted balance with legs wide then dropping to the floor, later reversing and then developing into a back arch. Riveted, I watch as he returns to gestures from initial movement after these investigations, fingers spreading, pauses of variable duration surprising me, new insights revealed through traces in the partial dark.

Then, light picking out the walls of the theatre, laid bare, he leans, slouching and falling as though someone, under the cover of darkness, removed his chair. But there never was a chair there and he chooses not to sit, but to fall into the wall. I watch dexterity, fluidity, articulation, shifting impulses and gestures, unfold and link into meaningful phrases, inviting engagement, thinking in movement. Interrupted by coughing or by an unanticipated cell phone call. Coincidences perhaps. But there are no gaps, no moments when I notice something else happening. He is now, only here, in this time. 'He decided this.'

Remnants of motifs, moments fulfilled by this or that gesture, waving good bye … and I am clapping wildly in the wings, swept up in the pleasure of performance, witnessing real-time composing.

Crafting a research project

With care I compile multiple copies of my application for research funding, preparing to submit my ideas to the scrutiny of our University research committee in the hopes of obtaining support.[2] With teaching finished for the year, I have the summer to focus on a new research project. I have written a brief overview of improvisation in dance, hoping that the diverse academics on the research committee will gain enough of an understanding of this (most likely) completely new area of creative practice in order to consider my application. As I staple pages together, I scan my introductory comments about the research.

Application for research funding

Improvisation in movement is practised by almost every contemporary dance practitioner in a wide variety of contexts (Gere 2003). Improvisation is also undertaken by most of us in our daily lives, as we negotiate traffic, speak in teaching contexts, converse with friends, meet deadlines, cook meals, play with our children and generally get on with being human. We all improvise in one way or another. 'Improvisation is everywhere in dance and … everywhere, every moment, in the world. It is present in every action and in every pregnant moment in between' (Gere 2003: xvi).

Within Western contemporary dance, movement improvisation is a common practice undertaken to generate movement material in response to particular stimuli, such as a piece of music, a theme, a sensation or an idea. Most contemporary choreographers, myself included, will begin with the practice of improvisation when starting on new movement for a choreographic work. As Susan Foster writes, improvisation is a form of 'generative play between corporeality and consciousness and between the dance of everyday life and dance as a theatrical practice' (cited in Hay 2000: ix).

For me, studio improvisation is usually a solitary process aimed at tricking myself out of movement habits by working from unusual stimuli and setting myself impossible tasks to respond to. For example, in a workshop with solo artist Deborah Hay, I was introduced to using 'meditations' to prompt investigation into my own corporeality, such as '"I" is the reconfiguration of my body into fifty-three trillion cells at once' (2000: 1). As Hay comments, it is impossible to attend to or process the possible feedback generated from this meditation, but asking the question and engaging in the meditation can generate movement (2000: xxiv).

Improvisation, in this context, becomes an initial research method in the choreographic process of creating a new dance work. Kent de Spain writes:

> Improvisation is a form of research, a way of peering into the complex natural system that is a human being. It is, in a sense, another way of 'thinking', but one that produces ideas impossible to conceive in stillness. (1993: 21–7)

There is a growing body of literature regarding the teaching of improvisation in the dance studio.[3] Drawing on this American and British literature and my previous dance training, I have developed an approach to improvisation as a tool for creating movement and choreographing my own dance work, and as a pedagogical method for introducing dance students to creating their own movement for choreography.

However, improvisation also provides a context for embodied ways of knowing to be shared in performance. While I use improvisation extensively in the dance studio, I have undertaken limited improvisation in performance myself. Performance improvisation is another experience entirely from the studio practice of improvisation focused around generating movement material for choreography. Rather more like the work of a proficient jazz musician, dance performance improvisation involves responding in the moment of performing to a range of environmental and personal stimuli, including the audience, other performers, emotional states, intentional drives and memories. Just as jazz musicians learn to create improvisational melodic and rhythmic variations based on knowledge of stock phrases, melodies and musical materials (Brown 2000; Foster 2002), dancers may agree upon a shared body of movement or set of tools that form the basis around which the performance hinges. In this sense, the 'improvising dancer tacks back and forth between the *known* and the *unknown*, between the familiar/reliable and the unanticipated/unpredictable' (Foster 2003: 3, italics in original). Known aspects include human behavioural conventions, structural guidelines, scores or rules agreed upon in advance, movement habits, collaboration with other people in the performance and previous experiences of improvisation in performance (Foster 2003).

Some American practitioners have explored and developed specific structures for performance improvisation, often called 'scores'. A score is a 'set of overarching structural guidelines that delimit the improvising body's choices' (Foster 2003: 4). Structuring improvisations gave dancers a method for relating to each other, as well as the freedom to make some choices and to potentially discover new movement (Foster 2002). Some historic examples within dance writing include Steve Paxton's 1967 work *Satisfying Lover* which involved walking, standing and sitting on a chair (Paxton, cited in Banes 2003a). Yvonne Rainer's work with the Grand Union group of dancers, *Continuous project – Altered daily*, was performed first in 1969 and included known movement material, scenarios, props and relationships between performers that evolved through many performances into a looser structure with more choices for each performer (Banes 1978 2003b). Richard Bull's 1985 score for *Making and doing* had a 'three-part structure of rehearsal, repetition to music, and second repetition' to guide each performance, requiring the dancers to remember what was improvised in the first part (Foster 2003: 5). Simone Forti began performing *News Animations* in 1989, starting her improvisations by carrying, placing and walking over newspapers before reading aloud selected news stories so that she could talk and move to animate (dance) the news stories (Forti 2003). This work evolved into *Logomotion*, a score based around talking and dancing three randomly chosen words from a dictionary (Hermann 2003). In each case, the specific movements the dancers performed were improvised, engaging in the known but with the resulting movement being unknown (Foster 2003).

Although, as the examples above illustrate, there is a history of practice, few practitioners other than Yvonne Rainer (1974) have published written accounts of their improvisational performance processes (Lepkoff and Paxton 2004). Notable dance writer Sally Banes published writing about the Grand Union and Judson Church group of dance practitioners working in New York City in the 1970s (see Banes 1978, 1987, 2003a, 2003b), and Susan Foster published an excellent book about improvisation practitioner Richard Bull (2002). In the last ten years, more practitioners internationally have begun to publish accounts of their practice in dance journals and to undertake graduate research. However, there remains limited academic research specifically focused on the creation of improvisational scores or structures that can be utilized to shift movement improvisation from a studio practice for choreography to a performance form in itself. Susan Foster summarizes the context of this limited research and points to the tendencies for misunderstanding the embodied knowledge and the intelligence of improvisational dance:

> Within the meager discourses describing the experience of improvisation that history has left us, the terms mind and body often stand in for the known and the unknown. We read of the improvisation as the process of letting go of the mind's thinking so that the body can do its moving in its own unpredictable way. But this description is an obfuscation, as unhelpful as it is inaccurate; surely all bodily articulation is mindful. Each body segment's sweep across space, whether direct or meandering, is thought-filled. Each corporeal modulation in effort thinks; each swelling into tension thinks; each erratic burst or undulation in energy thinks. Each accented phrasing or accelerating torque or momentary stillness is an instance of thought. Conceptualized in this way, bodily action constitutes a genre of discourse. (Foster 2003: 6–7)

In this exploratory research project I aim to work with another experienced improvisation practitioner[4] to develop skills and structures to allow movement improvisation to be taken into a performance context. Feminist and phenomenological methods, including embodied workshop activities, structured discussions and journal writing, will be utilized to engage in movement experiences, to discuss and to articulate the findings.

*   *   *

As I continue compiling my research funding application and the accompanying ethics submission, I reassure myself that my research, although perhaps foreign to my colleagues, does offer unique opportunities. I know that I am pushing some methodological boundaries in this research undertaken through creative practice. In previous research projects I made use of known qualitative methods: conducting interviews with women solos artists, collecting samples of student writing, keeping a journal to document my experiences and reflections, and creating solo dance choreography. By contrast, in this research project I venture into the unknown. While I have reviewed literature and I will undertake some structured discussions with my colleague, I want to workshop to immerse myself in improvisational methodology. I hope we can crystallize our embodied understandings together.

Letter to research participant

Tēnā koe, greetings to you Kristian

I am writing to follow up on our recent informal conversation regarding a research project in performance improvisation I am undertaking. I would like to invite you to come to work with me in December. We will be working on developing aspects of performance improvisation. In particular, my research interests are focused around the question: How can improvisational scores and/or structures be developed to support performance improvisation?

I invite you to work with me in structured discussions and in movement improvisation sessions. Discussions will likely focus around documentation of improvisation workshop activities and reflective responses, relevant research literature on performance improvisation, and the development of relevant scores and/or structures. I suggest we also work together in the dance studio to trial improvisation scores and/or structures. The opportunity may exist to trial our performance improvisation with a small invited audience. Performing is an option we may consider if you are interested, and we may also discuss the option to video any performance work ... Finally, I would like to ask you to consider being identified by name in potential research publications.

If you have any questions or concerns regarding the conditions of participation in this research project, please do not hesitate to contact myself as Principal Researcher to discuss and negotiate. I very much look forward to working with you on this research project.

Noho ora mai, may you remain well

Karen

Improvisation, choice and freedom

Finishing my sushi lunch, I relax back in my office chair. Across from me, Kristian is consuming a filled roll sandwich and declaring between mouthfuls that he does not count my sushi as food. We debate jokingly about the nutritional benefits and aesthetics of sushi and eventually agree to differ. One ankle crossed easily over his knee and arm slung along the back of the chair, his attire of loose pants, shirt and sneakers allows him to blend in with the student community here on campus. But Kristian is far from an average university student, as my dance students discovered over the last three days. We all participated in a workshop with Kristian in which he shared his approach to the practice of performance improvisation. He developed his approach through extended immersion in practice and a recent dance study trip to Europe, initially calling his work 'real time composition'[5] and later 'choreographic improvisation'.

During Kristian's workshop, I participated comfortably in some familiar activities, such as improvising with flow/continuous movement, and exploring the effect of stillness and breath on my movement dynamic (Larsen and Longley 2006). I appreciated the suggestions Kristian gave to pause, rather than following my first impulse to move. I noticed that I could better appreciate the value of the movement before and after the pause within this discipline. We worked also with the deliberate practice of making a clear, intentional movement proposition. These activities reminded me of how much I enjoy the state of total committment and immersion, and the sustained interest in moving that solo improvisational practice fosters. Yvonne Rainer's articulation of this experience remains useful to me:

> Improvisation, in my handling of it, demands a constant connection with some thing – object, action and/or mood – in a situation. The more connections are established the easier it is to proceed. The idea of 'more' or 'fewer' connections is related to one's degree of awareness of the total situation, including audience [...]. One must take a chance on the fitness of one's own instincts. (1974: 3)

The ideas of American artists like Rainer and Deborah Hay, as well as the teaching of my friend Alison East, contributed to my early improvisational practice.[6] Immersion in an experience, connection and attention, deepening awareness: these were all values I embodied as a dancer in my approach to improvisation. But I felt that these values and my skills in fulfilling them did not support me enough in ensemble improvisations. I often felt overwhelmed by information and caught between my desire to follow my own movement agenda and to respond to others.

As Kristian's workshop activities unfolded we progressed from solo activities to ensemble and my awareness opened to working more effectively with others. In 'the walking game' score, the movement options were reduced to simply walking through the space, changing direction and standing. Each dancer had choices to make about when to enter and exit the space, when to pause and where to walk. Even within this very simple structure or score in which there seemed to be limited options, many choices were available. When I observed the other dancers during the workshop, it was obvious that narrative, composition and interaction were revealed. Kristian also intimated to me that he had repeatedly observed as a teacher how individual expression immediately appears and how each dancer's behavioural tendencies become clear within the group.

We also practised skills that were new to me, such as 'not making anything up', and deliberately shifting focus with our eyes as we moved from close- to mid- to long-range focus.[7] A sense of enthusiasm and momentum built in me for a different approach to improvisation that might support me in performance. The more my awareness opened beyond my own movement and kinaesthetic interests (Martin 2007) and the more I attended closely to what was happening in the ensemble environment, the clearer my improvisational choices became.

Moments of choice

Workshop completed and now our lunch finished too, we sit around Kristian's Mp3 recording device on my office desk, with our coffees, journals and pens close at hand. Our conversation develops from general sharing of our improvisational experiences and values to discussing Katie Duck's comments about improvisation and choice (cited in Corbet 1999; Duck 2000). Kristian acknowledges Duck as a significant influence on his work, and he introduced some of her practices in the workshop. I have not met or danced with her myself, but reading about Duck's work stimulates many new questions for me.

With copies of a short published interview with Duck in front of us, I begin by asking Kristian specifically about her comments. 'Okay Kristian, so if I paraphrase Katie Duck, she is saying that dancers and choreographers use memorized combinations of movements and movement patterns, or what I would call "structured improvisations", so that the performer can "take a break" from the duration dilemma of the art form (Duck cited in Corbet 1999: 2). Is she saying that in improvisation you can use sections of choreography to help give you a break within the performance? Or perhaps provide some anchor within the time duration you have set for the performance?'

Thinking quickly, Kristian replies, 'You can, but it is only part of what she is saying. What interests me more is where she goes on to say "I am interested in memorized patterns up to the point that the performer still makes choice within the design" (Duck cited in Corbet 1999: 2). So in a structured improvisation, the dancers are using a score and set vocabulary. Katie is saying that she is more interested in the choices that they make as opposed to the score and the vocabulary. I really like what she says a little later on: "There is a kind of falling asleep at the wheel effect in structured improvisations where designs for dancers or musicians begin to work with the limit of time and duration" (Duck cited in Corbet 1999: 2). That is one of the things that I sort of intuitively get a bit wary of, because in some ways, you are not making any choices. In a way, what is left that is interesting is the choices made in the moment, as opposed to the score itself.'

Nodding slowly, I consider this point. I recall the ways in which, even using a stock melody that many people would recognize (a 'score'), different jazz improvisers can generate very different responses (Brown 2000). So, as Kristian is expressing, the score is a means to an end or, perhaps more accurately, a score is a means to the beginning of the improvised performance, but it is the choices the performer makes within the improvisation that are ultimately important.

Kristian continues: 'That is one of the reasons I don't think that scored improvisations are nearly as strong with regards to authorship, with regards to your consciousness of time and space and relationship ... It can be safer for sure, but for mature, experienced improvisers, there is something more. It is like being told you can wear any clothes you want to so long as it is from these two drawers. You know what I am saying?'

I agree, also knowing that sense of frustration that comes from very limited options, whether it is in dance, work, buying lunch or other areas of life. But I suppose that limitations can also be 'enabling constraints', offering a manageable range of choices.

I gesture to Kristian to encourage him to continue and he explains further: 'It is kind of like you've been given a choice but a very limited one. So scores for performance they become a little bit problematic. They become a little bit dry to actually do. It also removes choice in a way for the viewer – because it is removed from the performer it is removed from the viewer. They are not getting to see someone really making decisions, they are getting to see somebody remember the decisions that have been made for them and act upon them. For some people it is fine, that they want to get out there and be exploratory. But for me, I'm against it. You just watch an experiment for which the outcome is unspecified and there is no way of really knowing if it worked or not. I think sometimes there are different ways of looking at the word "experiment", and often people say, you know, "we were experimenting". There is experimenting with outcome and there is experimenting with no outcome. And quite often I feel like people are experimenting with no real outcome, just a "see what happens" kind of experiment. You might discover something, you might get lucky but ... maybe not.'

Perhaps this is why I usually shy away from performing improvisation myself. While I am able to accept that dancers are experimenting when improvising in the studio, I have been unsatisfied when I do not have a sense that some artistic resolution has been reached within a performance improvisation. I flash back to a performance I attended at Movement Research in New York City – an hour or so of experimentation that simply left me bored, despite the obvious talent, experience and reputation of the performers. I know I prefer to watch performances, improvised or choreographed, in which I am left with some sense of completion or resolution, and that I feel have moved me in some way. But there have been performances that, as Sally Banes describes in her writings about Grand Union, did discover something, that were experimental and that were successful without a real outcome:

The performances were without plan, without script, without a single pre-planned structure. There was no focal climax, no particular order, no illusions that were allowed to stand for more than a moment. And yet – illusion, order, climax, focus, presence, repetition, logic and structure were what the performances were always about, no matter what the surface material may have been. And somehow their performances were at their most magical when everyone on stage seemed intent on figuring out precisely what magic is, on deliberately denuding magic for themselves and for the audience [...]. Yet magic was not the goal of Grand Union. Rather than magic, they aimed at displaying the social and psychological conditions that make the 'magic' of performance possible. (Banes 1978: 48)

While not around to see Grand Union, I know that sometimes amazing, magical and revealing moments can arise spontaneously, perhaps seeming coincidental, like the phone ringing unexpectedly in a performance, for example. Such 'coincidences' can be grasped as opportunities by performers.

Coincidence

'Kristian, I recall that you were exploring coincidence in one of your earlier writings, commenting on how, if you are doing something and a phone rings, even these unplanned events have a kind of power in relation to the context or other things within the event.'

Kristian smiles, asking, 'Did I say "you can't beat reality"?'

'Yes, I think so' I reply. I riffle through my papers and locate the section he wrote:

This brings me to 'coincidence'. I was given a piece of advice about theatrical conventions by a Professor of choreography. I can't quote him precisely but he more or less said 'you can't beat reality'. He explained that if you are performing a rehearsed choreography and it is interrupted by a 'real time' event such as a dog or a child walking on stage then it doesn't matter what you are doing, the unexpected event will take precedence in the eye of the audience. That unplanned event has a certain kind of power. It is random, chance, coincidental in its nature. But it only has meaning and power in relationship to a context or another event. Coincidence has an extraordinary potential to provide meaning in a theatrical context. Also in day-to-day life. The mind perceives a coincidental event and does one of two things with it. It either associates a significant amount of meaning to it or dismisses the event as, well, mere coincidence. In improvisation we are looking to set up conditions where coincidence can occur. This is where real discovery and response to those discoveries can occur. Chance and coincidence can transform the banal and abstract into a meaningful and rewarding event to witness. (Larsen 2003a: 3)

I enjoy reading Kristian's words back to him, recalling that in one of his provocative writings, he promised a free ticket to his next show if readers read and quoted him. Largely a joke perhaps, but maybe I will get a free ticket ...

I continue, 'I like this idea that, in terms of generation or providing meaning "chance and coincidence can transform the banal and abstract into a meaningful and rewarding event"' (Larsen 2003a: 3).

'Yes, there is coincidence happening all the time. They are kind of a given, especially when ensemble composition is happening. Unless you are soloing in the space by yourself with no lights and no music and no audience, there are some co-incidences actually occurring.'

'So this is a kind of a statement of fact, in a sense? Coincidence provides meaning.'

'Yeah. Well … it provides patterns that the brain is going to put into meaning. Sometimes those interactions are very powerful, such as that dancer hurting her leg in our workshop yesterday. Essentially that was a coincidence and it was relatively banal. Someone bumped into her. But on stage it was very, very significant. It changed everything that happened before and everything after it. And, about that thing that you can't beat reality – that was reality.'

'It is tempting to say simply – improvisation is just life really, happening on stage in a specific here and now – and you can't beat that,' I muse.

Reflecting on our conversations so far, I wonder out loud where we should steer our discussion now, glancing at the pile of articles we have carefully collected over the last week and considering the list of questions in my journal arising from my workshop experiences. Kristian's approach to choreographic improvisation reveals that, just as meaning can come from the unexpected and coincidental aspects of living, meaning in performance can come from coincidence as much as from any intentions I have, or scores/structures that I might set up deliberately. I am intrigued by his comment about how coincidence can provide meaning, recalling also my solo choreographic practice of bringing together various objects and ideas from my everyday life, and movements in the studio to discover new connections, relationships and meanings. For me, the words of writer Gertrude Stein relate to these experiences, articulating the way in which life and composition (choreographed or improvised) relate, in her lecture 'Composition as explanation' (Stein 1926):

> Each period of living differs from any other period of living not in the way life is but in the way life is conducted and that authentically speaking is composition. After life has been conducted in a certain way everybody knows it but nobody knows it, little by little, nobody knows it as long as nobody knows it. Any one creating the composition in the arts does not know it either, they are conducting life and that makes their composition what it is, it makes their work compose as it does. (para 18)

Choreographic improvisation, in a sense, is living life in performance.

Some time ago, when I participated in workshops with the renowned American dance practitioner Deborah Hay, she stated 'my preparation for dancing today is my life' (1994). In that moment I became liberated as a dancer. I was released by these words from the effects of pressure to conform to technique and to demonstrate virtuosity, instead becoming free to play, to make my own choices and dance as I desired. Improvisation became an expression of freedom and choice for me.

Scores in performance

Kristian interrupts my wandering thoughts, making the decision about where to move our conversation easy. 'Let's go back to your research question because it seems pretty elusive.'

'Okay then. Can I ask you more directly: What do you consider scores to be and what do you see as the limitations in relation to scores?'

Kristian is remarkably quick to begin his answer to this supposedly elusive question. 'I tend to think of a score as appropriate in the educational context because the dancers need to experience some degree of safety, and a score or a script can offer them that. So in a way I think it's good introductory thing, so that's how would I use it. How it falls down is that it does not necessarily facilitate this quick decision making that Katie Duck is referring to' (cited in Corbet 1999).

I shuffle through our collected papers and scan the sections I highlighted. 'Hold on a minute. I want to re-read Katie's words to be sure I am with you.' Finding the marked passage, I read Duck's comments quietly to myself.

I think that the art form is defined by its use of time, space, communication and the elements. In the case of this art form (dance-choreography) body is the element. I am a strong believer in a combination of traditional techniques alongside bodywork. Intelligent dancers can make quick decisions because they not only understand the limits of their own bodywork but because they understand the limits of the body. They study body! Quick decision making comes out of understanding limit rather than potential. Edit is key! (Duck cited in Corbet 1999: 4)

I certainly relate to studying 'body', although I would say that my study is of 'embodiment' and embodied ways of knowing (rather than being about 'body' as distinct from 'mind' in the Cartesian dualistic sense). I also value the process of editing within composition, whether it is in editing my life into choreography, or editing as I live within the time of an improvisation. So some of Duck's comments resonate strongly for me. Understanding my own limitations is crucial for me within my dancing, writing and living in general. In Kristian's workshop, the walking game made understanding limitations very important. I remark to Kristian about the value of this game.

He responds, 'The walking game is a score as well as an exercise. It can be used informatively actually and probably could work in front of an audience too. But I also feel like it's an exercise. I don't want to be doing demonstrations of exercises for an audience, I want to be having some kind of active relationship with them.'

Inevitably in research, the intended focus I had for this research is shifting as I listen to Kristian identifying different issues in understanding performance improvisation that I had not considered. As he addresses the challenges of structured improvisations and scores, I open myself to other possibilities, searching for potential ways into performance improvisation for myself.

'One of the things about a score: it's a technical practice for the dancer, for the improvising dancer. What it can do is potentially offer choreographic knowledge and other kinds of compositional skills that can really illustrate things to a dance student, such as level changes and changes of direction. One can really get clever in there and try to work out how a canon can be part of a score, or spatial relationships, for example. You know, all these things I think are very, very important. And in my teaching, yeah, I use exercises that end up being scores, like the walking game.'

Recognizing my own experiences in teaching and learning in improvisation, I respond 'Oh, this makes sense to me. I've been considering scores as a starting point for performance improvisation because most of what I've done in terms of improvisation has been within my own training in an educational context. I use improvisation scores as part of the studio classroom context. So, yes, this might well be appropriate. But are you saying that this does not allow for the full range of what's possible in choreographic improvisation when you are a professional performer and you want an audience to see you.'

'Yeah. I just feel like with the way that I am working with the parameters and the skills and the ways of looking at the information and space, I feel that this offers so much more than a score and is applicable to choreography and it's composition. I feel like it's a more sophisticated set of tools than what a score can actually offer. And in a way, I am not *anti* the score; I just find that I would hate to perform it.'

As Kristian and I take a break from our discussion of choice and improvisation, I think back over the workshop this week. I remember many things – Kristian talking, gesturing with his hands, enthusiasm exuding from his pores. Then observing his passion in his practice as he taught, moved with us and later performed.

Throughout the workshop I started engaging my critical faculties more fully in choreographic improvisation, rather than simply responding to others and/or following my own movement sensations. As I worked with other dancers, I felt a sense of both co-authoring movement when we worked in ensemble, as well as 'writing' my own material, making propositions or statements clear, and being critically conscious. I felt encouraged to make such propositions, offering clear movements that others might pick up on and develop. I had choice and freedom and responsibility for what might happen in the moment, but not that idealized or weighty responsibility familiar to me as a choreographer. My role was not choreographer or dancer but instead 'composer-in-live-dialogue-with-other-artists'. So collaboration was critical in the ensemble. There needed to be dialogue and communication taking place within the moment of performance.

As I consider further our experiences in the workshop, a particular practice or score comes to mind. We participated in the ensemble practice of following a leader and stopping when we could not see the leader any more. We re-joined the group when the leader came back into peripheral vision, picking up what movement we could. There were definitely interesting and valuable compositional insights to be gained from watching the practice of 'follow-the-leader' in a studio setting and I made notes to adapt this score for my students. Kristian linked this practice to Duck's ensemble process of 'not making anything up', in which dancers take into their own body any movement they see other dancers doing, not making anything new up but gleaning movement from others. It is like a more sophisticated version of 'follow-the-leader'. I love these practices as a dancer and in working with the students I notice they embrace the opportunity to 'copy' and then adapt at will. In reflecting on his own teaching, Kristian has commented:

In my experience this process gets the dancer into a state of acute observation. They read very accurately what is happening in the ensemble and make decisions about what movements they will do based on what it is they see. What tends to happen is that beautiful, coherent ensemble integration occurs consistently and without effort. It also tends to produce new and interesting movement precessionally without the dancer having to focus on that as a conscious task. (Larsen cited in Larsen and Longley 2006: 2)

This opportunity to share responsibility prompts me to consider specifically feminist and collaborative approaches within ensemble improvisation. For me, these ideas connect directly to Jennifer Monson's work (cited in Galeota-Wozny 2005), in which she describes observing bird migration and flight patterns and how these suggested an egalitarian and sustainable approach of sharing leadership and responsibility within movement of the group. Nina Martin also comments 'this is the beauty of ensemble work – a division of labor' (Martin 2007: p. 15). There is certainly some interesting potential in these ideas for me to investigate in terms of feminist improvisational practices.

Hmm … I started this research with the question: How can improvisational scores and improvisational structures be developed to support performance improvisation? Already I am setting this question aside and beginning to consider new questions and other approaches to improvisation in performance.

I share my conclusions with Kristian and it seems we agree on this point – that there are many options in addition to the use of scores and structures in performing improvisation. Kristian is certainly enjoying explicating the detail of his practice, and I am excited by the direction our research is heading and by the way in which our discussion is creating links and relationships between our exploration of the literature and varied experiences of improvisational practice. What I need now is time in the studio to more fully explore these ideas about improvisation.

Improvising together

Begin … breath rushing out, wood under my forearms, thighs, toes … hurtling across the floor … to stillness. Eyes opening as though from dreamy depths, light freeing my imagination from the bounds of performing in the half-light of the studio. Toes walking legs along the floor. A creeping foot searching in the dark longing for another to rub against. Finger tips reaching back, as though from hands not my own, searching for comfort … baby touches in the dark. Rolling through the darkness, weight pouring from peak of hipbones to valley of pelvis, from height of shoulder to depth of sternum. Skull rotating, rope-like hair wrapping, breath rushing out. Wood an easy cradle for forehead, breasts, belly … then shoulder blades, pelvis, calves and heels. Light tracing easily over awakened skin. Sensation leading … then shift, repeat, edit. Pause …

Insert, another foot lands. A proposition in a careful step, rhythmic hopping and a slide, creeping feet walking legs, moving through shared space. Shift, develop, extend, replace foot. Listening, moving in the same time, ending at the same moment, open to observation, a dialogue beginning. Beyond sensation leading, active decision making, editing, together.

Feminism and performance improvisation

Bringing together my varied experiences of improvisation in the studio, my recent experience in choreographic improvisation with Kristian, and the literature I have reviewed on performance improvisation, I begin exploring my own interests. I regard improvisation in performance as (potentially) a demonstration of embodied ways of knowing – knowledge constructed and demonstrated in the here and now of the performance moment.

The sense of enthusiasm and momentum I gained from workshops with Kristian for a different approach to performance improvisation becomes stronger when I consider how these recent experiences and readings add to my feminist understandings of choreographic and compositional strategies. The words of Susanne, Ali and Raewyn (the solo contemporary dancers with whom I have previously discussed improvisation), reverberate too (see Chapter Four). Incorporating improvisation within performances, Susanne shared her lived experience as she desired in the moment, letting go of the need to present herself as carefully constructed and controlled 'product' to meet other people's expectations. All three approached improvisation playfully, as an expression of their freedom and their resistance to socio-cultural oppression – as a feminist strategy.

I recall how Ali expressed that 'in performance improvisation, we might understand a little more when we actually sense everything working together suddenly in the moment … You understand what integration means, or what that whole idea of mind/body/spirit means. And you can exhibit as a dancer, this fabulous organization in the moment, of intricate movement patterns, emotive expression, spiritual states of being, and qualities of energy.'[8]

Ali's comments align well with the experiences I have had of desiring to privilege freedom, choice and playful investigation in dance. I articulated these experiences as alternative modalities of feminine movement. In workshops, Kristian emphasized the value of practicing making clear movement propositions. While I could argue with Kristian that perhaps practicing making clear movement propositions might reinforce a masculine model of action (in that masculine movement must have an identifiable plan, singular intention and exhibit control (Young 1998b)), there are other aspects of his practice that align easily with my feminist understandings.

Opening my awareness in both solo and ensemble improvisation through these practices is useful in that I can continue to respond to environmental information in the moment-to-moment performing context, as I am used to doing in solo improvisation. But the seeming complexity of responding to the wider range of information offered by other dancers in the environment is balanced by understanding my limitations, using quick decision-making and

Photograph 7: In *Nightshade* (Cheesman et al. 2007). Photograph by Cheri Waititi.

practicing 'edit'. I realize that I need to limit my absorbtion in my own kinaesthetic experiences to some extent, forcing myself to focus more on awareness of the group and the composition we are creating together (Martin 2007). Opening my awareness to audience information and other dancers' cues while performing means that there is potential to develop a more responsive relationship with all in the moment. Potential for co-authoring movement both with other dancers and perhaps even with audience members is very exciting.

While able to utilize tools to make choices about responding to all of this rich environmental information, I am also already equipped as a choreographer/composer in the moment, to express specific movement intentions, and to subvert and re-create images of femininity within improvisational movement. Allowing for movement to have multiple intentions, to be responsive in the moment, and to be playful rather than 'controlled' also seem appropriate agendas for my own feminist performance impovisation, just as I find them to be for choreography.

Consequently, I can see that there is potential for me to develop personal practices for performance improvisation that embody a feminist perspective. The use of a score or structure may not be the most relevant way for me to approach performing improvisation. However, it is only through embodiment, through regular and focused practice that understanding and integrating these new practices will be possible.

Notes

1. *You Are Not Alone You Are Just In New Zealand* is the title of the solo dance Kristian Larsen performed in a shared season of dance with me in 2006.
2. In my role as an academic I regularly have to craft research applications and submissions for ethical approval. The writing of such applications and submissions has a particular style that is important for me to demonstrate competently, as the opportunity for me to pursue such research depends of providing clear information for my non-dancing colleagues.
3. For some texts on teaching improvisation, see Franklin (1996); Gere (2003); Lavender and Predock-Linnell (2001); Minton (2007); Morgenroth (1987); Nagrin (2001); Olsen (2002); Schneer (1994); Schrader (1997); Smith-Autard (2004); Spurgeon (1991).
4. Improvisation practitioner Kristian Larsen (2002, 2003a, 2003b, 2004, 2005, 2006, 2010a, 2010b; Larsen and Longley 2006).
5. Kristin eventually adopted the phrase 'choreographic improvisation' to describe his practice and to reference the traditions of improvisation in performance begun with Richard Bull's work (Foster 2002).
6. While improvisation in Contact Improvisation (CI) is a different practice from what I am discussing in this chapter, I acknowledge that I have integrated some aspects from the CI work of Nancy Stark Smith, Andrew Harwood and Martin Keogh, with whom I have also participated in workshops (Barbour 2000). To some extent, my experience in Butoh, training with Joan Laage and Gabrielle New also influenced my approach to improvisation.
7. Kristian attributes these technical practices to European dancer Katie Duck (noted in Larsen and Longley 2006).
8. This quote is linked to comments embedded in Chapter Five.

Chapter 8

Performing Identity: Tattoos, Dreadlocks and Feminism in Everyday Life

Prologue

The warm wooden floorboards beneath my shins and palms feel comfortingly familiar as I fold my legs underneath my torso and stretch my arms out in a pool of sunlight.[1] The sun's warmth seeps generously through my skin into my lower back. Reverberations from this morning's dance warm up resound through my flesh even in stillness now. I am resting, feeling easy in my bones as residual sensations stream through my consciousness. Snippets of conversation and the vibrations of others moving about in the dance studio provide a background to my quiet stretching ritual. Footfalls sound closer to me, and I am interrupted …

'Umm, excuse me, I just noticed your cool tattoo. Does it mean anything? Can I just take a photo of your back and your tattoo in the sun?'

'No.' Rolling over, hiding my back from curious eyes.

Performing everyday

That evening after the day of dancing, I am lying stretched out on the bed with the phone clutched to my ear, recounting my experiences to my partner at home.

'This is the same woman, who, before I even met her, was asking me why I got my tattoo and when I had it done?' I relate.

I hear a short intake of breath from my partner and he replies, 'Well, it's not her business. You don't have to tell her if you don't want to.'

'I know, I know!' I exclaim. 'But why do people think it is alright to ask these very personal questions or take photos? "Does it mean anything?" – what sort of question is that? As if I would endure the pain and change my body forever without any thought about what I was doing! And this is happening here at home in Aotearoa in a dance workshop in Auckland! I mean, I can understand that maybe I seem a bit odd to people in the States – remember how I told you about standing in line to board the plane in Arizona and realizing the person behind me in the queue was plucking at my t-shirt to look at my tattoo? How rude! But to get these questions from other Kiwis. Do people just think that tattooing is a sign that my body is publicly accessible? And if that's is not enough, when I was in Arizona random people walked up and tried to tell me that my hair had turned into dreadlocks because I didn't wash it!'

Breath short, sweaty in the summer heat, the frustration from the last few months of travelling and the pressure of these invasive gazes and assumptions almost spill down my cheeks.

'Karen you're ranting. Calm down. You know I know what you mean.'

I grapple with my layers of dance clothes, lifting them away from my body and gulping in deeper breaths. I wish we were talking together on the couch at home rather than in separate cities right now. I try to tune into my partner's voice.

'You have to admit that you do look different and people are just going to be curious. And underneath it all, maybe you even want that attention. Why is it that we mark our bodies anyway, if we don't accept it will draw attention?' he asks more gently.

My partner too is a tattooed person,[2] a wearer of *moko* (Māori tattoo). Moko is the traditional tattooing form of his ancestors and he is aware of the attention he receives from others for his marked skin. However, as a Māori man, his tattooing seems to be more socially acceptable, both to other Māori and to Pākehā.[3] Or maybe it is just that being a large male he just does not appear as approachable as I must seem to those who want to ask curious questions.

'It gets hard sometimes, to cope with people's interest. I guess that woman today in the dance studio was just interested in me. But you know, if she was perceptive, or if she knew me, she wouldn't have to look at, or to ask about the meaning of my tattoos. Because she'd realize that my tattoos are integral to who I am, or know what my commitments are already.'

'You expect a lot of others Karen,' he replies. 'And what do you offer back to people who are curious? Do you think it's okay to walk around confronting people's expectations, albeit with political or feminist or whatever you call your agendas, and then not engage with them? That's not like you.'

Dreadlocks

Later, lying alone in the hot summer night in this noisy city, I throw off my bed sheet and roll over. No position seems to encourage sleep. My thoughts keep returning to the woman who asked about my tattoo. Despite my desire to avoid her, during the lunch break today she sat cross-legged beside me in the sun and introduced herself as Jenny. Feeling a little embarrassed about my sharp refusal to let her look at my tattoo, I introduce myself and my apprehension begins to dissolve as we talk about dancing. As we talk and she massages her feet gently, I notice a delicate rose tattoo on Jenny's ankle.[4] In that moment I realize she must feel a connection to me because of having a tattoo herself. I discover that she is quite genuine and nice actually. I guess she is also Pākehā and she seems to be a similar age to me. I find myself listening and responding comfortably about dance for a while, and then Jenny comments that she likes my dreadlocks, asking how long I have had them. Accepting her interest in my hair, I reply that I had begun growing in my locks about ten years ago, for the second time.

Running her hands through her own straight blonde hair, she comments, 'That's cool. I've thought about doing my hair too, but I don't know if it would work because my hair is really fine. Maybe I could get my hair braided,' she reflects. 'So where did you get your dreads done? Are they difficult to maintain?'

I often get this question, dreadlocks having become a popular style in Aotearoa following the election of a Minister of Parliament with dreadlocks. This man, a member of the Green Party, stimulated much interest in the media and helped to promote further acceptance of dreadlocks through his visibility as a 'dread in the house'. Previously dreads had been reasonably uncommon in New Zealand and mostly associated with Bob Marley and Rastafarians, or with Māori activists who tended to be represented by the media as radicals (Edmonds 2003). This mirrors the international attitudes towards dreadlocks and Rastafarians, as Ennis Edmonds describes:

> Before 1970, the very proclamation of oneself as a Rasta was a militant and challenging gesture. The wearing of dreadlocks, the repeated enunciations of 'blood and fire' and other vitriolic outbursts by Rastas, and the combative lyrics of the popular songs were likely to create panic in non-Rastas and to set the establishment on alert. Today, dreadlocks have become a trendy hairstyle among many non-Rastas, verbal outbursts by Rastas are regarded as comical (non-Rastas are also likely to clothe their verbal outbursts in Rastafarian terms), and protest in reggae lyrics is commonplace, hardly regarded as anything but an outlet for pent-up frustration. The movement has therefore become less threatening as it has become more familiar to wider society. (Edmonds 2003: 124)

While the popularity of our Green Minister of Parliament prompted trendy teenagers to suddenly get dreadlocks at the hairdressers, like any fashion, it did not last long and the trendsetters soon swapped their locks for another style. Nevertheless, there still remain plenty of dreads in Aotearoa. Whilst some are Rastafarian and some are radicals, there are plenty of surfers and sports stars and musicians too. Perhaps not so many academics or dancers, but there are at least some of us.

Over the last couple years I have worked out a standard answer to the question about where I got my hair 'done', which I share with Jenny.

'I didn't go to a hair shop to get my hair locked. Personally I don't think dreadlocks are really about fashion and hair styling, but more a rejection of fashion. Plus the hair shops fill your hair with lots of wax and hair product, which seems a bit weird to me. I have dreadlocks because my hair is naturally curly and it just starts locking up on its own. I gave up trying to comb it out and let my hair revert to a more organic state. But I do tidy my hair to keep the locks from all growing together. I wash my hair like normal, with tea tree shampoo so my scalp doesn't get itchy. Otherwise, having dreadlocks is pretty easy. You would probably find your hair doesn't easily lock though, being straight and fine. It looks good as it is.'

Jenny digests my response and then asks 'Umm, what do you mean about rejecting fashion? I think dreadlocks are a cool style.'

Photograph 8: In *Fluid Echoes Dance* (Barbour et al. 2007). Photograph by Cheri Waititi.

'Well, you know how much women are influenced, maybe even indoctrinated, by body image, fashion magazines, cosmetics and projects to lose weight, become fitter, do make-overs, therapy and all those things?'

Jenny nods knowingly.

'Well, I'm a feminist and I try to be conscious of the huge influence of these industries and social attitudes on me. Rejecting the beauty and hair product industry is a kind of feminist political statement I suppose. Wearing my hair in dreadlocks is, I guess, an embodiment of this.'

'Oh, so are you sort of protesting against that "beauty myth" stuff?' Jenny asks.

'Well, sort of … But maybe it's not really a protest or, at least, I doubt many other people would see a protest in me wearing dreadlocks.'

I laugh and tell her 'Most people just seem to think I smoke marijuana – which I don't, that I am Rastafarian – which I am not, although I like reggae music, and some even think that my hair is dirty or that I am lazy – neither of which are typically true.' Chuckling about this to myself, I watch for Jenny's response.

Jenny laughs too, a little uncomfortably maybe. I wonder fleetingly if I just answered one of her next questions. I do not share this with her, but I am aware that Rastafarians and others regard dreadlocks as a symbol of the rejection of European beauty values and/or an assertion of African aesthetics (Chevannes 1994; Dash 2006; Edmonds 2003). Some wearers cite biblical teachings forbidding trimming or shaving hair and others consider it a symbol of a return to valuing 'naturalness'. Dreadlocks can also mark someone who has chosen a 'righteous path' (Chevannes 1994; Edmonds 2003). But instead of giving Jenny these arguments, I continue with my personal reasons.

'I suppose for me it is more about walking the talk. You know, embodying my commitments, expressing feminist beliefs in living. Does that make any sense to you?'

Jenny nods non-committally and goes on to talk about her workshops with women and how many are constantly working to improve the way they look through gym training and makeovers. She finishes by asserting that many women are really empowered by these experiences. I nod tentatively back, speculating about how to respond. But our discussion ends abruptly when we both hear the dance teacher giving a 5-minute call for the start of the next session. Jenny walks with me back into the studio and we begin the next dance session warming up together. But I tie my T-shirt around my waist, deliberately hiding my back where some of my tattoo is visible.

* * *

Restless in the hot night, something that has been niggling at me surfaces into a question: how can I, as a feminist, artist and educator, ignore the opportunity to engage in discussion and provide alternative perspectives about tattooing? I do find it a bit of an insult when random people ask me questions like 'Does your tattoo mean anything?' But I also get the question 'Doesn't your hair feel dirty?' and this should be equally insulting. I manage to cope better with this question somehow. Do I need to feel insulted by questions like 'Does it mean anything?' Maybe I could see this question as a positive opportunity for a conversation instead? Perhaps I need some other strategies for dealing with the way in which my personal, private choice to be a tattooed person seems to become a public and political statement.

Being a tattooed person in Aotearoa

A colleague of mine in the department of psychology, Mohi Rua, has been researching the experiences of wearers of *moko kauae* and *pūkanohi* (traditional Māori facial tattoo for women and men). He discovered that the people he interviewed with facial moko (far more visible than my own tattoo of course) developed a range of coping strategies to deal with the varied responses of others (Nikora et al. 2005; Rua 2003; Te Awekotuku and Nikora 2007). Rua writes that while generally experiencing positive affirmation for their marked faces, most also had some experiences of negative judgment or ignorance. If they anticipated negative judgments, some would choose to avoid public settings, but many directly confronted curious questions, attempting to modify attitudes through discussion and promoting alternative perspectives. Most often 'they insist that the decision to take the marking is about continuing affirmation, identity and commitment' (Nikora et al. 2005: 203). Thus, many wearers acknowledge moko as reclamation of cultural identity and celebrate the survival of Māori aesthetics, values and design (Nikora et al. 2005; Pritchard 2001; Rua 2003; Te Awekotuku et al. 2007).

Clearly, moko is something different to Western forms of tattooing; moko being an enduring and recently revitalized Polynesian tradition. When my partner undertook moko, he shared with me why knowledge of his own genealogy and of te reo Māori and tikanga were integral to wearing moko. Subsequently, we have had many conversations about other people's responses and our own growth as a result of being tattooed people. As young people, we had both read about moko, viewing paintings and photographs of *kuia* and *koroua* (female and male elders) with moko (Blakely and Bateman 1997; King 1992; Te Awekotuku 1997). We were both excited by the designs, and while I knew that moko was not something I could wear, he understood that moko was a potential choice for him.

There were some Pākehā people with tattoos around me when I was a child, including a schoolteacher who rode motorbikes, an old sailor and some women with bracelet tattoos or roses in 'secret' places. There certainly was a tradition of Pākehā people and their European ancestors becoming tattooed as a result of living in Aotearoa and in the South Pacific. Historically, as European settlers and Māori communities engaged over land and under the covers, there were many different cross-cultural exchanges. For some,

becoming tattooed in indigenous fashion was a fundamental outcome of their residence in Pacific communities, a product of the social relationships that were established, or which individuals attempted to forge in order to become assimilated. The permanent markers that ensued from these relationships became a source of spectacle in non-Pacific contexts. (White 2005: 88–9)

The most well-known example (outside Aotearoa) of a settler who received facial tattoos is 'Baines' in Jane Campion's feature film *The Piano* (1993). While a fictional character (played by Harvey Keitel), this man was nevertheless based on real settlers whose immersion in Māori communities resulted in them becoming tattooed. However, in the film (arguably), Baines is represented as an exotic other (although not a Māori character) and he becomes a fetish object of the new female immigrant Ada's desire. While offering much filmic beauty and opportunity for feminist debate, Campion nevertheless portrays Baines' character from a colonizer's perspective, making him a spectacle for the other characters in the film and for international film audiences.[5]

Fictional film characters aside, what I mostly remember about Western tattooing from my childhood was the skit my Mum and her friend did in a local theatre evening. Singing *Lydia the tattooed lady*, they painted their skin and performed a short stylized act. As the song goes, 'Lydia' had historical scenes, such as the Battle of Waterloo, depicted on her back (Groucho Marx 1939, cited in Braunberger 2000: 8). I did not know about these historical events but I loved watching my Mum, seeing her very differently with her painted body.

Quite recently, reading an article by Christine Braunberger (2000), I realize that tattooed women apparently toured around the United States with the circus, exhibiting themselves as 'freaks'. Analyzing Western tattooed women like 'Lydia' as 'bodies in revolt', Braunberger comments that such women 'complicate recent body theory by staging an aesthetic revolution in "feminine" beauty' (2000: 1; Mifflin 1997). 'As symbols demanding to be read, tattoos on women produce anxieties of misrecognition' (Braunberger 2000: 1). This is an argument that resonates with my experiences. However, the potential for a revolutionary feminine aesthetics may always be unrealized, Braunberger comments, because 'It would seem that whatever manifold meanings women attach to their tattoos are culturally written over to simply and only punctuate meanings already attached to their bodies within a larger cultural domain' (Braunberger 2000: 2). Whether or not women personally feel they can 'configure radical difference in rewarding, self-confirming ways' (Braunberger 2000: 3) through tattooing, the risk is that you simply remain an object of public curiosity, speculation and judgment.

This is a very different experience from the cloak of affirmation that is usually placed on the shoulders of Māori moko wearers. I am personally inclined to both believe in the transformative power and the aesthetic beauty of tattooing and, simultaneously (though reluctantly), to acknowledge that public fascination also results in me being viewed as an oddity.

Sometime in the midst of all this late-night personal reflection, I eventually fall asleep. Returning to the University the next week after my dance workshop, I realize that there is a story I can tell here as a researcher. The ending to the story is unclear right now, but I have at least small glimpses of different personal narratives that, through writing, might help me to understand my experiences differently. Perhaps writing might help me cope with the public curiosity relating to the way in which my markings of gender, culture and identity seem to confront others' stereotypes, and lead to both negative encounters and insults, as well as positive affirmations.

Feminism and tattooing

I begin writing to understand my experiences, remembering that it was during my doctoral research that my childhood interest in tattooing began to resolve into a specific desire. My feminist convictions gained clarity through research and my embodied commitments found expression in solo dance performance (Barbour 2001c). I came to appreciate how knowledge is developed from actually experiencing knowledge as constructed, contextual and embodied as a dancer. Such embodied knowledge arose in the dance studio as I experimented with different ideas, engaged in 'combinatory play' (Einstein 1952), resolved challenges and tensions, and danced out the possibilities. I understood more clearly how I lived creatively, through articulating embodied ways of knowing as an epistemological strategy (as discussed in Chapter Five). So, my feminist choreographic research helped me focus on my embodied convictions, adding momentum to my interest in becoming tattooed.

Reading feminist theory supported my rejection of the 'beauty myth', leading me to submit to my hair's natural predisposition to unify in dreadlocks (Greer 1999). I really attempted to embody Australian feminist Germaine Greer's provocation (1999) to critique the ways in which patriarchy has become enacted even within my understanding of my own body. My interest in tattooing gained momentum, but feminine 'pretty in ink' designs held no interest for me (Atkinson 2002), and I was no 'Lydia' either. Careful discussions with my family and close friends led me to tentatively search out possibilities.

So it was that I found myself one afternoon gazing at photographs of skin resplendent in moko on the inside of a local shop window. I could see fresh swelling welts around the incised black edges of the curving patterns. Lingering outside the shop, I glanced down, unfolding and refolding the paper on which I had laboured over ideas. Realizing that my drawings were becoming blurred by sweat, I thrust my hands in my pants pockets and tried to innocuously wander into the shop. There was a long-haired man working at a computer and a couple of people talking quietly, all uninterested, I hoped, in me.

Surreptitiously I studied the images framed on the walls, pondering the way in which the bare unmarked skin of the people photographed seemed as integral to the design as the shaded black areas. Unlike the Western tattoo style of rendering a pictorial image on the skin, moko is design-based, and, in the instances I most admired, created for individuals and for the specifics of their embodiment. Patterns followed the curves of muscle and bone, and the lines and textures of the skin.

Fascinated, I battled internally with the desire to look closer, held back by the awareness that I was looking at someone's actual back or leg or face. This was no book of 'flash' standard images from which I could or would choose. I knew I was looking at representations of each person's *whakapapa* (genealogy and tribal affiliations) and that I was a Pākehā who clearly did not whakapapa (trace and represent genealogy) in this way.

Standing by the photos, I suddenly become aware of a discussion behind me. A young woman is arguing in whispers with a man, her boyfriend I guess, emphatic that she wants a Māori tattoo on her arm to remind her of their New Zealand trip. I listen to their accents, German I think, and eavesdrop.

'Darling, think what your parents will say. Why don't you just get something sexy on your arm like Kathrin has?'[6]

I am suddenly reminded of the public debate that raged in the media over the decision of a respected moko artist who agreed to give the British pop music star Robbie Williams a moko. Summarizing the concerns Thomas writes:

> It is undoubtedly the case that many in America and Europe who acquire pseudo-Oceanic or for that matter pseudo-Celtic designs in tattoo studios are influenced by naive and one-dimensional New Age romanticization of indigenous culture and spirituality. It may be argued also that such people appropriate elements of living indigenous cultures, ignorant and indifferent to indigenous notions of cultural property. Just as tattoo transactions have in fact proceeded for a long time, debates about what should be transacted and who are appropriate recipients will inevitably carry on as contentiously as they do now. (Thomas 2005a: 29)

Although I was curious to hear how the German girl's request for a 'Māori tattoo' would be met, I remember suddenly doubting that I should actually be there myself. Was I being a 'tourist' in the moko studio too, and, even if I was not asking for moko, was I guilty of appropriating? I started to leave, but a deep voice spoke.

'*Kia ora e hoa*, (hi) can I help? Are you interested in a tattoo?'

The long-haired man who had been at work on the computer, the moko artist, stood beside me.

I mumbled about loving the photographs, and touched the paper deep in my pocket. He waited patiently beside me as I wrestled internally, and then hesitantly extended my drawings, folded and sweaty though the paper was.

'Umm, I think I need something like this.'

He studied my drawings carefully, for rather too long I felt. I stretched my hand out, intending to grab the paper back and bolt out the door.

But the man simply said, 'I think you need to talk with the woman who works here.'

That was the beginning of a year-long process and collaboration with a Pākehā woman tattooist. It was a journey of personal discovery and reflection that took me further into the murky, sometimes uncomfortable, and always challenging territory of personal and cultural identity, genealogical research, personal imagining, reclamation and affirmation. Along the way I became substantially tattooed.

Researching tattooing

In the years since my tattooing was completed, I have read some of the literature on Western tattoo traditions. I discovered a range of interpretations of tattooed bodies in the West that pointed to very different values and experiences from those I understood related to moko.[7] Some research suggests that wearing tattoos constitutes an act of resistance against dominant Western culture, or reveals a desire for identification with so-called 'primitive' peoples (Atkinson and Young 2001; Howson 2004; Klesse 2000; Rosenblatt 1997; Thomas et al. 2005; Turner 2000). Other researchers discuss the assumption that tattoos are markings of membership in alternative subcultures or non-mainstream contemporary 'tribes', or are markers of deviance, criminal behaviour and gang membership (De Mello 2005; Falk 1995; Irwin 2001). Some writers suggest that tattooing is a bodily self-improvement project that is consistent with Western bodily ideals rather than being a form of resistance, and is used to mark conventional achievements, pursuits and aesthetics, rather than independence (Atkinson and Young 2001, 2002, 2004; Irwin 2001). Still other researchers argue that tattoos are an ironic fashion (Kosut 2006), and many argue that tattoos celebrate rites of passage in the establishment of identity and expression of agency.[8] I was particularly interested in feminist arguments that women's tattooing is an expression of a new feminist aesthetic (Braunberger 2000; De Mello 2005; Mascia-Lees and Sharpe 1992; Pitts 1998).

Each argument is contextual of course, and while I relate to some aspects, I find that my experiences as Pākehā and feminist living in the South Pacific sit uncomfortably with many of these Western understandings. The socio-cultural, political and historical context of Aotearoa New Zealand is obviously a different context from Europe or America. My era is also a very different one from those in which indigenous peoples first encountered and began exchanges with colonialists, and from the eras in which tattoos became a fashion or marker of deviance.

Thus the challenge remains for me to critique my own experiences and begin to articulate my embodied knowledge as a tattooed woman. I recognize that issues in understanding and interpreting the choices of tattooed people 'can be adjudicated only by talking about which people, when, in the contexts of what cross-cultural dealings' (Thomas 2005b: 226). I acknowledge that understandings of tattooed peoples must be concerned

> with the ways in which identity and difference are constituted in culturally and historically specific ways, and at the same time, performatively affect the possibility of problematizing the material conditions of (un)becoming in and through processes that provoke further discussion. (Sullivan 2001: 185)

This sense of needing to interpret personal expressions of and choices about identity in relation to the specific embodied people and their cultural contexts is a good reminder to me in relation to my attempts to articulate being Pākehā.

Identity

So here I am. I have undertaken the process of becoming a tattooed person. It took over a year to complete the design and, yes, my tattoos do have significant meaning. Growing in dreadlocks took a little longer, but dealing consciously with public responses to my embodied commitments is ongoing. Both dreadlocks and tattoos are embodied manifestations of my own reclamation of personal and cultural identity and my attempt to affirm my feminist, political subjectivity (Brunt 2005). Tattooing is not simply a form of protest or resistance for me, nor is it based on a desire to transform my body into something more feminine or attractive in relation to public expectations.

I find it impossible not to reflect consciously on identity, surrounded as we are in Aotearoa by provocative debates about cultural appropriation, self-determination, environmental and cultural property. Perhaps given all of this, it is not surprising I am a Pākehā and a feminist who wears dreadlocks and is a tattooed person. What is more surprising I suppose is that I find it challenging to speak about being tattooed. Dealing consciously with public responses to my embodied commitments is the ongoing challenge I live with. Sometimes, being a performer and especially a dancer seems to justify my 'unusual' embodiment in others' eyes. So along with being Pākehā and a feminist writer, researcher, teacher and mother, being a dancer is integral to my identity.

In a complex and transformative way, I suspect I am the embodiment of my era in Aotearoa, a child who grew up proud of our status as the first country in the world to achieve the vote for women and living through recent years under a strong woman Prime Minister.[9] I grew up a feminist and a Greenpeace supporter, aware of the need to witness social, political and environmental change and to initiate protest action. I grew up in the midst of the era of Māori land reclamation under Te Tiriti o Waitangi and I support the ongoing process of gaining government compensation for the wrongs of colonization. I was a child who grew up to become a woman who lives biculturalism, professionally, politically and personally every day.

Notes

1. A version of this paper called '"Does it mean anything?" and other insults. Dreadlocks, tattoos and feminism' was presented to *The Third International Congress of Qualitative Inquiry*, 2–5 May 2007, at The University of Illinois, Urbana-Champaign, IL.
2. Following Bell (1999) and others, I distinguish between people who have tattoos that are discreet and able to be hidden, and tattooed people, who have more obvious, larger tattoos and are likely to face public curiosity or marginalization as a result.
3. For discussion of experiences of moko wearers, see Nikora and Te Awekotuku (2002); Nikora et al. (2005); and Te Awekotuku and Nikora (2007).
4. See Atkinson (2002, 2004) for a discussion of women's feminine tattoos.

5. Obviously a full discussion of the portrayal of tattoos and moko in New Zealand film is beyond the focus of my discussion in this chapter. However, for interesting discussion of these and other issues relating to colonization in *The Piano*, see Bruzzi (1995); Dyson (1995); hooks (1994); and Pihama (2000).
6. See Irwin (2001) for a discussion of first-time tattooees' behaviour.
7. For insightful discussion, see Atkinson (2002); Braunberger (2000); De Mello (2005); Mascia-Lees and Sharpe (1992); Rosenblatt (1997); and Sullivan (2001).
8. See Atkinson (2001); Bell (1999); Brunt (2005); Irwin (2001); Kosut (2006); Mansfield (1999); Mascia-Lees and Sharpe (1992); Pitts (1998); Pritchard (2001); Rosenblatt (1997); Schildkrout (2004); and White (2005).
9. All women gained the right to vote in New Zealand in 1893, some years after Māori men in 1867 (King 2003). Helen Clark was the New Zealand Labour Government Prime Minister from 1999 to 2008. (Clark won the 1999 election, taking leadership from Prime Minister Jenny Shipley.) Clark moved on from New Zealand politics to take the position of head of the United Nations Development Programme.

Chapter 9

Imaginings: Reaching for a Vision

Backs of hands open and resting on crossed legs, spine lengthening into the air, a quiet behind closed eyes, breath soft and deep here. Cool marble beneath sit bones and ankles, warm sun sinking through skin and down into bones. Touch of a light breeze offering the delicate scent of flowers. Now that familiar sensation of sun seeping into lower back as forehead rests here on the marble, arms stretching away and spine curving over folding legs. Pressing into hands, energy ascending from crown to tailbone, sun caressing down the backs of legs, gravity drawing heels and head down. Tinkling accompaniment, water splashing lightly from a central fountain, racing down the rills of marble into the channels bisecting the garden. Stepping a foot between hands, rotating and opening from hip joint as legs lengthen, allowing spine to align horizontally and spiral easily from pelvis through to skull. Eyes searching into the open blue of the sky, arms extending above and below in vertical lines. Folding again now to sit here, legs crossed, finding connection between thumb and index tips, circle complete. Drinking in vibrant orange and red, highlights of white and yellow flowers rising out of the green, giving life and inspiration to circling butterflies. White marble, tiles and stone walls surrounding blue water. The smiling eyes that light my heart, my son watching Mama dance, my family enjoying his small boy play alongside me. Dancing Through Paradise.

The touch of cool stone under slow steps, under my palms and then under my pelvis and shoulder blades as I roll, pressing one foot flat into the wall, other leg reaching away. Eyes resting on torso, sense of my dance partner's movement next to me and we roll to stand here on hands, feet sliding apart and down the wall, finding footing, moving to extend through lunge now. Then stepping to lean shoulder to the stone, knee hugged in to chest as sternum and throat open. Moving closer together, the touch of her hands pressing into my lower back, my forearms bearing weight as I swing into a balance, reassurance in her fingertips on my calves. Stillness. Then releasing down and curving through, the heat of her body near mine as we mirror each other's movements and then confidently accepting her weight as she rests against me. Trust and support, turning in to clasp hands and countering our weights evenly, suspended here momentarily. Calves resting into my hands as she balances now, then moving through again sensing each other's proximity and speed. Dancing in duet.

Calmly balancing, arching, stepping, opening, curving, progressing along the narrow marble channels, water and flowers just below spreading feet. Movements familiar from

Photograph 9: Emma Goldsworthy in *Dancing Through Paradise* (Barbour 2010). Photograph by Marcia Mitchley.

years of investigation, now even more satisfying, sustaining and energy giving. Aligning legs, arms, spine and gaze with the edges and angles of the formal garden. Reflecting architectural choices and structural possibilities within my skeleton, organic softness offering moments of contrast with the solidity of stone. Meeting together, claiming a corner each around the chattering fountain, breath settling into a shared rhythm. A unison prayer for peace, palms pressing together across heart, then releasing above, diving up into the blue sky. Thumbs creasing to find home between eyes and nose, then drawing fingertips down to rest. Bowing fully, forehead on marble between the triangle of index fingers and thumbs. A meditation of hope, trust embodied, experiencing freedom. Savouring a moment of calm in the midst of multiplicity as mother, dancer, teacher, writer, friend, and performer. Dancing hope and peace.

Sliding steps across the stone tiles, crossing to sink into a roll, moving in canon, peripheral vision linking our timing. Music adding a quiet melody to the water, breeze drifting up from the river and carrying the flowers' subtle scent. Drawing focus from movement to movement in situ, opening, opening and opening awareness. Progressing towards the audience, some reclining on cushions on the stone, others seated or standing, joining us. Sharing joy in sensation, in moving, in the experience of the garden here. The brush of breath, the touch of a smile, the hope in a child's face, a sigh from a grandparent. Hearts expanding, muscles softening, releasing now. Hands meeting in applause, warmth reflected, moments shared. Small boy running into waiting arms, precious trust given completely. Dancing family and community.

Moving meditations

Recording specific dancing sensations is a pleasurable experience today. As I write my way through *Dancing Through Paradise*, I respond unconsciously, my spine lengthening and tensions unwinding as I visualize dancing. Concern for our well-being as dancers is at the centre of this creative process and I find a sense of renewal even in analyzing the process now. To deepen my descriptions of sensations, I look through the rich selection of images in my photo library. These images and my memories provide much information and I integrate them with choreographic and discussion notes in my journal. Journaling is ongoing, still providing a repository of sketches and text that chart aspects of my creative dancing and writing processes, and to which I can refer in writing my research.

Like much of my work, *Dancing Through Paradise* is framed as creative practice as research and I integrate exploration of specific research questions within the process of choreographing and performing the work.[1] The research focus in this work is to enhance well-being for us within the dance-making process; a practice I have been interested in for some time (Barbour 2008, 2010; Barbour and Mitchley 2005; Barbour et al. 2007). In this research, I deliberately included yoga-based movement motifs, developed a considered choreographic process that fostered collaboration with the dancers as well as pursuit of choreographic agendas (Butterworth 2009) and a meditative performance practice. Of course, part of my motivation for this research project is my personal desire for focus, stillness and balance in my life, as well as my enthusiasm for providing opportunities for integration through moving for other dancers. I find personally that yoga is a complimentary embodied practice for me as a dancer – a moving meditation. Beginning training with Sondra Fraleigh recently in her somatic yoga practice (2009), I decided to integrate her approach within my dance research and choreography.[2]

Consequently, there are many drawings and notes in my journal about the yoga poses I select to develop as motifs in the choreography. Inserted quotes from Sondra Fraleigh's book *Land to Water Yoga* (2009) remind me of specific rehearsals and points of discussion too. I have noted next to my drawing of the 'dancer pose': beneficial in 'developing courage in a challenging posture and practicing self-forgiveness in occasional loss of balance' (Fraleigh 2009: 14). In discussion with the dancers about this pose, we agree that it might actually be easier to balance than to forgive ourselves for losing balance and much laughter follows this realization.

I dedicate time to considering the implications of including yoga-based movement motifs within choreography. The dancers express their concerns about performing 'well' and dancing these movements with integrity. I am reminded that my own yoga practice, spanning 15 years or so, means that I have a comfort and familiarity working within this vocabulary that my dancers do not all share. The dancers have varied experiences with yoga, seldom attending regular classes but willingly engaging in the yoga I typically integrate into my dance exercises and activities.

'I see yoga as a journey rather than an end,' I share with them, 'just like our lives are journeys. So integrity for me in yoga is about working where I am at, and not being afraid to be honest in the movement. And, well, obviously breathing is pretty important too!'

Next to my sketches of 'downward facing dog' pose, I have noted the obvious benefits that the dancers identify readily, like lengthening the spine, releasing the neck, stretching hamstrings and strengthening in the upper body. Again I quote Fraleigh's insight to them: 'It is more important to start where you are. Learning as you go, build capacity along the way. Perfect line is not the goal. Feeling whole and integrated in the movement is the goal' (2009: 28).

I am not surprised to discover, through discussion with the dancers, that their sense of well-being is contingent on dancing. I know this so clearly myself. Many of the aspects of well-being that we identify together relate to activities we practice in dancing, whether learning in classes, spending time together as a small community or performing choreography and improvisation. We share our experiences of well-being, expressing that it means, to us, feeling generally happy and whole, making embodied sense of our lives, being open, ready and able to respond, finding balance in the varied things we are doing, being present and able to notice what is happening, having some freedom within daily activities, feeling connected to family, being confident in reaching out while having a sense of home to come back to. We talk about our need for times of solitude and for self-forgiveness, about relationships and love, and about peace. We are imagining together, reaching for a vision of how we can be, as dancing women, response-able and capable of contributing to our community.

Photograph 10: Patti Mitchley in *Dancing Through Paradise* (Barbour 2010). Photograph by Marcia Mitchley.

Perspective

While my most recent performance experiences in *Dancing Through Paradise* are fresh in my memory, traces of movement from dancing my solo *This Is After All the Edited Life* are still present. This morning I also recall a story I told in that solo as an expression of my positioning and reflectivity as a feminist, dancing researcher. Locating this story in my doctoral research files from 10 years ago, and re-reading it now, I am surprised at how much of my life today can be read in these words.

Script from *This Is After All the Edited Life*

I want to tell you a story. It is a story about a discussion I was having with a friend of mine as we drove along in the car recently.

My friend was asking me about my doctoral research work. He said, 'How do you do research in dance?'

I get this question quite a lot actually … I reply, 'it's really like doing any other sort of research. You start with a research question, something that interests you passionately, and you clarify what your theoretical perspective is. Then you find out about the relevant literature in the area, and you develop a methodology for doing your research. Then you go out and do your research, make some discussion and draw some conclusions. So really it's like doing any research. And for me, I'm trying to embody feminist theory in my dance making.'

'Hmmm' my friend says. 'But why do you need to be a feminist? Why do you need to work with feminist perspective?'

I am wondering how to answer this, looking out the window and thinking how to reply. My friend must be wondering if I understand him and, perhaps thinking, 'Well, she's one of those "arty types"', he uses a metaphor to explain his question further. 'It seems to me that feminism is like a hill you've climbed and it gives you a particular perspective on the world. I can see how that is useful for your research,' he says. 'But you know, it only gives you one perspective.'

'Mmm …'

Again, looking at the hills outside the car, I say, 'Better to know the hill you've climbed. Better to know your perspective, and the journey you have taken. Do you know what I mean?' I ask him. He looks a little perplexed. Knowing I have got a captive audience in the car, I try to explain more clearly.

'I think it is important to know your own perspective, to know where you stand and where you've come from. And all of us have a perspective. Sitting here now I have a perspective because I am embodied in the world. I think that is important. Better to know your own perspective than try to find some sort of universal "God's eye" view, which I think is unattainable anyway. And for me dancing is my way of expressing my feminist perspective. It is a way of embodying my feminist ideas!'

A rather long silence follows. I can see my friend glance out the window as he drives, looking at the hills rushing by, like I am. And I realize we see different things, and that is okay.[3]

* * *

As dancer, writer, researcher, teacher and mother, I still belong within the wider contemporary dance communities of Aotearoa as well as within my family and my community of academic colleagues. I believe there is rich potential for me as a Pākehā contemporary choreographer to assert a stronger voice, to articulate more clearly the concerns I feel about being Pākehā through my creative practices. While there are still many Pākehā dancers who choose, like Susanne, to live and work as artists in Europe, the value of remaining in Aotearoa must surely be in the ability to investigate Pākehā 'representations of gender, race, sexuality and physical ability' (Albright 1997: xiii). Just as my dancing body is surely shaped by conflicting notions of being a Pākehā woman, I am also able to assert some resistance as a choreographer, to challenge stereotypes about personal and cultural identity and re-create myself in dance and in everyday life. Deliberately exploring questions of femininity and masculinity, articulating the politics of the personal and the local, critically investigating biculturalism and expressing an embodied relationship to and responsibility for this *whenua* (land) seem relevant agendas for me in Pākehā contemporary dance (Buck and Barbour 2007; East 2007).

I believe I can articulate these concerns through movement material that leaps beyond merely demonstrating movement techniques imported from Europe, the United States and elsewhere. As my friend and colleague Kristian asks, I too am curious to consider Pākehā movement aesthetics (Larsen 2010b). I recognize the typical descriptors of New Zealand dancers as being athletic, energetic and physical, with an 'easy relationship with the floor', fluid spines and spiralling movement, and expressive through both refined gestures and everyday movement (Barbour 2007b; Larsen 2010b: 9). While these are very general descriptions, I do believe it is possible to personally and deliberately articulate sensuous and conscious movement vocabularies that arise directly from walking the fertile and changeable land of these South Pacific islands. Using relevant improvisational and choreographic strategies I believe I can integrate these personalized movement vocabularies with everyday performativity, and express myself as a Pākehā woman 'speaking' of emerging culture.

I know who I am and my perspective is clear, as a Pākehā woman living here now in Aotearoa. I consciously assert my cultural identity as Pākehā while living in relationship with ngā iwi Māori, attempting to expand my professional, political and personal understandings and practices. I imagine the future for my son, competent in both te reo Māori and the English language, knowing his place to stand in the embrace of his whānau, marae, hapu, iwi, and tūpuna[4] as well as sharing a home with my family, confident in his right to speak as both Māori and Pākehā, and strong in his embodiment of biculturalism.

I live in the embrace of my family and in touch with my communities. I value my personal, embodied, local and specific experiences, while searching for links and relationships with the swirling mass of voices in this postmodern, globalizing world. Every time I travel, my own positioning is brought into sharp relief, whether through the anxieties of misrecognition I experience as I engage with others, or in my sensuous responses to different landscapes and cultures. My narrative and embodied ways of knowing provide the rationale and the confidence for me to pursue my feminist research through dancing.

Concluding thoughts for today

A familiar steady flame resides in my chest, setting alight my heart, spreading throughout my cells, reaching to my fingertips and dropping into the keys of my computer as I write. The gentle breeze stirs the curtains and beyond the wooden window frame the grape vine sags under the weight of ripe fruit. Wide green leaves seem to contrast perfectly with blue of the clear sky today. Sighing, I stretch my legs and release them from the confines of the chair and table. Around me is the reassuring comfort of my home and this day set aside for writing is a welcome respite from my busy academic life.

Opening this file called 'Imaginings' this morning, I am struck by the chapter title I gave myself some time ago when I first began writing this book.[5] I am still imagining, still reaching for a vision and constantly engaging my embodied ways of knowing. Somehow I have come to feel a sense of peace in this imagining. My life has become a moving meditation, a dance of being and becoming dancer, writer, researcher, teacher and mother.

On this late summer morning, safe in my home, I am remembering dancing as I write. My research, my dancing and my family all come together in the here and now of today's writing. In moments like these, my experiences are informed by the many voices of my research participants, colleagues and friends. Their voices help locate me here in the unique and thriving communities of dancers in Aotearoa. While I may be living on a small island in the South Pacific, far south of most of the world's population and many flying hours from the inspiring academics I avidly read, I have become attuned to searching for links to others, for moments of contact between us, for voices on the wind and islands in the vast oceans. We dancers are engaged in very human concerns, professionally, politically and personally enhancing well-being, engaging with community and cultivating responsiveness.

My friends demonstrate how to set aside time and space for renewal, for rest and to allow my accumulating experiences to resolve. They remind me to be patient with others and with myself too, as life is continually unfolding.

My family teaches me about love and care. My son teaches me the value of being here and now, reminding me at once of the visceral shortness of a lifetime and the fullness of every moment. We improvise in our lives, constantly balancing and falling, delighting in our experiences together. Love is here and now, together.

In the moment of dancing, it is my family that makes it possible for me to share the magic of embodied knowing and the mystery of love. My performing births a specific embodied joy – a momentary dance of peace.

I release my experiences, sharing them with you as my words dance across the page.

Notes

1. At the time of writing this chapter, my yoga and dance choreography research is ongoing. I acknowledge with love my research participants and dancing friends involved: Patti Mitchley, Emma Goldsworthy, Marie Hermo Jensen and Alex Hitchmough.

2. Previous to beginning work with Sondra Fraleigh, I had focused on Iyengar yoga for about 15 years. I experienced many insights in this yoga form and I used my knowledge in the dance studio, but working without the (arguably) complex equipment required for a strict Iyengar (2001) approach. I chose not to train as a certified Iyengar teacher because I prefer the freedom to adapt yoga teachings for contemporary dance. I acknowledge my formative yoga teacher Sharon Lightfoot (a student of Felicity Green. Both were students of BKS Iyengar.)

3. This script comes from my solo dance *This Is After All The Edited Life* and can be found in Barbour (2002).

4. Family, traditional settlement, extended family or clan, tribe or group of people, and ancestors (Ngata dictionary 2007).

5. The narratives in this book span 10 years of dancing and writing. While I have taken some liberties in positioning the chapters and unfolding events, my writings are loosely chronological.

References

Abram, D. (1996), *The Spell of the Sensuous*, New York: Vintage Books.

Albright, A.C. (1997), *Choreographing Difference: The Body and Identity in Contemporary Dance*, Hanover, NH: Wesleyan University Press.

Armstrong, N. and Du Plessis, R. (1998), 'Shifting certainties, complex practices: Reflections on feminist research', in R. Du Plessis and L. Alice, (eds), *Feminist Thought in Aotearoa, New Zealand. Connections and Differences*, Auckland, New Zealand: Oxford University Press, pp. 104–10.

Ashley, L. (2002), *Essential Guide to Dance*, 2nd ed., London: Hodder & Stoughton.

Atkinson, M. (September 2002), 'Pretty in ink: Conformity, resistance, and negotiation in women's tattooing', *Sex Roles*, 47:5/6, pp. 219–235.

—— (2004), 'Tattooing and civilizing processes: Body modification as self-control', *The Canadian Review of Sociology and Anthropology*, 41:2, pp. 125–46.

Atkinson, M. and Young, K. (2001), 'Flesh journeys: neo primitives and the contemporary rediscovery of radical body modification', *Deviant Behaviour: An Interdisciplinary Journal*, 22, pp. 117-146.

Balkin, A. (May 1990), 'What is creativity? What is not?', *Music Educator's Journal*, 76:9, pp. 29–32.

Banes, S. (Spring–Summer 1978), 'Grand union: The presentation of everyday life as dance', *Dance Research Journal*, 10:2, pp. 43–9.

—— (1987), *Terpsichore in Sneakers: Post-modern Dance*, 2nd ed., Middletown, CN: Wesleyan University Press.

Banes, S. (ed.). (2003a), *Reinventing Dance in the 1960s: Everything was possible*, Madison, WS: University of Wisconsin Press.

—— (2003b), 'Spontaneous combustion. Notes on dance improvisation from the sixties to the nineties', in A.C. Albright & D. Gere, (eds.), *Taken by Surprise. A Dance Improvisation Reader*, Middletown, CT: Wesleyan University Press, pp. 77–85.

Bannon, F. (April 2004), 'Towards creative practice in research in dance education', *Research in Dance Education*, 5:1, pp. 25–43.

Barbour, K.N. (June 2000), 'Contact improvisation: Thinking in movement', *Proximity*, 4, 3. http://proximity.slightly.net/index2.htm Accessed 4 May 2010.

—— (2001a), 'Writing about lived experiences in women's solo dance making', in P. Markula (ed.), *Proceedings of the 3rd Dance Aotearoa New Zealand Research Forum: Critical Reflections on Dance Research*, , Hamilton, New Zealand: University of Waikato, pp. 1–9.

—— (August 2001b), 'Journeys in dance-making and research', in J. Bolwell (ed.), *Tirairaka. Dance in New Zealand*, Wellington, New Zealand: Wellington College of Education, pp. 5–11.

—— (February 2001c), *This Is After All the Edited Life*, (dance performance), Hamilton, New Zealand: WEL Energy Trust Academy of Performing Arts, Hamilton, 10 October.

—— (2002), 'Embodied ways of knowing in women's solo contemporary dance in Aotearoa New Zealand', Ph.D. thesis, Waikato: The University of Waikato, New Zealand.

—— (December 2003), 'Researching embodied ways of knowing in women's solo dance', in J. Bolwell (ed.), *Tirairaka. Dance in New Zealand*, Wellington, New Zealand: Wellington College of Education, pp. 14–23.

—— (2004a), 'Embodied ways of knowing', *Waikato Journal of Education, 10*, pp. 227–38.

—— (2004b), 'Dream yourself anew: Choreographic strategies in women's solo contemporary dance making', in *Proceedings of the International Dance Conference, Taiwan: Dance, Identity and Integration*, Taipei, Taiwan: World Dance Alliance/Congress on Research on Dance, pp. 31–9.

—— (June 2005), 'Beyond "Somatophobia": Phenomenology and movement research in dance', *Junctures. The Journal for Thematic Dialogue*, 4, pp. 35–51.

—— (2006a), 'Embodied engagement in arts research', *The International Journal of Arts in Society*, 1:2, pp. 85–91.

—— (2006b), 'Dancing across the page: Representing research findings from interviews and journal entries', in *Proceedings of the 38th Annual Conference: Continuing Dance Culture Dialogues – Southwest Borders and Beyond*, pp. 24–9, Tempe, AZ: Congress on Research in Dance.

—— (2007a), 'Creative research in the arts: Introduction to the special section'. *Waikato Journal of Education*, 13, pp. 3–5.

—— (2007b), 'Understanding contemporary dance in Aotearoa, New Zealand', *Side step. New Zealand dance writings online*, http://www.danz.org.nz/sidestep.php?article_id=246&type_id=1 Accessed 4 May 2010.

—— (2007c), '"Does it mean anything?" and other insults: Dreadlocks, tattoos and feminism', in *3rd International Congress of Qualitative Inquiry*, The University of Illinois, Urbana-Champaign, IL, 2–5 May 2007.

—— (June 2008), 'Sustainable dance making: Dancers and choreographers in collaboration', *Brolga*, 28, pp. 40–51.

—— (2009), 'Standing strong. Pedagogical approaches to affirming identity in dance', in C. Stock (ed.), *Dance Dialogues: Conversations across Cultures, Artforms and Practices: Proceedings of the 2008 World Dance Alliance Global Summit*, Brisbane, Australia: QUT Creative Industries and Ausdance, 2009. http://www.ausdance.org.au/resources/publications.html Accessed 4 May 2010,

—— (2010), *Dancing Through Paradise*, (dance season), Hamilton, New Zealand: Indian Char Bagh Garden, Hamilton Gardens Arts Festival, Hamilton, 20–22 February.

—— (2010), 'Engaging delight: A case study of site-specific dance in public city gardens', *International Journal of Arts in Society*, 5:3, pp. 119–135.

Barbour, K.N., Davies, J., Homan, R., May, H., Mitchley, P., and Nakayama, A. (2007), *Fluid Echoes Dance*, (dance season), Hamilton, New Zealand: Japanese Garden, Hamilton Gardens Summer Festival, Hamilton, 17–18, 21–22 February.

Barbour, K.N. and Mitchley, P. (2005), 'Staying real': Issues in choreographing from lived experience in *You know how I feel*', in *Proceedings of the 4th Dance Aotearoa New Zealand Research Forum: Tuanui Whakamaru – Dance Canopy 05*, pp. 7–14, Auckland, New Zealand: Dance Aotearoa New Zealand.

Barbour, K.N., Ratana, D., Waititi, C. and Walker, K. (2007), 'Researching collaborative artistic practice', *Waikato Journal of Education*, 13, pp. 49–76.

Barbour, K.N. and Thorburn, R. (2002), 'Reconstructing stereotypical femininity in women's solo dance-making', *Australia New Zealand Dance Research Society Journal*, pp. 6–13.

Barbour, K.N. and Whyte, R. (1998), 'Limbs dance company', in T. Benbow-Pfalzgraf (ed.), *The International Dictionary of Modern Dance*, Detroit, MC: St James Press.

Barrett, E. and Bolt, B. (eds) (2007), *Practice as Research: Approaches to Creative Arts Enquiry*, London: I. B. Tauris.

Belenky, M.F., Clinchy, B.M., Goldberger, N.R., and Tarule, J.M. (eds), (1986), *Women's Ways of Knowing. The Development of Self, Voice and Mind*, New York: Basic Books.

Bell, A. (2004), '"Half-castes" and "White natives": The politics of Māori-Pākehā hybrid identities', in C. Bell and S. Matthewman (eds.), *Cultural Studies in Aotearoa New Zealand: Identity, Space and Place*, Oxford & New York: Oxford University Press, pp. 121–38.

—— (June 2006), 'Bifurcation or entanglement? Settler identity and biculturalism in Aotearoa New Zealand', *Continuum: Journal of Media and Cultural Studies*, 20(2), 253–68.

Bell, C. (2002). 'The big 'OE': Young New Zealander travellers as secular pilgrims'. *Tourist Studies*, 2:2, pp. 143–58.

Bell, S. (1999), 'Tattooed: A participant observer's exploration of meaning', *Journal of American Culture*, 22, pp. 53–8.

Bentley, S. (2000), 'Someone else's weirdo', in *Red Shift*, (dance season), Wellington, New Zealand: Bats Theatre, Wellington, 1–4 March.

Bigwood, C. (1991), 'Renaturalizing the body (with the help of Merleau-Ponty)', *Hypatia*, 6:3, pp. 54–73.

Blakely, R. and Bateman, D. (eds), (1997), *Goldie*, Auckland, New Zealand: David Bateman.

Bolwell, J. (1998), 'Into the light: An expanding vision of dance education', in S.B. Shapiro (ed.), *Dance, Power, and Difference: Critical and Feminist Perspectives on Dance Education*, Champaign, IL: Human Kinetics, pp. 11–21.

—— (2000a), *Off My Chest*, (dance performance), Dunedin, New Zealand: Mary Hopewell Theatre, Dunedin College of Education, Dunedin, 15 September.

—— (2000b), 'The pink nude', in M. Clark (ed.), *Beating our Breasts. Twenty New Zealand Women tell their Breast Cancer Stories*, Auckland, New Zealand: Cape Catley Ltd, pp. 11–21.

Bordo, S.R. (1988), 'Anorexia nervosa: Psychopathology as the crystallization of culture', in I. Diamond and L. Quinby (eds), *Feminism and Foucault: Reflections on Resistance*, Boston, MA: Northeastern University Press, pp. 87–117.

—— (1989), 'The body and the reproduction of femininity: A feminist appropriation of Foucault', in A.M. Jagger and S.R. Bordo (eds), *Gender/Body/Knowledge. Feminist Reconstructions of Being and Knowing*, New Brunswick, NJ & London: Rutgers University Press, pp. 13–33.

Braidotti, R. (1994), *Nomadic Subjects. Embodiment and Sexual Difference in Contemporary Feminist Theory*, New York: Columbia University Press.

Braunberger, C. (Summer 2000), 'Revolting bodies: The monster beauty of tattooed women', *National Women's Studies Association Journal*, 12:2, pp. 1–23.

Brew, A. (1998), 'Moving beyond paradigm boundaries', in J. Higgs (ed.), *Writing Qualitative Research*, Sydney, Australia: Hampden Press, pp. 29–45.

Bright, D. (July 2005), 'Reflective practice in dance making', in *Proceedings of the 4th Dance Aotearoa New Zealand Research Forum: Tuanui Whakamaru – Dance Canopy 05*, pp. 15–23, Auckland, New Zealand: Dance Aotearoa New Zealand.

—— (2010), 'Exploring female art-making through reflective practice: A multi-dimensional cultural, spiritual and embodied experience'. Ph.D thesis, Waikato: University of Waikato, New Zealand.

Brown, C. (1994), 'Inscribing the body: Feminist choreographic practice'. Ph.D thesis, Surrey: University of Surrey, United Kingdom.

—— (1999), 'Unpacking the body', *Dance Theatre Journal*, 14:4, pp. 12–16.

Brown, L.B. (Spring 2000), '"Feeling my way": Jazz improvisation and its vicissitudes-a plea for imperfection', *The Journal of Aesthetics and Art Criticism*, 58:2, pp. 113–23.

Bruce, T. (1998), 'Postmodernism and the possibilities for writing "Vital" sports texts', in G. Rail (ed.), *Sport and Postmodern Times*, Albany, New York: State University of New York Press, pp. 3–19.

—— (2003), 'Pass', in J. Denison and P. Markula (eds), *Moving Writing*, New York: Peter Lang Publishing, pp. 130–46.

Brunt, P. (2005), 'The temptation of Brother Anthony: Decolonization and the tattooing of Tony Fomison', in N. Thomas, A. Cole and B. Douglas (eds), *Tattoo. Bodies, Art, and Exchange in the Pacific and the West*, London: Duke University Press, pp. 123–7.

Bruzzi, S. (1995), 'Tempestuous petticoats: Costume and desire in the Piano', *Screen*, 36:3, pp. 257–66.

Buck, R. and Barbour, K.N. (2007), 'Experiential learning: A narrative of a community dance field trip', *Waikato Journal of Education*, 13, pp. 149–60.

Burroway, Janet. (1996), *Writing Fiction: A Guide to Narrative Craft*, 4th ed., New York: Harper Collins.

Butler, J. (1990), *Gender Trouble: Feminism and the Subversion of Identity*, New York: Routledge.

Butterworth, J. (2009), 'Too many cooks? A framework for dance making and devising', in J. Butterworth and L. Wildschut (eds), *Contemporary Choreography: A Critical Reader*, London & New York: Routledge, pp. 177–94.

Butterworth, J. and Wildschut, L. (eds) (2009), *Contemporary Choreography: A Critical Reader*, London & New York: Routledge.

Byatt, A.S. (1990), *Possession*, London: Vintage.

Campion, J. (Director) (1993), *The Piano*, Australia and United States: Miramax.

Cheesman, S., Barbour, K.N., Jackson-Gough, J.J., May, H., and Mitchley, P. (2007), *Nightshade*, (dance performance), Hamilton, New Zealand: lakeside at The University of Waikato, Hamilton, 30 March.

Chevannes, B. (1994), *Rastafari. Roots and Ideology*, Syracuse, New York: Syracuse University Press.

Code, L. (1991), *What can she Know? Feminist Theory and the Construction of Knowledge.* New York: Cornell University Press.

Coe, D. (1999), 'The challenge, tension and passion of researching dance', in *Proceedings of Dance Research Forum 1999*, Wellington, New Zealand: Dance Aotearoa, pp. 1–10.

—— (2003), 'Dance has connected me to my voice: The value of reflection in establishing effective dance pedagogy', *Waikato Journal of Education*, 9, pp. 39–49.

Corbet, D. (December 1999), 'Katie Duck: An interview', *Proximity*, 2:4, pp. 7–10. http://proximity.slightly.net/index2.htm Accessed 4 May 2010.

Daly, A. (1993), 'Unlimited partnership: Dance and feminist analysis', *Writings on Dance*, 9, pp. 4–8.

Dann, C. (1991), 'In love with the land', in M. King (ed.), *Pākehā. The Quest for Identity in New Zealand*, Auckland, New Zealand: Penguin Books, pp. 46–60.

Dash, P. (January 2006), 'Black hair culture, politics and change', *International Journal of Inclusive Education*, 10:1, pp. 27–37.

De Beauvoir, S. (1972), *The Second Sex* (trans. H.M. Parshley), London: Cape. (First published 1953).

De Mello, M. (2005), *Bodies of Inscription: A Cultural History of the Modern Tattoo Community*, Durham & London: Duke University Press.

De Spain, K. (1993), 'Dance improvisation: Creating chaos', *Contact Quarterly*, 18:1, pp. 21–7.

Denison, J. and Markula, P. (eds) (2003), *Moving Writing. Crafting Movement in Sport Research*, New York: Peter Lang Publishing.

Denison, J. and Rinehart, R. (2000), 'Introduction: Imagining sociological narratives', *Sociology of Sport Journal*, 17, pp. 1–4.

Denzin, N.K. and Lincoln, Y.S. (eds) (2000), *Handbook of Qualitative Research*, 2nd ed., Thousand Oaks, CA: Sage.

Dewey, J. (1934), *Art as Experience*, New York: Minton Balch & Co.

Diprose, R. (1994/1995), 'Performing body-identity', *Writings on Dance*, 11/12, pp. 6–15.

Du Plessis, R. and Alice, L. (1998), 'Feminisms, connections and differences', in R. Du Plessis and L. Alice, (eds), *Feminist Thought in Aotearoa, New Zealand. Connections and Differences*, Auckland, New Zealand: Oxford University Press, pp. xv–xx.

Duck, K. (November 2000), 'A manifesto', *Proximity*, 3:4, pp. 3–4. http://proximity.slightly.net/index2.htm Accessed 4 May 2010.

Dyson, Lynda. (1995), 'The return of the repressed? Whiteness, femininity and colonialism in *The Piano*', *Screen*, 36:3, pp. 267–76.

East, A. (1996), 'How being still is still moving', in *Four women dance*, (dance season), Auckland, New Zealand: Watershed Theatre, Auckland, 29 May–1 June.

—— (2007), 'Interweaving philosophies of dance teaching and dance-making: What can one practice teach the other?', *Waikato Journal of Education*, 13, pp. 123–38.

Edmond, L. (1986), 'Camellias I: Femme de Lettres', in L. Edmond (ed.), *Seasons and Creatures*, Auckland, New Zealand: Oxford University Press, p. 49.

Edmonds, E.B. (2003), *Rastafari. From Outcasts to Culture Bearers*, Oxford & New York: Oxford University Press.

Einstein, A. (1952), 'Letter to Jacques Hadamard', in B. Ghiselin (ed.), *The Creative Process. A symposium*, New York: Mentor Books, pp. 43–4.

Eisner, E.W. (1998), *The Enlightened Eye: Qualitative Inquiry and the Enhancement of Educational Practice*, Upper Saddle River, NJ: Merrill.

—— (2002a), 'What can education learn from the arts about the practice of education?', *the Encyclopedia of Informal Education*, www.infed.org/biblio/eisner_arts_and_the_practice_of_education.htm Accessed 4 May 2010.

—— (2002b), 'From episteme to phronesis to artistry in the study and improvement of teaching', *Teaching and Teacher Education*, 18:4, pp. 375–85. http://www.sciencedirect.com/ Accessed 5 May 2010.

Ellis, C. (1999), 'Heartfelt autoethnography', *Qualitative Health Research*, 9:5, pp. 669–83.

—— (June 2000), 'Creating criteria: An ethnographic short story', *Qualitative Inquiry*, 6:2, pp. 273–77.

—— (2004), *Ethnographic I: A Methodological Novel about Autoethnography*, Walnut Creek, CA: AltaMira Press.

—— (January 2007), 'Telling secrets, revealing lives. Relational ethics in research with intimate others'. *Qualitative Inquiry*, 13(1), 3–29.

—— (October 2008), 'Do we need to know?', *Qualitative Inquiry*, 14:7, pp. 1314–20.

Ellis, C. and Bochner, A.P. (2000), 'Autoethnography, personal narrative, reflexivity. Researcher as subject', in N.K. Denzin and Y.S. Lincoln (eds), *Handbook of Qualitative Research*, 2nd ed., Thousand Oaks, CA: Sage, pp. 733–68.

——. (August 2006), 'Analyzing analytic autoethnography: An autopsy', *Journal of Contemporary Ethnography*, 35:4, pp. 429–49.

Falk, P. (1995), 'Written in the flesh', *Body and Society*, 1:1, pp. 95–106.

Fleras, A. and Spoonley, P. (1999), *Recalling Aotearoa. Indigenous Politics and Ethnic Relations in New Zealand*, Auckland, New Zealand: Oxford University Press.

Foster, S.L. (1986), *Reading Dancing: Bodies and Subjects in Contemporary American Dance*, Berkeley, CA: University of California Press.

—— (1995), 'Choreographing history', in S.L. Foster (ed.), *Choreographing History*, Bloomington, IN: Indiana University Press, pp. 3–21.

—— (2002), *Dances that Describe Themselves: The Improvised Choreographies of Richard Bull*, Middletown, CT: Wesleyan University Press.

—— (2003), 'Taken by surprise', in A.C. Albright and D. Gere (eds.), *Taken by Surprise: A Dance Improvisation Reader*, Middletown, CT: Wesleyan University Press, pp. 3–10.

Forti, S. (2003), 'Animate dancing. A practice in dance improvisation', in A.C. Albright and D. Gere (eds), *Taken by Surprise. A Dance Improvisation Reader*, Middletown, CT: Wesleyan University Press, pp. 53–63.

Fraleigh, S.H. (1987), *Dance and the Lived Body: A Descriptive Aesthetics*, Pittsburg, PA: University of Pittsburg Press.

—— (Summer 2000), 'Consciousness matters', *Dance Research Journal*, 32:1, pp. 54–62.

—— (2004), *Dancing Identity. Metaphysics in Motion*, Pittsburgh, PA: University of Pittsburgh Press.

—— (2009), *Land to Water Yoga. Shin Somatics Moving Way*, Bloomington, IL: iUniverse.

Franklin, E. (1996), *Dance Imagery for Technique and Performance*, Champaign, IL: Human Kinetics.

Fraser, D. (2004), 'Creativity: Shaking hands with tomorrow', in D. McAlpine and R. Moltzen (eds), *Gifted and Talented: New Zealand Perspectives*, 2nd ed., Palmerston North, New Zealand: Kanuka Grove, pp. 145–69.

Fraser, N. and Nicholson, L.J. (1990), 'Social criticism without philosophy: An encounter between feminism and postmodernism', in L.J. Nicholson (ed.), *Feminism/ Postmodernism*, New York: Routledge, pp. 19–38.

Galeota-Wozny, N. (Summer/Fall 2005), 'Following Jennifer follow the birds: Interview with Jennifer Monson on BIRD BRAIN DANCE – A navigational dance project', *Contact Quarterly*, 30:2, pp. 12–24.

Gamble, S. (ed.) (1999), *The Icon Critical Dictionary of Feminism and Postfeminism*, Cambridge, United Kingdom: Icon Books.

Gannon, S. (2005), '"The tumbler": Writing an/other in fiction and performance ethnography', *Qualitative Inquiry*, 11:4, pp. 622–27.

Gardner, H. (1999), *Intelligences Reframed. Multiple Intelligences for the 21st Century*, New York: Basic Books.

Gardner, S. and Dempster, E. (1990), 'Moving about the world. An interview with Elizabeth Dempster', *Writings on Dance*, 6, pp. 41–8.

Gatens, Moira (1995), *Imaginary Bodies. Ethics, Power and Corporeality*, London & New York: Routledge.

Gere, D. (2003), 'Introduction', in A.C. Albright and D. Gere, (eds), *Taken by Surprise: A Dance Improvisation Reader*, Middletown, CT: Wesleyan University Press, pp. xiii–xxi.

Gibbons, E. (September 2004), 'Feedback in the dance studio', *Journal of Physical Education, Recreation and Dance*, 75:7, pp. 38–43.

Goldberger, N.R., Tarule, J.M., Clinchy, B.M. and Belenky, M.F. (eds) (1996), *Knowledge, Difference and Power: Essays Inspired by Women's Ways of Knowing*, New York: Basic Books.

Graham, B.T. (1995), 'Riding in someone else's waka: Academic theory and tribal identity', in S Perera (ed.), *Asian and Pacific Inscriptions: Identities/ Ethnicities/ Nationalities: A Special Issue of Meridian*, Bundoora, Australia: La Trobe University, pp. 45–63.

Green, J. (1996), 'Choreographing a postmodern turn: The creative process and somatics', *Impulse*, 4, pp. 267–75.

Greer, G. (1999), *The Whole Woman*, London: Anchor.

Grosz, E. (1994), *Volatile Bodies. Toward a Corporeal Feminism*, Australia: Allen & Unwin.

Grove, R., Stevens, C. and McKechnie, S. (2005), *Thinking in Four Dimensions: Creativity and Cognition in Contemporary Dance*. http://web.mup.unimelb.edu.au/e-store Accessed 4 May 2010.

Hamalainen, S. (2004), 'Ethical issues of evaluation and feedback in a dance class', in L. Rouhiainen, E. Anttila, S. Hamalainen and T. Loytonen (eds), *ACTA Scenica 17, The Same Difference? Ethical and Political Perspectives on Dance*, Helsinki, Finland: Theatre Academy, pp. 79–108.

Hartsock, N.C.M. (1983), 'The feminist standpoint: Developing the grounds for a specifically feminist historical materialism', in S. Harding and M.B. Hintikka (eds), *Discovering Reality. Feminist Perspectives on Epistemology, Metaphysics, Methodology and Philosophy of Science*, Dordretch, Holland, Boston and London: D. Reidel Publishing Co., pp. 283–310.

Hay, D. (1994), *Lamb at the Alter*, Durham & London: Duke University Press.

—— (2000), *My Body the Buddhist*, Middletown, CT: Wesleyan University Press.

Hermann, C. (2003), 'Learning to speak. An apprenticeship with Simone Forti in logomotion', in A.C. Albright and D. Gere (eds), *Taken by Surprise: A Dance Improvisation Reader*, Middletown, CT: Wesleyan University Press, pp. 65–74.

Himmelmann, N. (1998), 'Documentary and descriptive linguistics', *Linguistics*, 36:1, pp. 161–95.

hooks, b. (1994), 'Gangsta culture–sexism and misogyny: Who will take the rap?' in *Outlaw Culture: Resisting Representations*, New York: Routledge.

Hong, C.M. (2003), 'Taking the road less travelled: Developing dance literacy in Aotearoa New Zealand', in E.M. Grierson and J.E. Mansfield (eds), *The Arts in Education: Critical Perspectives from Aotearoa New Zealand*, Palmerston North, New Zealand: Dunmore Press, pp. 137–59.

Howson, A. (2004), *The Body in Society: An Introduction*, Cambridge, United Kingdom; Malden, MA: Polity Press.

Huata, N. (2000), *The Rhythm and Life of Poi*, Auckland, New Zealand: Harper Collins.

Humphreys, M. (2005), 'Getting personal: Reflexivity and autoethnographic vignettes', *Qualitative Inquiry*, 11:6, pp. 840–60.

Irwin, K. (2001), 'Legitimating the first tattoo: Moral passage through informal interaction', *Symbolic Interaction*, 24:1, pp. 49–73.

Iyengar, B.K.S. (2001), *Light on Yoga: Yoga Dipika*, London: Thorsons.

Jahn-Werner, T. (2008), *The Illustrated History of Dance in New Zealand*, Auckland, New Zealand: Random House.

Janesick, V.J. (2000), 'The choreography of qualitative research design. Minuets, improvisations, and crystallization', in N.K. Denzin and Y.S. Lincoln (eds), *Handbook of Qualitative Research*, 2nd ed., Thousand Oaks, CA: Sage, pp. 379–99.

Jones, S.H. (1999), 'Torch', *Qualitative Inquiry*, 5:2, pp. 280–304.

—— (2002), 'Emotional space: Performing the resistive possibilities of torch singing', *Qualitative Inquiry*, 8:6, pp. 738–59.

—— (2010a), 'Singing it the way she hears it', *Cultural Studies – Critical Methodologies*, 10:4, pp. 267–70.

Judge, B. (1998), *Housework*, (dance video), (Available from Bronwyn Judge, PO Box 351, Oamaru, New Zealand, 1998).

Jutel, A. (Dec 2006), 'On cartwheels and other things', *Junctures. Journal of thematic dialogue*, 7, pp. 107–12.

Jutel, T. (2004). '*Lord of the Rings*: Landscape, transformation, and the geography of the virtual', in C. Bell and S. Matthewman (eds), *Cultural Studies in Aotearoa New Zealand: Identity, Space and Place*, Oxford and New York: Oxford University Press, pp. 54–65.

Kaiwai, H. and Zemke-White, K. (2004), 'Kapa Haka as a "Web of cultural meanings"', in C. Bell and S. Matthewman (eds), *Cultural Studies in Aotearoa New Zealand: Identity, Space and Place*, Oxford and New York: Oxford University Press, pp. 139–60.

Karetu, T. (1993), *Haka: The Dance of a Noble People*, Auckland, New Zealand: Reed Publishing.

Kealiinohomoku, J. (1983), 'An anthropologist looks at ballet as a form of ethnic dance', in R. Copeland and M. Cohen (eds), *What is Dance?*, London: Oxford University Press, pp. 533–49.

Kellor, K. (1999), 'Her-story: Life history as a strategy of resistance to being constituted women in academe', in L.K. Christian-Smith and K. Kellor (eds), *Everyday Knowledge and Uncommon Truths*, Boulder, CO: Westview Press, pp. 25–44.

King, M. (ed.) (1991), *Pākehā. The Quest for Identity in New Zealand*, Auckland, New Zealand: Penguin Books.

—— (1992), *Moko. Māori Tattooing in the 20th Century*, Auckland, New Zealand: David Bateman.

—— (1999), *Being Pākehā Now. Reflections and Recollections of a White Native*, Auckland, New Zealand: Penguin Books.

—— (2003), *The Penguin History of New Zealand*, Auckland, New Zealand: Penguin Books.

Klesse, C. (2000), '"Modern primitivism": Non-mainstream body modification and racialized representation', in M. Featherstone (ed.), *Body Modification*, London: Sage, pp. 15–38.

Kolb, D.A. and Fry, R. (1975), 'Toward an applied theory of experiential learning', in C. Cooper (ed.), *Theories of Group Process*, London: John Wiley.

Kosut, M. (December 2006), 'An ironic fad: The commodification and consumption of tattoos', *Journal of Popular Culture*, 39:6, pp. 1035–48.

Landis, J. (Director) (1983), *Thriller*, United States: Columbia Pictures.

Larsen, K. (July 2002), 'Conjecture 2.0 The state we're in', Sidestep archive of New Zealand dance writing. http://www.danz.org.nz/sidestep.php?article_id=79&type_id=2 Accessed 4 May 2010.

—— (September 2003a), 'Conjecture 5.0 – Improvisation as a value shift in contemporary dance', Sidestep archive of New Zealand dance writing. http://www.danz.org.nz/sidestep.php?article_id=111&type_id=2 Accessed 4 May 2010.

—— (October 2003b), 'Conjecture 3.0. Or your money back', *Dance Aotearoa New Zealand*, 17, pp. 9–11.

—— (March 2004), 'Conjecture 4.0. Audience participation and contemporary dance', Sidestep archive of New Zealand dance writing. http://www.danz.org.nz/sidestep.php?article_id=116&type_id=2 Accessed 4 May 2010.

—— (January 2005), 'Conjecture 6.0 – Kristian Larsen reviews John Smythe', Sidestep archive of New Zealand dance writing. http://www.danz.org.nz/sidestep.php?article_id=164&type_id=2 Accessed 4 May 2010.

—— (September 2006), 'You are not alone you are just in New Zealand', (dance performance), Hamilton, New Zealand: WEL Energy Trust Academy of Performing Arts, 29–30 September.

—— (2010a), 'Performing the studio. Articulating a practice of dance improvisation in New Zealand', M.A. thesis: Auckland, New Zealand: University of Auckland.

—— (Winter 2010b), 'Looking like we do', *DANZ Quarterly*, 20, p. 9.

Larsen, K. and Longley, A. (2006), 'Kristian Larsen's Teaching: Tuanui Whakamaru – Dance Canopy July 2005', *Proximity*, 9:1, pp. 7–13.

Lavender, L. and Predock-Linnell, J. (2001), 'From improvisation to choreography: The critical bridge', *Research in Dance Education*, 2:2, pp. 195–209.

Leijen, A., Lam, I., and Simons, P.R-J. (2008), 'Pedagogical practices of reflection in tertiary dance education', *European Physical Education Review*, 14:2, pp. 223–41.

Liu, J.H. (2005), 'History and identity: A system of checks and balances for Aotearoa/New Zealand', in J.H. Liu, T. McCreanor, T. McIntosh and T. Teaiwa (eds), *New Zealand identities*, Wellington, New Zealand: Victoria University Press, pp. 1–19.

Lepkoff, D. and Paxton, S. (Winter/Spring 2004), 'Between the lines. Representing improvisation', *Contact Quarterly*, pp. 42–9.

Lyne, A. (Director) (1983), *Flashdance*, United States: Paramount Pictures.

Macdonald, M. (1995), *Representing Women. Myths of Femininity in the Popular Media*, London & New York: Edward Arnold.

Madison, D.S. (2007), 'Performing ethnography: The political economy of water', *Performance Research*, 12:3, pp. 16–27.

Mane-Wheoki, J. (2003), 'Culturalisms and the arts curriculum', in E.M. Grierson and J.E. Mansfield (eds), *The Arts in Education: Critical Perspectives from Aotearoa New Zealand*, Palmerston North, New Zealand: Dunmore Press, pp. 81–91.

Mansfield, S. (January–March 1999), 'The indelible art of the tattoo', *Japan Quarterly*, 46:1, pp. 30–2.

Markham, A.N. (2005), '"Go ugly early": Fragmented narrative and Bricolage as Interpretive Method', *Qualitative Inquiry*, 11:6, pp. 813–39.

Markula, P. (1995), 'Firm but shapely, fit but sexy, strong but thin: The postmodern aerobicizing female bodies', *Sociology of Sport Journal*, 21:4, pp. 424–53.

—— (1998), 'Dancing within postmodernism', *Waikato Journal of Education*, 4, pp. 73–85.

—— (2003), 'Bodily dialogues: Writing the self', in J. Denison and P. Markula (eds), *Moving Writing: Crafting Movement in Sport Research*, New York: Peter Lang, pp. 27–50.

—— (2005), 'Introduction', in P. Markula (ed.), *Feminist Sports Studies: Sharing Experiences of Joy and Pain*, New York: State University of New York Press, pp. 1–21.

—— (November 2006), 'Body-movement-change: Dance as qualitative performative research', *Journal of Sport and Social Issues*, 30:4, pp. 353–63.

Markula, P. and Denison, J. (2000), 'See spot run: Movement as an object of textual analysis', *Qualitative Inquiry*, 6:3, pp. 406–31.

—— (2005), 'Sport and the personal narrative', in D.L. Andrews, D.S. Mason and M.L. Silk (eds), *Qualitative Methods in Sports Studies*, Oxford & New York: Berg, pp. 165–84.

Martin, N. (Summer/Fall 2007), 'Ensemble thinking: Compositional strategies for group improvisation', *Contact Quarterly*, pp. 10–15.

Mascia-Lees, F.E and Sharpe, P. (eds) (1992), *Tattoo, Torture, Mutilation, and Adornment: The Denaturalization of the Body in Culture and Text*, Albany, New York: State University of New York Press.

Masica-Lees, F.E., Sharpe, P. and Cohen, C.B. (1989), 'The postmodern turn in anthropology: Cautions from a feminist perspective', *Signs*, 15:1, pp. 7–33.

Matthews, N. (December 2004), 'The physicality of Māori Message transmission – Ko te Tinana, He Waka Tuku Kōrero', *Junctures. Journal of Thematic Dialogue*, 3, pp. 9–18.

May, S. (ed.) (1999), *Critical Multiculturalism: Rethinking Multicultural and Antiracist Education*, London, Philadelphia PA: Falmer Press.

McRobbie, A. (1997), 'The Es and the anti-Es: New questions for feminism and cultural studies', in M. Ferguson and P. Galding (eds), *Cultural Studies in Question*, London: Sage, pp. 170–86.

Mead, H.M. (2003), *Tikanga Māori: Living by Māori Values*, Wellington, New Zealand: Huia.

Merleau-Ponty, M. (1962), *The Phenomenology of Perception* (trans. C. Smith), London: Routledge & Kegan Paul.

—— (1964), *The Primacy of Perception*, Evanston, IL: Northwestern University Press.

Mifflin, Margot (1997), *Bodies of Subversion: A Secret History of Women and Tattoo*, New York: Juno Books.

Minton, S.C. (2007), *Choreography: A Basic Approach using Improvisation*, 3rd ed., Champaign, IL: Human Kinetics.

Morgenroth, J. (1987), *Dance Improvisations*, Pittsburgh, PA: University of Pittsburgh Press.

Nagrin, D. (2001), *Choreography and the Specific Image*, Pittsburgh, PA: University of Pittsburgh Press.

Ness, S.A.A. (2004), 'Being a body in a cultural way: Understanding the cultural in the embodiment of dance', in H. Thomas and J. Ahmed (eds), *Cultural Bodies, Ethnography and Theory*, Oxford UK: Blackwell Publishing, pp. 123–44.

Nettleton, S. and Watson, J. (eds) (1998), *The Body in Everyday Life*, London: Routledge.

Ngata Dictionary. (2007), 'Learning media: H.M. Ngata English-Māori Dictionary'. http://www.learningmedia.co.nz/ngata/ Accessed 4 May 2010.

Nikora, L.W. and Te Awekotuku, N. (2002), 'Cultural tattoos: Meanings, descriptors, and attributions', in Proceedings of the *National Māori Graduates of Psychology Symposium*, Hamilton, New Zealand: The University of Waikato, pp. 129–32.

Nikora, L.W., Rua, M., and Te Awekotuku, N. (2005), 'Wearing Moko: Māori Facial Marking in today's world', in N. Thomas, A. Cole and B. Douglas, (eds), *Tattoo. Bodies, Art, and Exchange in the Pacific and the West*, London: Duke University Press, pp. 191–204.

Olsen, A. (2002), *Body and Earth. An Experiential Guide*, Lebanon, NH: University Press of New England.

O'Loughlin, M. (1995), 'Intelligent bodies and ecological subjectivities: Merleau-Ponty's corrective to postmodernism's "Subjects" of education. http://www.ed.uiuc.edu/EPS/PES-Yearbook/95_docs/o'loughlin.html Accessed 4 May 2010.

Orange, C. (1987), *The Treaty of Waitangi*, Wellington, New Zealand: Allen & Unwin.

—— (1989), *The Story of a Treaty*, Wellington, New Zealand: Allen & Unwin.

Osumare, H. (Winter 2002), 'Global breakdancing and the intercultural body', *Dance Research Journal*, 34:2, pp. 30–45.

—— (2007), *The Africanist Aesthetic in Global Hip-Hop: Power Moves*, New York: Palgrave Macmillan.

Pakes, A. (2009), 'Knowing through dance-Making: Choreography, practical knowledge and practice-as-research', in J. Butterworth and L. Wildschut (eds), *Contemporary Choreography: A Critical Reader*, London & New York: Routledge, pp. 10–22.

Pearson, D. (2000), 'The ties that unwind: Civic and ethnic imaginings in New Zealand', *Nations and Nationalism*, 6:1, pp. 91–110.

Phelan, P. (1993), *Unmarked: The Politics of Performance*, New York: Routledge.

Pihama, L. (2000), 'Ebony and ivory: Constructions of Māori in *The Piano*', in H. Margolis (ed.), *Jane Campion's The Piano*, Cambridge: Cambridge University Press, pp. 114–34.

Piccini, A. (2002), 'An historiographic perspective on practice as research'. http://www.bris.ac.uk/parip/t_ap.htm Accessed 4 May 2010.

—— (2005), 'Practice as research in performance'. http://www.bris.ac.uk/parip/introduction.htm Accessed 4 May 2010.

Pinney, A. (2005), 'Ethics, agency, and desire in two strip clubs: A view from both sides of the gaze', *Qualitative Inquiry*, 11:5, pp. 716–23.

Pitts, V. (1998), '"Reclaiming" the female body: Embodied identity work, resistance and the grotesque', *Body & Society*, 4:3, pp. 67–84.

Ponifasio, L. (2002), 'Creating cross-cultural dance in New Zealand', in Creative New Zealand (ed.), *Moving to the Future. Ngā Whakanekeneke atu ki te Ao o Apōpō*, Wellington, New Zealand: Creative New Zealand, pp. 52–6.

Preston-Dunlop, V. (1998), *Looking at Dances: A Choreological Perspective on Choreography*, Ightham, UK: Verve Publishing.

Pringle, R. (2001), 'Competing discourse. Narratives of a fragmented self, manliness and rugby union', *International Review for the Sociology of Sport*, 36:4, pp. 425–39.

Pritchard, S. (2001), 'An essential marking: Māori Tattooing and the properties of identity', *Theory, Culture & Society*, 18:4, pp. 27–45.

Rainer, Y. (1966), *Trio A: The Mind as a Muscle*, (dance season), New York: Judson Church.

—— (1974), *Work 1961–1973*, New York: New York University Press.

Rambo, C. (October 2005), 'Impressions of grandmother. An autoethnographic portrait', *Journal of Contemporary Ethnography*, 34:5, pp. 560–85.

—— (2006), 'Reflecting on reflexivity: Me, myself and *The Ethnographic I*', *Symbolic Interaction*, 29:2, pp. 271–6.

Reinharz, S. (1992), *Feminist Methods in Social Research*, New York: Oxford University Press.

Richardson, L. (1997), *Fields of Play: Constructing an Academic Life*, New Brunswick, NJ: Rutgers Press.

—— (1998a), 'Writing. A method of inquiry', in N.K. Denzin and Y.S. Lincoln (eds), *Collecting and Interpreting Qualitative Materials*, Thousand Oaks, CA: Sage, pp. 345–71.

—— (2000a), 'New writing practices in qualitative research', *Sociology of Sport Journal*, 17, pp. 5–20.

—— (2000b), 'Evaluating ethnography', *Qualitative Inquiry*, 6:2, pp. 253–5.

—— (2005). 'Writing: A method of inquiry', in N.K. Denzin and Y.S. Lincoln (eds), *The Sage Handbook of Qualitative Research*, 2nd ed., Thousand Oaks, CA: Sage, pp. 959–78.

Rinehart, R. (2003), 'On "Sk8ing": Reflections on method', in J. Denison and P. Markula (eds), *Moving Writing. Crafting Movement in Sport Research*, New York: Peter Lang, pp. 150–66.

Risner, D. (2000), 'Making dance, making sense: Epistemology and choreography', *Research in Dance Education*, 1:2, pp. 155–72.

Ritchie, J. (1992), *Becoming Bicultural*, Wellington, New Zealand: Huia Publishers.

Roberston, N. and Masters-Awatere, B. (2007), 'Community psychology in Aotearoa/New Zealand: Me Tiro Whakamuri a kia Hangai Whakamua', in S.M. Reich, M. Reimer, I. Prilleltensky and M. Montero (eds), *International Community Psychology: History and Theories*, New York: Springer, pp. 142–65.

Ronai, C.R. (September 1998), 'Sketching with Derrida: An ethnography of a researcher/erotic dancer', *Qualitative Inquiry*, 4:3, pp. 405–40.

Rosenblatt, D. (August 1997), 'The antisocial skin: Structure, resistance, and "Modern primitive" adornment in the United States', *Cultural Anthropology*, 12:3, pp. 287–334.

Royal Commission on Social Policy (1988). *The April Report: Report of the Royal Commission on Social Policy*. Wellington, New Zealand: The Commission.

Rua, M.R. (2003), 'Moko: Māori facial tattoos. The experiences of contemporary wearers', M.SocSci thesis, Hamilton, New Zealand: The University of Waikato.

Schildkrout, E. (2004), 'Inscribing the body', *Annual Review of Anthropology*, 33, pp. 319–44.

Schneer, G. (1994), *Movement Improvisation: In the Words of a Teacher and her Students*, Champaign, IL: Human Kinetics.

Schrader, C.A. (2005), *A Sense of Dance. Exploring your Movement Potential*, 2nd ed., Champaign, IL: Human Kinetics.

Shapiro, S.B. (ed.) (1998), *Dance, Power and Difference: Critical and Feminist Perspectives on Dance Education*, Champaign, IL: Human Kinetics.

Sheets-Johnstone, M. (1999), *The Primacy of Movement*, Amsterdam & Philadelphia: John Benjamins Publishing Co.

Sklar, D. (Summer 2000), 'Reprise: On dance ethnography', *Dance Research Journal*, 32:1, pp. 70–7.

Smith, L.T. (1999), *Decolonizing Methodologies. Research and Indigenous Peoples*, Dunedin, New Zealand: University of Otago Press.

Smith-Autard, J.M. (2004), *Dance Composition: A Practical Guide to Creative Success in Dance Making*, London: AC & Black.

Snyder, A.F. (2006), 'Allegra fuller Snyder's Keynote address on humanism and the body', in *Proceedings of the 38th Annual Conference: Continuing Dance Culture Dialogues – Southwest Borders and Beyond*, pp. 7–8, Tempe, AZ: Congress on Research in Dance.

Spry, T. (January 2000), '*Tattoo Stories*: A postscript to *Skins*', *Text and Performance Quarterly*, 20:1, pp. 84–96.

—— (2001), 'Performing autoethnography: An embodied methodological practice', *Qualitative Inquiry*, 7:6, pp. 706–32.

—— (2006), 'A "Performative-I" copresence: Embodying the ethnographic turn in performance and the performative turn in ethnography, *Text and Performance Quarterly*, 26:4, pp. 339–46.

—— (2010), 'Call it swing: A Jazz blues autoethnography', *Cultural Studies – Critical Methodologies*, 10:4, pp. 27–282.

Spurgeon, D. (1991), *Dance Moves: From Improvisation to Dance*, Sydney, Australia: Harcourt Bruce Jovanovich.

Stanley, L. (ed.). (1990), *Feminist Praxis: Research, Theory and Epistemology in Feminist Sociology*, London: Routledge.

Stein, G. (1926), 'Composition as explanation', London: Hogarth Press. Reprinted in *What are Masterpieces?* (New York, 1970). http://74.125.155.132/scholar?q=cache:RCjRwt3eCp0J:scholar.google.com/+gertrude+stein&hl=en&as_sdt=2000 Accessed 4 May 2010.

Stinson, S.W. (1995), 'Body of knowledge', *Educational Theory*, 45:1, pp. 43–54.

Sullivan, N. (2001). *Tattooed Bodies: Subjectivity, Textuality, Ethics and Pleasure*, Westport, CI: Praeger.

Taouma, L. (2002), 'Gettin' Jiggy with it', in S. Mallon and P.F. Pereira (eds), *Pacific Art: Niu Sila*, Wellington, New Zealand: Te Papa Press, pp. 133–45.

Te Awekotuku, N. (1997), 'Ta Moko: Māori Tattoo', in R. Blakely and D. Bateman (eds), *Goldie*, Auckland, New Zealand: David Bateman, pp. 109–14.

Te Awekotuku, N. and Nikora, L.W. (2007), *Mau Moko: The World of Māori Tattoo*, Auckland, New Zealand: Viking, Penguin Group.

Tertiary Education Commission (2004), *Performance-Based Research Fund Quality Evaluation: Creative and Performing Arts Panel – The 2003 Assessment*, Wellington, New Zealand: Tertiary Education Commission.

Thomas, N. (2005a), 'Introduction', in N. Thomas, A. Cole and B. Douglas (eds), *Tattoo: Bodies, Art, and Exchange in the Pacific and the West*, London: Duke University Press, pp. 1–29.

—— (2005b), 'Epilogue: Embodied exchanges and their limits', in N. Thomas, A. Cole and B. Douglas (eds), *Tattoo: Bodies, Art, and Exchange in the Pacific and the West*, London: Duke University Press, pp. 223–6.

Thomas, N., Cole, A., and Douglas, B. (eds) (2005), *Tattoo: Bodies, Art, and Exchange in the Pacific and the West*, London: Duke University Press.

Thorburn, R. (1997), 'Sensual Ensemble', in *Dress Sense*, (dance season), Auckland, New Zealand: Lopdell House, Auckland, New Zealand, 10 August.

Tsang, T. (2000), 'Let me tell you a story: A narrative of identity in high-performance sport', *Sociology of Sport Journal*, 17:1, pp. 44–59.

Turner, B.S. (2000), 'The possibility of primitiveness: Towards a sociology of body marks in cool societies', in M. Featherstone (ed.), *Body Modification*, London: Sage, pp. 39–50.

United Nations. (2004). The concept of indigenous peoples. Background paper prepared by the Secretariat of the Permanent Forum on Indigenous Issues. Workshop on data collection and disaggregation for indigenous peoples, New York, 19–21 January 2004.

—— (2010), 'Health of indigenous peoples'. http://www.who.int/mediacentre/factsheets/fs326/en/index.html Accessed 8 December 2010.

Van Dijk, B. (2006), *Devised Theatre: A Devising Model*. http://www.theater-tools.com Accessed 4 May 2010.

Van Manen, M. (1997), *Researching Lived Experience: Human Science for an Action Sensitive Pedagogy*, 2nd ed., London, Canada: Althouse Press.

Warren, K.J. (1988), *The Power and the Promise of Ecological Feminism*. http://www.dhushara.com/book/renewal/voices2/warren.htm Accessed 4 May 2010.

—— (1996), *Ecological Feminist Philosophies*, Bloomington, IN: Indiana University Press.

Weedon, C. (1987), *Feminist Practice and Poststructuralist Theory*, Oxford: Basil Blackwell.

Weiss, G. (1999), *Body Images: Embodiment as Intercorporeality*, New York & London: Routledge.

White, J. (2005), 'Marks of transgression: The tattooing of Europeans in the Pacific Islands', in N. Thomas, A. Cole and B. Douglas (eds), *Tattoo: Bodies, Art, and Exchange in the Pacific and the West*, London: Duke University Press, pp. 72–89.

Williams, S.J. and Bendelow, G. (1998), *The Lived Body: Sociological Themes, Embodied Issues*, New York: Routledge.

Wolf, N. (1991), *The Beauty Myth: How Images of Beauty are used Against Women*, London: Vintage.

Woolf, V. (1929), *A Room of One's Own*, London: Hogarth Press.

Young, I.M. (1980), 'Throwing like a girl', in I. Young (ed.), *Throwing like a Girl*, Bloomington, IN: Indiana University Press, pp. 141–59.

—— (1998a), 'Situated bodies: Throwing like a girl', in D. Welton (ed.), *Body and Flesh: A Philosophical Reader*, Oxford: Blackwell, pp. 259–73.

—— (1998b), '"Throwing like a girl": Twenty years later', in D. Welton (ed.), *Body and Flesh: A Philosophical Reader*, Oxford: Blackwell, pp. 286–90.

29
37
90 - 6